FAITH, FREEDOM, AND RATIONALITY

FAITH, FREEDOM, AND RATIONALITY

Philosophy of Religion Today

edited by
JEFF JORDAN
and
DANIEL HOWARD-SNYDER

ROWMAN & LITTLEFIELD PUBLISHERS, INC.

ROWMAN & LITTLEFIELD PUBLISHERS, INC.

Published in the United States of America
by Rowman & Littlefield Publishers, Inc.
4720 Boston Way, Lanham, Maryland 20706

3 Henrietta Street
London WC2E 8LU, England

British Cataloging in Publication Information Available

Library of Congress Cataloging-in-Publication Data

Faith, freedom and rationality : essays in the philosophy of religion /
edited by Jeff Jordan and Daniel Howard-Snyder.
p.   cm.
Includes bibliographical references and index.
1. Religion—Philosophy.   I. Jordan, Jeff, 1959–   .   II. Howard
-Snyder, Daniel.
BL51.F315   1996   210—dc20   96-19272   CIP

ISBN 0–8476–8152–1 (cloth : alk. paper)
ISBN 0–8476–8153–x (pbk. : alk. paper)

Printed in the United States of America

∞ ™ The paper used in this publication meets the minimum requirement of
American National Standard for Information Sciences—Permanence of
Paper for Printed Library Materials, ANSI Z39.48–1984.

To William L. Rowe
with affection, gratitude, and respect

Contents

Preface

The past two decades have seen the field of philosophy of religion flourish. This may surprise anyone familiar with the field's status as recently as just some forty years ago. At mid-century philosophical circles dismissed philosophy of religion as an uninteresting area of which Hume and Kant had already had the last say. Logical positivism and existentialism, both descended from Hume and Kant via vastly different lineages, were the prevailing movements of the time and neither held any tolerance for rational argument concerning the existence and nature of God. Logical positivists asserted that theological and metaphysical claims were one and all nonsensical; while existentialists rejected the idea that one should investigate theological claims as one would the claims of science, law, or history in favor of the idea that a radical subjectivism was more apropos.

But, things change. Today philosophy of religion is a vibrant and exciting area of philosophical research with four academic journals and at least three professional societies devoted to the field. One of these, the Society of Christian Philosophers with over a thousand members, is the largest single-interest group in the American Philosophical Association. Indeed, many of the most influential philosophers at work today publish regularly on topics in this particular field. For these reasons a collection of essays on topics central to philosophy of religion is timely.

The title of this collection, *Faith, Freedom, and Rationality: Philosophy of Religion Today,* is significant for two reasons. First, it reflects a threefold classification of the essays. The first section discusses the religious attitudes of belief, acceptance, and love; the second section is about human and divine freedom; and the third section examines the rationality of religious belief. All the essays contain arguments and analyses that extend on far beyond the purview of philosophy of religion, into areas such as epistemology, agency theory, moral theory, philosophy of mind, and history of philosophy.

Those interested in epistemology will find much in the initial chapter, William Alston's "Belief, Acceptance, and Religious Faith." Alston explores the important distinction between belief, the disposition to feel that such and such is the case, and acceptance, the act of committing to the truth of a proposition. He argues that acceptance, as well as belief, is properly employable within the context of a full-blooded religious faith. Chapter 2, Philip Quinn's "The Divine Command Ethics in Kierkegaard's *Works of Love*" looks into the nature and possibility of the sort of love that is commanded of Christians, that of loving one's neighbors as oneself. Kierkegaard is, Quinn suggests, the best source from which to inquire into the commanded love and Quinn contrasts the commanded love with erotic love and friendship.

"Free Agency and Materialism," chapter 3, coauthored by Jan Cover and John O'Leary-Hawthorne, argues that the thesis of agent causation is compatible with the thesis of microphysical determinism. However, the compatibility of agent causation and microphysical determinism is purchased at the high price of introducing many theoretical complexities within materialism.

Eleonore Stump investigates in chapter 4, "Libertarian Freedom and the Principle of Alternative Possibilities," a recent attempt to show that a proponent of libertarian freedom and moral responsibility must accept the principle of alternative possibilities. According to this principle, a person is morally responsible for doing such and such only if she could have done something other than she did. Stump finds that the recent attempt is implausibly tied to an extreme Cartesian dualism; but, significantly, she suggests that, apart from the extreme Cartesian dualism, a libertarian need not endorse the principle of alternative possibilities as long as the ultimate source of one's actions is found within one's own will and not in some external source, whether or not one has alternative possibilities open to one.

The nature of divine freedom as well as human freedom is the subject of James Ross's "Real Freedom" (chapter 5). Ross's chapter is interesting not only for *what* it says, but also for *how* it says it. The form of the essay is something like the Tenebrae service held during the Christian Holy Week and commemorating the suffering of Christ: the essay has repeated antiphonies, nine lessons, and several lamentations. Ross argues that divine freedom is understandable only by examining human freedom, but integral human freedom was lost in the fall of humanity. Thus, we can understand our freedom, and by extension divine freedom, only through God's redemption.

In his trenchant essay, "Jonathan Edwards, William Rowe, and the Necessity of Creation" (chapter 6), William Wainwright critiques the claim of the great American theologian Jonathan Edwards that God created the world in order to display God's glory. Edwards's views committed him to two other claims: that God must create and that God must create this world. Wainwright argues that the first claim is defensible, but the second is not since it is incompatible with God's being free. Wainwright offers a way of avoiding Edwards's second claim by arguing that every creatable world is surpassable. Wainwright notes that his solution succeeds only if an argument formulated by William Rowe is unsound; and that argument, he further argues, is indeed unsound.

Epistemology is again brought to the foreground with Peter van Inwagen's analysis of what might be dubbed Cliffordian evidentialism in chapter 7," 'It Is Wrong, Everywhere, Always, and for Anyone, to Believe Anything upon Insufficient Evidence.' " According to Cliffordian evidentialism (CE), one should possess adequate evidence in support of any proposition that one believes. Van Inwagen does not argue that CE is false, but he does argue that CE, if widely accepted, would have extensive and undesirable consequences for what we ordinarily think ourselves justified in believing. If CE were correct, our political beliefs, for one, would be severely pruned back since most of us lack adequate evidence for these beliefs. Moreover, religious belief has been held to a double standard regarding CE: CE is often taken to hold decisively against religious beliefs, but not against beliefs in science or politics or law. Van Inwagen argues that this double standard is unseemly and indefensible.

Robert Audi takes a look in chapter 8, "Theism and the Mind-Body Problem," at a rather neglected argument of the current age. According to it, theistic belief and the scientific orientation of our time is at least disharmonious and, perhaps, more ominously, even incompatible. Looking at this contention is important since, although one does not find the argument articulated often, it is clearly assumed by many people, even those who would otherwise consider themselves friends of the pious, and it is something of a modern sentiment in its pervasiveness. Audi focuses upon the question of whether there is a scientifically acceptable conception of mind that coheres with a plausible theistic view of personhood—whether human or divine. Audi argues that theism is compatible with the predominant views of mind that are currently discussed. Theism enjoys a considerable elasticity regarding its view of personhood and is, thereby, compatible with several competing views of mind. Regarding whether scientific views render theism implausible, Audi offers four strategies that the theist might adopt in order to incorporate within his or her worldview both traditional theistic beliefs and scientific claims. As mentioned earlier, the idea that science and theism are in some sense mutually exclusive is widespread and, consequently, a close look at the idea is important.

The idea of the miraculous is an example of the tension between the scientific and the religious, at least insofar as a miracle is taken to be a violation of a natural law. Martin Curd notes in "Miracles as Violations of Natural Law" (chapter 9) that the standard analysis of the concept of miracle is that an event is miraculous if and only if it is a violation of a law of nature and it is caused directly by a supernatural agent. These two conditions, Curd argues, must be epistemically independent—one can justifiably believe one without thereby believing the other—if the purported occurrence of a miracle can be a reason for thinking that God exists. It has been argued by some that no miracle could occur since it is logically impossible for an event to violate a law of nature. Curd examines three attempts to refute this contention and he concludes that the three attempts succeed only by forfeiting the epistemic independence between the two conditions of the miraculous and, as a consequence, the miraculous cannot be used as a reason for thinking that God exists.

In chapter 10, which is significant both for its historical treatment and its philosophy of religion, Norman Kretzmann analyzes a cosmological argument found in chapter 15 of Aquinas's *Summa Contra Gentiles*, that he suggests is richer in philosophical import than even Aquinas realized. Kretzmann argues that Aquinas's sixth argument succeeds: although it is not an argument for the existence of God as classically defined, it is an argument for there being a single universal and ultimate explanation of existing things. Kretzmann suggests, however, that the following volumes of the *Summa Contra Gentiles* supply the identifying link between something being the single universal and ultimate explanation of what exists and something being God.

A parity defense consists in arguing that one class of propositions is relevantly similar to another class of propositions such that, if the latter class of propositions was taken to be rationally permissible, so too should the former class. Chapter 11, "On Plantinga's 1967 and 1983 Parity Defenses," is a detailed and vigorous probe of the parity defense in support of theistic belief. Here George Nakhnikian argues that such a defense is doomed to failure since there is an inverse relation between the plausibility of the compared classes of propositions and the cogency of the parity defense: the more plausible the propositions in the compared classes are, the less cogent the similarity between the propositions will be. Nakhnikian focuses upon the parity defense as it has been deployed by Alvin Plantinga in *God and Other Minds* (1967) and "Reason and Belief in God" (1983), arguing that both fail to deliver the promised epistemic succor to theistic belief.

As mentioned earlier, there is a second reason why the title *Faith, Freedom, and Rationality* is significant: it reflects and parallels the interests and writings of William Rowe. This volume is intended by the editors and the contributors as a tribute to him. Bill Rowe, in both his writings and in his professional relationships, has proved again and again an estimable model of philosophical acuity and eminent graciousness that is altogether too rare. His civility and his respect for the views of his opponents are invaluable qualities.

Three of the contributors to this volume were Bill Rowe's teachers— William Alston, James Ross, and George Nakhnikian. Nakhnikian remembers that early professor/student relationship this way:

> Bill Rowe appeared in one of my classes a year or so after I began teaching at Wayne State University in the Fall of 1949. I was a thirty-year old neophyte philosopher, eager to learn and to be a good teacher. I had convictions stronger than the warrant I had for them. I was a logical positivist, and I lost no opportunity to voice my alienation from religion in any form. Bill was a twenty-year old neophyte intellectual. Like me, he was eager to learn. Like me, he had convictions stronger than the warrant he had for them. He came from a conservative Christian environment, and he lost no opportunity to voice his wholehearted commitment to that style of Christianity. We two were a match. I spent more time outside the classroom with him than with any other undergraduate or graduate student in my nearly forty years of teaching. Most of our talk was about religion. Sometimes we would go on until midnight. We had a great deal of contact in the classroom as well. Bill enrolled in every course that I taught during his undergraduate years.
>
> His belief and my unbelief were matters of deep importance for both of us, and we battled without letup. During those hours of dialogue, we forged a bond. We became life-long friends. I was struck by, and loved, his passion, his integrity, his uncommon purity of heart, his incisive intelligence, clearly in need of stimulation and refinement, but there unmistakably. We trusted and admired each other. We disagreed with respect and love for each other. We gladly accepted each other as we were and we still do. There came a time, in 1953, I believe, when Bill turned to me for advice and guidance about what to do after finishing his undergraduate philosophy major. I advised him to go to Ann Arbor to study with Bill Alston, but before that

to go to the theological school at the University of Chicago and explore systematically, with a professor whom Bill admired, some of the ins and outs of Christian faith. I thought that he needed to do that before undertaking the philosophical scrutiny of religion with Alston. Bill found this plan greatly to his liking, and decided to implement it. We all know the outcome. Contemporary American philosophy is enriched by a large number of well-trained, able, clear-thinking practitioners. Bill Rowe is among the best of them.

And because he is a human being of exceptionally fine character, Bill has been also a good influence on the life of the institutions where he has served. Purdue has been the most fortunate beneficiary.

I do not remember the first day I became aware of Bill's presence in my class. Even if I had, I would not have known that this young stranger was to become one of the people I love most. Life is like that. When it is good.

A good part of the reason that philosophy of religion is today a vivacious area is due to the work of Bill Rowe. That reason alone is good cause to dedicate this volume to him.

Part I

Faith

1

Belief, Acceptance, and Religious Faith

William P. Alston

The Distinction between Belief and Acceptance

My aim in this chapter is to use the distinction between *belief* and *acceptance* to throw light on some of the complexities of the cognitive aspect of religious faith. Before doing so, I must explain the distinction as I understand it, and explain my conception of religious faith as involving various aspects, including a cognitive one. The distinction between belief and acceptance I will employ was mainly inspired by L. Jonathan Cohen's *An Essay on Belief and Acceptance*. My way of putting it is my own, however, and Cohen should not be held responsible for it.[1]

The concept of belief that I will be setting out, is, I believe, a familiar commonsense concept, though, as in many cases, a philosophically unreflective subject will not be explicitly aware of its constitution. There are several salient features of the concept. But before getting to that I should make it explicit that the concept I will be dealing with is the concept of *propositional belief*, *belief that so and so*. This is to be distinguished from *belief in*, for example, belief in acupuncture and *believing a person*, as when I say to someone who has just told me something, "I believe you." I will say a bit about *belief in* after laying out the concept of propositional belief. It is also worth pointing out that "belief" is ambiguous between *the psychological state of believing something*, and *what is believed*, the propositional content of that state. It is the former with which I am concerned.

3

(1) Belief is *dispositional.*

I have believed for years that outlining a philosophical article helps one to get clear as to its structure, though this has not been on my mind during all my waking hours (not to mention my sleeping hours) through all those years. Nor is it the case that for every moment during that period some manifestation of the belief has been evoked. Whatever it is to have that belief, it is not to be in a certain episodic conscious state or to perform any action or undergo any process. Thus, it is clear that belief is something that one can have in a *latent* state as well as in an *active* state. A disposition of a suitable sort nicely satisfies this constraint.

But what disposition is it? A disposition to do what under what conditions? We can begin to answer this question by thinking of the various outcomes we would expect, under certain conditions, if a subject, S, believes that *p*. Here is a partial list.

1. If S believes that *p*, then if someone asks S whether *p*, S will have a tendency to respond in the affirmative.
2. If S believes that *p*, then if S considers whether it is the case that *p*, S will tend to feel it to be the case that *p*, with one or another degree of confidence.
3. If S believes that *p*, then S will tend to believe propositions that he or she takes to follow from *p*.
4. If S believes that *p*, then S will tend to use *p* as a premise in theoretical and practical reasoning where this is appropriate.
5. If S believes that *p*, then if S learns that not-*p*, S will tend to be surprised.
6. If S believes that *p*, then S will tend to act in ways that would be appropriate if it were the case that *p*, given S's goals, aversions, and other beliefs.[2]

Note that in each case, it is only a *tendency* to a certain manifestation that is specified in the consequent of the conditional. That is because a given belief by itself does not necessitate a certain outcome. What eventuates is also influenced by other psychological states and attitudes of S. The most that can be said to follow from the belief that *p* alone is a *tendency* to a certain outcome in the relevant conditions. To say that one has a tendency to A is to say that A will be forthcoming in the absence of sufficient contravening influences, where we have some conception of what counts as such an influence.

If we ask whether all these conditionals form part of the *meaning* of "believe" (part of the concept of belief), and whether any other conditionals have an equal claim to that status, it would seem that the answer is not at all clear. Even if, as I think, Quine is mistaken in supposing that no analytic-synthetic distinction is viable, there are cases in which the distinction is not sharp and there is a largish boundary region that cannot be confidently assigned to either side. This is a strong candidate for such a case.[3] Some of the items on this list are much stronger candidates for being part of the meaning than others, particularly 1, 2, 4, and 6; but I don't think it is possible to draw a sharp line between the ones that hold by virtue of what "believe" means, and those that we confidently believe to be true of belief.

Cohen gives pride of place to 2. His version of that component is the "disposition, when one is attending to issues raised, or items referred to, by the proposition that *p*, normally to feel it true that *p* and false that *not-p*" (4). Notice that Cohen's "normally" has the same role as my "tendency"—to take account of the fact that one may have the disposition even though the typical manifestations are blocked. Cohen points out that "feelings that would have exemplified the belief that *p* sometimes do not occur . . . because you have difficulty in remembering that *p* or because you need or want to concentrate on other relevant matters. Or they may just be crowded out because you have too many relevant beliefs for them all to be activated within the same span of consideration" (7–8). He mentions other factors as well. It is not all clear to me how to understand "feel it *true* that *p*." If it involves deploying the concept of truth, then the suggestion is mistaken. One can have beliefs without possessing the concept of truth at all. Hence I take it that the same basic idea can be more felicitously expressed as "feel it to be the case that *p*" or "have the sense that *p*."

I have used the term "feel" for the manifestation in 2 in order to convey the idea that it possesses a kind of *immediacy*, that it is something one *experiences* rather than something that one *thinks out*, that it is a matter of one's being *struck by* (a sense of) how things are rather than deciding how things are.[4] This is also connected with the second basic feature of belief, to be introduced shortly, its *involuntary* character. I am not suggesting that "feeling it to be the case that *p*" is some kind of sensation or some kind of emotional state. I take "feel" to be a broad enough term to range over a great variety of inner experiential states.[5]

My formulation of 2 is designed to allow for degrees of belief, belief that is more or less firm, assured, confident, certain. We may think of the different degrees of assurance that *p* is the case as a handy measure of degrees of belief. We ordinarily regard it as such. We ask questions like

"How sure are you that *p*?", "How confident are you that *p*?", "How certain do you feel of it?", when we want to know how strong or firm the belief is. But we should not suppose that degree of belief simply consists in the degree of confidence with which *p*'s being the case strikes one. It is certainly *part* of what constitutes that degree, but it is used as the indication of choice because (1) it is easily accessible and (2) it is assumed to vary with parallel variations in the other dispositional components of belief. Consider 4. One may use *p* as a premise where appropriate more or less often; and when one does so, this may be with greater or lesser alacrity, and with greater or lesser confidence. Similar points apply to 6. All the manifestations of belief are subject to variations in degree, and it is plausible that they usually do so in lockstep. But this is not always the case. One can feel very certain that *p* but (frequently) not act as if one believed it and seldom use it in one's reasonings where appropriate. And the reverse also happens. In these cases we have to qualify the belief attribution in some way if we are not to withhold it altogether. Just how we do this depends on the relative emphasis we give to the different components of the complete package. I won't have time to go into all this in this essay. I will be concerned here with cases in which the various components match up in a neat fashion.

I must confess to some uneasiness about the whole notion of degrees of belief. I am inclined to think that unqualified, flat-out belief that *p* requires that it seem unquestionable to S that *p*. On this view, belief excludes any doubts or uncertainty. To be sure, one can find oneself feeling positive about the proposition that *p* without feeling at all certain about it. But we have other terms (than "believe") for such states. One may "think *p* to be more or less likely," "think it to be more likely that *p* than not," "be inclined to suppose that *p*," "be of the opinion that *p*," and the like. If I were to set things up this way, I would have to recognize that in addition to belief and acceptance there is a variety of belieflike states that present basically the same configuration as belief except for differences of degree of confidence. That would considerably complicate my discussion.[6] Hence I will go along with the common view that beliefs come in all degrees of strength, from complete certainty at the top all the way to down to a mere inclination to suppose that *p*. Below a certain degree of felt sureness, practically everyone will withhold the (unqualified) term "believe" and say instead that the person "is inclined to think" or something of the sort. But I won't try to say just where that minimum requirement is to be located; I doubt that any sharp line can be drawn. In any event, my concern in this essay is with beliefs that exhibit a high degree of felt certainty.

Cohen gives 2 pride of place in a very strong way, by regarding it and only it as embodying the meaning of "believe." There are reasons for this. It seems that feeling sure that p is more intimately connected to belief than the *behavioral* manifestations. Clearly one can act as if one believes that p when in fact one does not. One can dissemble. (This does not, of course, show that a *tendency* to such manifestations does not enter into the meaning of the term.) Moreover, it is also *possible* to deceive oneself into thinking that one is sure of something when one is not. But belief would seem to involve a much stronger tendency to feeling it to be the case that p than to any behavioral manifestations.[7] When I come to discuss acceptance, we will see that 2 plays a central role in distinguishing belief from acceptance. Nevertheless, I can't go along with Cohen in identifying belief with 2 alone. It seems the better part of wisdom to recognize that a variety of dispositions is involved.

(2) Belief is not under direct voluntary control.

Beliefs are items we *find* ourselves with, not items we *choose* to have. I cannot decide to believe that the Blue Jays will win the pennant or that Sam is trustworthy. In saying they are not under *direct* voluntary control, I am not only denying that we cannot believe that p at will, just by choosing to do so. To deny that is just to deny that believing is a *basic* act, one that can be done without doing it by doing something else. But belief is also not under direct voluntary control in the way opening a door or going to the office is. These are not basic acts either. I can't open a door just by willing that it be open (unless I have extraordinary telekinetic powers), nor can I go to the office just by choosing to do so; I have to make a variety of movements, and enjoy some environmental support, to do so. Believing is not under voluntary control in the way these nonbasic acts are, either. In their case, I can perform various basic acts that I can rely on to bring about the intended result, but this is not possible with respect to belief. If I were to try to do something that will bring it about, right away, that I believe that Salem is the capital of Massachusetts, I wouldn't know what button to push. In some cases I can perform voluntary acts that will have some *effect* on what I believe on certain matters, by, for example, selectively exposing myself to pro or con considerations; but that is a long way from being able to exercise effective, much less immediate, voluntary control.[8]

The concept of belief in question here is neutral between knowledge and what we might call "mere belief." So long as I have the right dispositions, then I can be said, in this sense, to believe that p, whether or not I also know that p. The supposition that belief contrasts with knowledge is encouraged by conversations like the following.

Jane: Go out and see what's making that noise in the kitchen.
Husband (returning): I believe the faucet is leaking.
Jane: You believe it's leaking?! Can't you see whether it is or not?

In most contexts, when one *says*, "I believe that p," that is taken to imply that the speaker is disavowing knowledge that p. But that can be explained in terms of H. P. Grice's "conversational implicatures," without supposing that non-knowledge is part of the meaning of "believe."[9] The conversational rule involved here is "Don't make a weaker statement than you are prepared to make." Because this rule is generally observed, when one says (in most contexts) "I believe that p," the hearer takes the speaker to be observing that rule, and *hence* infers that the speaker is not also prepared to say that he or she knows that p. But despite that, on the concept of belief under discussion here, belief is not incompatible with knowledge, and, for reasons just given, I take this to be true of the ordinary concept of propositional belief.

I could go much further into the concept of belief, but these points will suffice as a basis for the contrast I want to draw with *acceptance*. Acceptance differs from belief in each of the two respects I have mentioned.

The First Respect. Acceptance is, in the first instance, an act, more specifically a mental act. Like belief, it involves what we might call, in neutral terms, a "positive attitude" toward a proposition, but the mode of involvement is quite different. Whereas belief is a disposition to various reactions involving the proposition, the act of acceptance is the *adoption*, the *taking on*, of a positive attitude to the proposition. It is something one *does* at a particular time. In characterizing it as a mental act, I distinguish it from the verbal act of *assent*, which can be taken to be the overt expression of acceptance. But we must note that "assent" is not infrequently itself used for the mental act I call "acceptance." For examples, see the quotations below from Aquinas and Locke.

But just what positive attitude toward p does one adopt in accepting p? Cohen's capsule characterization is this: "to . . . adopt a policy of deeming, positing, or postulating that p—i.e., of including that proposition . . . among one's premises for deciding what to do or think in a particular context" (4). I take this to be along the right lines. To accept that p is to "take it on board," to include it in one's repertoire of (supposed) facts on which one will rely in one's theoretical and practical reasoning and one's behavior.

But though the act of acceptance is not a disposition, it typically engenders a complex dispositional state, which in the passage just cited Cohen calls a "policy." Indeed, if no such policy were engendered, if acceptance were just a momentary act that left no residue, it would have no point. The point lies precisely in the fact that to accept a proposition is to be prepared to make use of it in reasoning and in guiding one's behavior. Hence, we could attach "acceptance" to the *possession* of that policy, or, alternatively, let it spread over both adoption and possession. The latter is Cohen's choice. Here is the sentence cited above, with the omissions filled in. "More precisely, to accept that *p* is *to have* or adopt a policy of deeming, positing, or postulating that *p*—i.e., of including that proposition or rule among one's premises for deciding what to do or think in a particular context, whether or not one feels it to be true that *p*" (emphasis added).[10] It is, to be sure, infelicitous to use "accept," which is obviously an act term and moreover a term for *taking on* a "policy," for *having* and acting on a policy as well as adopting it. Nevertheless, there are sometimes sufficient reasons for overriding linguistic felicity. When I come to my thesis that *accepting basic Christian doctrines* can undergird a full-blown Christian commitment, I don't want to restrict myself to the act of initial adoption. If one "accepted" the doctrines and then promptly forgot all about them, if no further use were made of them or attention paid to them, this clearly would not serve as a foundation for a robust Christian life. We need the full package of accepting the propositions *and* thereby being disposed to *use* them in one's thinking, feeling, and behavior.[11] I could spell all this out every time I have occasion to discuss Christian acceptance, but it would be tedious to do so. Hence I will go along with Cohen's practice of using "accept" for the full package—(actively) having the policy as well as adopting it.

But what are the components of the complex dispositional state involved in acceptance? They will largely overlap those involved in believing that *p*. Specifically, they will include 1, 3, 4, 5, and 6 from the list I gave for belief. (In 3, substitute "tend to accept" for "tend to believe.") There will be some differences. Belief, at least firm belief, will involve more confident, unhesitating manifestations of these sorts than acceptance will. But in the main, the story on these components will be the same. By far the largest difference is the absence of 2. The complex dispositional state engendered by accepting *p* will definitely not include a tendency to feel that *p* if the question of whether *p* arises. That is, indeed, one of the main distinctions between the two. This gives us the reason foreshadowed earlier for taking 2 to be especially crucial for the nature of belief. It constitutes one of the main respects in which believing *p* differs from accepting that *p*.[12]

So accepting that *p* does not entail believing that *p*. But does it allow it? Can one accept a proposition one believes? The end of the quote from Cohen, "whether or not one feels it to be true that *p*," indicates that he takes them to be compatible. This is partly because of a feature of his position in which I am not following him, namely, taking it that the disposition to use propositions as premises in theoretical and practical reasoning is restricted to acceptance and is no part of belief. Hence, if he is to recognize the obvious fact that we do reason from premises that express beliefs, he has to allow a very considerable overlap. But since I take dispositions to use *p* as a premise to be partly constitutive of belief itself, I lack that reason for supposing an overlap to be possible. Indeed, if we concentrate on the upper part of the dimension of strength of belief, I see no point in one who believes that *p* also accepting that *p*. The believer already has everything that accepting it would give him or her and then some. To find any reason for adding acceptance to the picture, we have to go to beliefs of a weaker strength. There the dispositions, including dispositions to taking *p* as a basis for inferences and behavior, are themselves weaker. Hence, they may be shored up by a deliberate acceptance of *p*. In any event, in this chapter I will be concerned with the contrast between one who feels sure that *p* and one who, lacking that, accepts that *p*.[13]

To put some flesh on this skeleton, let's think of some familiar examples of accepting propositions one does not (firmly) believe. Suppose it is not at all clear what is the case or what one should do, but the relevant considerations seem to favor one alternative over the others. As the captain of the defensive team I am trying to figure out what play the opposing quarterback will call next. From my experience of playing against him and his coach, and given the current situation, it seems most likely to me that he will call a plunge into the middle of the line by the fullback. Hence I accept that proposition and reason from it in aligning the defense. Do I *believe* that this is the play he will call, unqualifiedly believe it, as contrasted with thinking it likely? No. I don't find myself feeling sure that this is what he will do. Who can predict exactly what a quarterback will do in a given situation? My experience prevents me from having any such assurance. Nevertheless I accept the proposition that he will call a fullback plunge and proceed on that basis.

Moving up to loftier heights, I survey the reasons for and against different positions on the free will issue. Having considered them carefully, I conclude that they indicate most strongly an acceptance of libertarian free will. Do I flat-out believe that we have that kind of free will? There are people who do feel sure of this. But I am too impressed by the arguments against the position to be free of doubts; it doesn't seem clear to me that this is the real situation, as it seems clear to me that I am now sitting in front of a computer, that I live in Central New York, and that I teach at Syracuse University. Nevertheless, I accept the proposition that we have libertarian free will. I announce this as my position. I defend it against objections. I draw various consequences from it, and so on.

The Second Respect. Acceptance differs strongly from belief on the voluntariness issue as well. Accepting a proposition is a voluntary act. I have effective voluntary control over my acceptances and abstentions therefrom. That is not to say that I can accept any proposition I can envisage, whatever my epistemic situation. In my first case, the defensive captain could not have accepted the proposition that the quarterback will take the ball and run in the opposite direction. And my philosopher, given her assessment of the relevant considerations, could not accept the proposition that human beings are unconscious automata. Nevertheless, she does have a choice *even if* libertarian free will is the only position that is a live option for her acceptance. Another course she could voluntarily choose is withholding acceptance of any of the alternatives until she sees the relevant reasons pointing more unambiguously in one direction. That is always an option where one of the alternatives does not seem clearly to be the correct one.

But we don't always have the luxury of postponing a decision in this way. When the press of affairs requires us to act on one assumption or another, we cannot wait for more evidence. This is the situation of our defensive captain. He must dispose his forces in one way rather than another, based on one or another assumption as to what the offense will do. But he still need not accept a particular hypothesis on this point. He can adopt an *assumption*, a *working hypothesis*, for the sake of action guidance without accepting it. Accepting *p* involves a more positive attitude toward that proposition than just making the assumption that *p* or hypothesizing that *p*. The difference could be put this way. To accept that *p* is to regard it as true, though one need not be explicitly deploying the concept of truth in order to do so. But one can *assume* or *hypothesize* that *p* for a particular limited purpose, as our captain might have done, without taking any stand on truth value. Again, one can assume or hypothesize that *p* for the sake of testing it, trying it out in practice, so as to help one decide whether to accept it. Thus, whenever it is not clear to one that *p*, and one is able to accept that *p*, one always at least has a choice between accepting that p and refraining from doing so. And often the area of choice will be wider. My view of the reasons for and against positions on the free will issue might be such that more than one position seems viable to me and, hence, a live option for acceptance.

Faith In and Faith That

Now I turn to a brief consideration of faith, first in general and then religious faith in particular. As with belief we have a distinction between "faith in" and "faith that." "Faith that," though like "belief that" in being a positive attitude toward a proposition, is most clearly distinguished from the latter by two features. (1) It necessarily involves some pro-attitude toward its object. If S is said to have faith that democracy will eventually be firmly established everywhere, that implies not only that S believes that this will happen but that S looks on this prospect with favor. If S were strongly opposed to universal democracy, it would be somewhere between inapt and false to represent S as having *faith* that democracy will triumph. Whereas one can truly and unproblematically be said to *believe* that democracy will win out even if one views the prospect with horror. (2) "Faith that" has at least a strong suggestion of a weak epistemic position vis-à-vis the proposition in question. One would say that one has faith that Jim will be promoted only when one's evidence is less than conclusive. One is said to "take it on faith" that this will happen. But this feature is less tightly connected semantically to "faith that" than the pro-attitude feature. This can be seen by considering cases in which we have one feature without the other. Suppose I definitely want you to get the job but also have strong reasons for supposing that you will, and contrast that with the case in which I don't want you to get the job but lack strong reasons one way or the other. It seems much more felicitous to speak of my having faith that you will get the job in the first case than in the second. Indeed, that way of putting it seems quite out of order in the second case.

Be this as it may, the central paradigmatic cases of "*faith that*" exhibit both of the features we have been discussing. This is classically exhibited in the famous passage from the Epistle to the Hebrews. "Faith is the assurance of things hoped for, the conviction of things not seen" (11:1). Here we have the pro-attitude in the first phrase, the relatively weak epistemic situation in the second.

Now for "faith in." Paradigmatically one has faith in a *person*. I believe that when one is said to have faith in a group, a social institution, or a movement, either these are being personified or we are thinking of a person or persons as being involved in them in some crucial way. In any event, let's concentrate on faith in a person. Here the crucial feature would seem to be *trust*, reliance on the person to carry out commitments, obligations, promises, or, more generally, to act in a way favorable to oneself. I have faith in my wife; I can rely on her doing what she says she will do, on her remaining true to her commitments, on her remaining attached to me by a bond of love. To return to the eleventh chapter of Hebrews, the "heroes of faith" celebrated there are said to have faith by virtue of trusting in the goodness and providence of God, even when they could not see how it would all turn out. "By faith Noah, being warned by God concerning events as yet unseen, took heed and con-structed an ark for the saving of his household" (verse 7). "By faith Abraham obeyed when he was called to go out to a place which he was to receive as an inheritance; and he went out, not knowing where he was to go" (verse 8). "By faith the people crossed the Red Sea as if on dry land" (verse 29). Note that in these attributions we have weak epistemic status as well as trust prominently displayed.

How is "faith in" related to "faith that"? Obviously, faith in a person presupposes that one has some positive attitude toward the proposition that the person exists and that he or she has various characteristics that provide a basis for one's faith. But it is not obvious that this attitude has to be properly characterizable as a case of "*faith* that". On the other hand, there are reasons for accepting a dependence in the other direction. It seems plausible that wherever it is clearly appropriate to attribute "*faith that*," there is a "*faith in*" in the background. If I have faith that Joe will get the job, I thereby have faith in Joe, of some sort. If I have faith that the church will rebound from recent setbacks, I thereby have faith in the church and its mission.

Here is an interesting linguistic point. Think of *faith in* as a mode of relationship between the one who has faith and the one in whom he or she has faith. Call the occupants of these two roles the *subject* and the *object*, respectively. Now think of the adjective "faithful." One might naturally be led to suppose that this means "full of faith," so that a faithful person is one who is outstanding in the subject role of the relationship, one who often, or readily, or fully has faith in others. But, as a moment's reflection will assure us, the use of the word is quite different. It has to do with the object role. A *faithful* person is one who is *worthy* of faith being reposed in him or her, *trustworthy*, reliable, loyal, steadfast, constant, and so on. It is as if the genius of the language puts the emphasis on the characteristics that inspire one to have faith in another, rather than in the having of that faith itself.[14]

This is an appropriate place at which to say something about "belief in" and its relation to the other concepts I have been discussing. I don't see a great difference between "belief in" and "faith in," certainly much less than between "belief that" and "faith that." "Belief in" would seem to carry an implication of a pro-attitude, though perhaps not as strongly as "faith in." Think of some typical cases. One believes in the public school system, foreign language study, regular exercise, the sacraments, one's plumber, one's adviser, manufacturers' guarantees, free enterprise. In all these cases it would be incoherent to express opposition to, for example, foreign language study in the same breath as expressing belief in it. This is vividly brought out in the old joke Q: "Do you believe in infant baptism?" A: "Believe in it! I've seen it done!" Even if belief in infant baptism presupposes that it is practiced (and we will soon see reasons for doubting this), it also essentially involves favoring it in some way.

As for the relation of "belief in" and "belief that," it is tempting to suppose that "belief in X" presupposes a belief that X exists. They often go together. But here too we must remember that, among positive propositional attitudes, acceptance is an alternative to belief. As I will be suggesting shortly, I can believe in God (trust in his providence) while *accepting* that He exists, rather than firmly believing this. Moreover, as Price points out, belief in X does not always presuppose any sort of positive attitude toward X's existence.[15] One can believe in equal pay for equal work even if one realizes that there has never yet been a society in which this is observed. Perhaps there is a difference here between things and states of affairs, such that believing in a "thing" presupposes its existence, while believing in a state of affairs does not presuppose that it is realized.

Religious Faith

Let this suffice as a survey of some salient aspects of faith in general. I now turn to religious faith. Since "faith" is a highly loaded positively evaluative term in religion, there is a tendency to attach it to whatever a particular thinker deems most important or central in a religious response to the divine. Thus we find Tillich characterizing faith as the "state of being ultimately concerned," where "ultimate concern" about X is, in turn, characterized as involving a number of elements—commitment to

X, taking X as a center of orientation for one's life, devotion and surrender to X, trusting X to provide ultimate salvation, and so on.[16] Clearly, Tillich has inflated the term so as to be a catchall for anything he deems to be centrally important in religion.[17] When this happens, "faith" loses its distinctive meaning as one element in religion among others. I want to think of religious faith in a more specific way as one important aspect of a total religious response, not the whole package. Since the concept exhibits somewhat different contours in different religions, I can keep the discussion manageable only by considering faith as it figures in a particular religious tradition.[18] For this purpose I consider the Christian tradition. What, then, is faith in Christianity?

It will be sufficient for our purposes here to point out that Christian faith essentially involves both cognitive and affective-attitudinal elements. The general discussion of faith foreshadows how this goes. On the cognitive side it involves some positive attitude toward the fundamental Christian doctrines as revealed to us by God. Thus, St. Thomas Aquinas says, "The act of faith is an act of the intellect assenting to divine truth at the command of the will moved by the grace of God."[19] Six centuries later at the First Vatican Council, the Roman church was saying the same thing, characterizing faith as "A supernatural virtue, by which, guided and aided by divine grace, we hold as true what God has revealed, not because we have perceived its intrinsic truth by our reason, but because of the authority of God who can neither deceive nor be deceived."[20] This latter formula makes explicit something that Aquinas elsewhere stresses, that faith does not count as *knowledge* because it, for the most part, does not concern matters that we can "see" to be true.[21] With respect to the Trinity and the Incarnation, for example, we would have no basis for believing these truths had God not revealed them to us, and moved us by a supernatural act of grace to accept them.

John Locke, writing in the seventeenth century and not as a theologian but as a philosopher, lays out a similar concept. He characterizes faith as "the assent to any proposition, not thus made out by the deductions of reason, but upon the credit of the proposer, as coming from God, in some extraordinary way of communication."[22]

It would appear from these passages that Aquinas's, and more generally the Roman Catholic, conception of faith is purely intellectual, a matter of a certain way of accepting certain propositions. But room is made for an affective-attitudinal aspect as well, though it is not given as much stress as in Lutheran and other Protestant formulations. Aquinas makes it explicit that faith is a virtue only if it is informed by love, which directs the will to the supreme end, namely, God.[23] So *love* of God must play a central role if faith is to be complete. In Luther and many other Protestant thinkers we find a stress on *trust* in God, complete reliance on the goodness and mercy of God who wills our salvation.

Much more could be said about the affective-attitudinal aspect of Christian faith, but since this essay is concerned with the cognitive side, I have made only a perfunctory bow in the former direction so as to set our central concern in its proper context.

Belief and Acceptance in Religious Faith

I now turn to the question for which all the above has been a propaedeutic, namely, how we are to think of the cognitive aspect of faith, and in particular, how the belief-acceptance distinction bears on this.

Contemporary discussions of religious faith on its cognitive side are almost entirely in terms of belief, especially philosophical discussions. I take it that the concept of belief used there is the one I adumbrated in the first section. I now want to explore the possibility that this exclusive concentration on belief is unfortunate and unrealistic, and that an adequate picture of the situation would allow an important place for acceptance in Christian faith.

The first point is that propositional belief and propositional acceptance are both to be found in Christianity. Some Christians have firm *beliefs* that, for example, Jesus of Nazareth was an incarnation of the second person of the Trinity, that he was resurrected after being crucified and buried, and that he is alive today and in personal relationship with the faithful. For them these are facts about which they have no more doubts than they do about their physical surroundings and the existence of their family and friends. Even if they can see how one *could* doubt or deny these doctrines, they are not themselves touched by this. Perhaps this has been part of their repertoire of constant belief for as long as they can remember, and nothing has come along to shake it.[24]

But not all sincere, active, committed, devout Christians are like this, especially in these secular, scientistic, intellectually unsettled times. Many committed Christians do not find themselves with such an assurance. A sense of the obvious truth of these articles of faith does not well up within them when they consider the matter. They *are* troubled by doubts; they ask themselves or others what reasons there are to believe that all this really happened. They take it as a live possibility that all or some central Christian doctrines are false. How, then, can they be sincere, committed Christians?

There are two ways. First, they may believe these doctrines but with less than full, undoubting confidence. But, second, they may *accept* them. The difference between these alternatives follows the earlier explanation of the distinction. To accept them is to perform a voluntary act of committing oneself to them, to *resolve* to use them as a basis for one's thought, attitude, and behavior. (And, of course, it involves being disposed to do so as a result of this voluntary acceptance.) Whereas to believe them, even if not with the fullest confidence, is to *find* oneself with that positive attitude toward them, to *feel* that, for example, Jesus of Nazareth died to reconcile us to God. That conviction, of whatever degree of strength, spontaneously wells up in one when one considers the matter. And so, at bottom, it is a difference between what one finds in oneself and what one has deliberately chosen to introduce in oneself.

Let's elaborate a bit on the acceptance alternative for Christian faith. Just as the philosopher described previously accepted the thesis of libertarian free will, though she did not spontaneously feel it to be the case, so it is with our (quasi) skeptical Christians. This can take several different forms. Perhaps such a person, having carefully considered the evidence and arguments pro and con, or as much of them as she is aware of, judges that there is a sufficient basis for *accepting* the doctrines, even though she does not find herself in a state of belief. Or perhaps she has been involved in the church from her early years, from a preskeptical time when she did fully believe, and she finds the involvement meeting deep needs and giving her life some meaning and structure.[25] And so she is motivated to accept Christian doctrines as a basis for her thought about the world and for the way she leads her life. Or perhaps the person is drawn into the church from a condition of religious noninvolvement, and responds actively to the church's message, finding in the Christian life something that is deeply satisfying, but without, as yet, spontaneously feeling the doctrines to be true. Such a person will again be moved to *accept* the doctrines as something on which she will build her thought and action.

In view of the concentration on belief in thought about religion, it is important to realize that the person who *accepts* the doctrines is not necessarily inferior to the *believer* in commitment to the Christian life, or in the seriousness, faithfulness, or intensity with which she pursues it. The accepter may pray just as faithfully, worship God just as regularly, strive as earnestly to follow the way of life enjoined on us by Christ, look as pervasively on interpersonal relationships, vocation, and social issues through the lens of the Christian faith. She will undoubtedly receive less comfort and consolation from her faith than the unquestioning believer to whom the whole thing seems certain. She will feel less assured of the life of the world to come, and in what she takes to be her interactions with God she will not be wholly free of nagging suspicions that it is all in her own mind (though such suspicions need not always arise). But the accepter can be as fully involved in the form of life, and not just on an "as if" basis. This is not a matter of resolving to act *as if* the doctrines are true, while not really taking seriously the idea that they are true. To *accept* the doctrines is to *accept* them as true. Since *Jesus was resurrected* is true *if and only if* Jesus was resurrected, I can't accept the latter without at least being committed to accepting the former. It is only the unthinking assumption that *belief* exhausts the possibilities for a positive attitude toward the articles of faith that gives rise to the judgment that the accepter is engaging in an elaborate make-believe or pretense.

Neither the believing nor the accepting groups are confined to cases like those I have indicated. As for the latter, I have already suggested some of the variety to be found there, but I need to give the former some attention too. One can be a believer, even a firm believer without having preserved intact an unquestioning faith from early childhood; converted believers are legion. St. Paul is a familiar paradigm, and if anyone has ever felt certain of the truth of Christian doctrine it was he. Again, as I pointed out above, it is possible for acceptance to turn into belief as one gets deeper and deeper into the religion one has accepted. Neither the believer nor the accepter is necessarily frozen forever into that stance. And I will point out once more that one can be in a condition that can be called belief even if it is a lesser degree of certainty or firmness than the strong belief on which I have been concentrating.

It is my distinct impression that a significant proportion of contemporary sincere, committed, devout Christians are accepters rather than believers. I have no direct statistical evidence to establish this. Gathering such evidence would require considerably more conceptual sophistication than one can expect from sociologists. And even if the sociologist had the distinction straight, it would be tricky to devise questionnaires that would elicit the information from a wide range of church goers. When we look at sociological surveys of "religious belief," we do not find our distinction in evidence. But there is considerable literary evidence, in spiritual autobiographies, for both the *belief* and the *acceptance* alternative among committed Christians. Consider, for example, two collections of faith stories of philosophers, Clark's *Philosophers Who Believe* and Morris's *God and the Philosophers*.[26] I will present a few samples from the latter. Some of the contributors clearly fall on the side of *belief*. Jerry L. Walls, for example, says "I was sure that I had met God and that He had granted me salvation" (103). "My relationship with God was very real to me" (103). "I had no doubt that it was God encountering me, speaking to me, forgiving me, and so on" (106). "I still believe I encountered God when I was eleven years old and have walked in His grace—often very imperfectly—ever since" (111). Marilyn Adams's contribution is filled with testimony such as "In my earliest years, a vivid sense of the reality of God came with mother's milk, with green grass and blue sky" (137). "I *knew* that God was an empirical entity; I had tasted and seen" (150). This is not to say that these people enjoyed an uninterrupted and untroubled enjoyment of their faith. Quite the contrary. The last quote from Adams, for example, continues, "I felt I was in a religious rut, but I didn't know what to do." But despite these ups and downs, the grasp of what is taken as Christian truth is one of feeling sure.

With other contributors it is a different story. William Wainwright tells us that "to this day I find it difficult to embrace *any* controversial belief without *some* hesitation" (78). The general picture is one of acceptance, rather than one of firm belief. "I have long thought that even if Christian theism isn't more probable than not, it is still reasonable to *embrace* it" (80, my emphasis). Most explicitly

> My attitude is in many ways similar to T. S. Eliot's. Eliot appears to have combined a deeply serious faith with both irony and skepticism. (When asked why he *accepted* Christianity, he said he did so because it was the least false of the options open to him . . .) I do not regard my stance as exemplary. If Christianity (or indeed any form of traditional theism) is true, a faith free from doubt is surely better. I suspect, however, that my religious life may be fairly representative of the lives of many intelligent, educated, and sincere Christians in the latter part of the twentieth century. (85, my emphasis)

Again, Jeff Jordan writes

> I should note, first, that my faith is perhaps best described as a hope rather than as a belief . . . I hope that the Christian message is true, and I try to act in the light of that hope. While I *assent* to the propositions of Christianity, I think it best to describe my faith as a hope rather than as a belief because I do not think I have rationally decisive evidence for the truth of Christian claims, and I realize that it is a real, but to my mind not a very likely, possibility that Christianity could turn out to be false. (134, my emphasis)

No doubt, philosophers are more articulate at bringing out distinctions than many other people, but it is my sense that the differing cognitive components of faith brought out so clearly in these passages are widely distributed among contemporary "believers."

If my impression is correct that acceptance as well as belief is common among committed Christians, it raises a question as to why this fact has so completely escaped notice in the mountain of literature on faith.[27] How is it that I can advance my thesis as a startling discovery? I think the answer is that the term "belief" has been allowed to spread over any positive propositional attitude. It has been used to apply indifferently to both sides of the distinction I have been emphasizing. This is reflected in dictionary entries. In the *Oxford English Dictionary*, we find among the entries for "believe"—"To give credence to, to accept (a statement) as true." And one of the main entries for "belief" reads, in part—"mental acceptance of a proposition . . . assent of the mind to a statement." It is also reflected in the widespread use of the term "believer" for an adherent of a religion.

There are many indications in the philosophical literature of this inflated use of "believe." I will mention one of the most striking. Philosophers who discuss the question of whether belief can be voluntary regularly take certain thinkers to give a positive answer to this question, where the passages cited in support of this clearly have to do with something in the area of acceptance, rather than with belief. For example, Louis Pojman in his generally excellent treatment of belief and the will, takes both Aquinas and Descartes to be voluntarists with respect to belief.[28] But in the material on which he bases these attributions, though these thinkers do clearly take something in the area of positive propositional attitudes to be voluntary, they are speaking about a mental act of the acceptance sort, rather than belief. We have already seen Aquinas characterize faith as "an act of the intellect assenting to divine truth at the command of the will moved by the grace of God." What is said here to be "at the command of the will" is a mental act of assent, what I have been calling "acceptance." And when he argues that faith can be meritorious because it proceeds from free choice, it is mental *assent* that is freely chosen.[29] As for Descartes, it is clear in the primary source for his voluntarism, Meditation IV, that it is some mental act that is said to be voluntary, rather than belief in the contemporary sense.[30]

. . . the will simply consists in our ability to do or not do something (that is, to *affirm* or *deny*, to pursue or avoid). . . . (40, my emphasis)

. . . If, however, I simply refrain from *making a judgement* in cases where I do not perceive the truth with sufficient clarity and distinctness, then it is clear that I am behaving correctly and avoiding error. But if in such cases I either *affirm* or *deny*, then I am not using my free will correctly. (41, my emphasis)

. . . it is surely no imperfection in God that he has given me the freedom to *assent* or *not to assent* in those cases where he did not endow my intellect with a clear and distinct perception; but it is undoubtedly an imperfection in me to misuse that freedom and *make judgements* about matters which I do not fully understand. (42, my emphasis)

Descartes consistently uses act terms, in the acceptance family, to specify what he is saying to be under the control of the will.

One thing that sometimes makes it difficult, though not in these cases, to determine whether a pre–twentieth century author is speaking of belief or acceptance is the widespread practice before our century of thinking of belief itself as an act. But when one uses "believe" for a mental *act*, that is clearly not the contemporary sense of "believe" with which I have been dealing.

Does Christianity Require Belief Rather Than Acceptance?

To resume the main line of the discussion, if we may take it that in fact many sincere, committed, devout Christians accept rather than believe many central Christian doctrines, that still leaves us with a normative question. Are they, by virtue of this, in violation of some basic Christian injunction? Even if they are heavily involved in the Christian way of life, are they still missing something that is essential to being a Christian in the fullest sense? Does Christianity require its devotees to *believe* the articles of faith, and not just to accept them?

If the question concerned what is the most desirable state possible (in this life) for a Christian, then it seems clear, as we saw Wainwright acknowledge, that this would include *believing* the claims of Christianity, rather than just *accepting* them. But that is not my question. I am asking whether the church *requires* of its adherents that they *believe* central Christian doctrines. Is one in violation of authoritative injunctions if one does not believe those propositions? Or is one in the clear, as far as what is required of a follower of Christ, if one *accepts* the doctrines in question?[31]

Obviously, what is taken as authoritative will differ somewhat for different denominations. And where acceptance or belief of certain doctrines is required, those doctrines will differ for different denominations. I can't go into all such variations in this chapter. What I will do is to look at some pronouncements that are widely recognized as authoritative and consider their bearing on our issue.

The first thing to note is that many formulations that are frequently read as involving propositional belief are better construed in terms either of acceptance or of "belief in" or of faith. First look at a couple of biblical passages that seem to require belief. In the Epistle to the Hebrews, we read, "For whoever would draw near to God must believe that he exists and that he rewards those who seek him" (11: 6). But the Greek verb translated "believe" in the Revised Standard version, from which I quote, and in many other translations, is *pisteuo*, the verbal form of the noun *pistis*, "faith." In English we lack a verb cognate of "faith," and this leads translators to settle on "believe" as the nearest English verb. But once we come to realize that it is not always belief that constitutes the cognitive aspect of faith, we can see that a better translation would be "have faith that he exists" (as in the Good News translation). Propositional *"faith"* can involve either belief or acceptance. Again, in Mark 16:16, typically translated as "he who does not believe will be condemned," the verb rendered "believe" is once more *pisteuo*.[32]

The formulations outside the Bible most widely accepted as authoritative are the Nicene and the Apostle's creeds. Here "believe" appears only in the "believe in" form. In the Apostle's Creed, "I believe *in* God, the Father almighty, maker of heaven and earth, And *in* Jesus Christ his only Son our Lord . . . I believe *in* the Holy Ghost, the holy catholic Church, the communion of saints." It is the same story with the Nicene Creed. "I believe *in* one God, the Father Almighty . . . and *in* one Lord Jesus Christ . . . And I believe *in* the Holy Ghost the Lord and Giver of Life . . . And I believe *in* one holy Catholic and Apostolic Church." Of course, believing *in* God the Father, Christ, and the Holy Ghost, and believing *in* the church, presupposes various propositional commitments, that God exists and did create heaven and earth, that Jesus Christ is His son who came down from heaven, and so on. But there is nothing in the language of the creeds that requires these commitments to be *beliefs* rather than *acceptances*.

For another example, look at the Baptismal Service in the Episcopal *Book of Common Prayer*, a form that in its essentials goes far back in the Christian tradition.[33] Here no propositional *beliefs* are required of the candidates (or their sponsors in the case of infants). They are required to renounce various things, for example, "Satan and all the spiritual forces of wickedness that rebel against God"; they are required to affirm that they accept Jesus Christ as their Savior and put their whole trust in his grace and love; they are required to promise to follow Jesus Christ and obey him as their Lord. They are required to affirm the Apostle's Creed, and to commit themselves to various lines of action, for example, proclaiming by word and example the Good News of God in Christ. But nowhere is the candidate required to make a statement of the form "I believe that _____."

This last example may lead readers of a Reformed or Baptist or old-line Roman Catholic persuasion to reply that this is what might be expected of a wishy-washy liberal crew like the Episcopal Church and the Anglican Communion in general. But if we look at some of the classic "confessions" of groups like these, it is still not clear that propositional *belief*, rather than *acceptance*, is required. Consider the "Profession of the Tridentine Faith" (1563), faith in the doctrines propounded by the Council of Trent. Except for the opening, which speaks of believing every one of the things contained in the Nicene Creed (and we have seen how belief enters there), the terms used with "that" clauses are "admit" (*admitto*), "embrace" (*amplector*), "profess" (*profiteor*), "receive" (*recipio*), "confess" (*fateor*), "assert" (*assero*), and "acknowledge" (*agnosco*). These are all terms that belong on the *acceptance* side of our contrast. And if we look at the major Protestant confessions, such as the Augsburg Confessions (1530), the Thirty-Nine Articles of the Church of England (1571), or the Westminster Confession (1647), we find that they consist of doctrinal statements without any explicit injunction to any one to believe any propositions.[34] Naturally, in putting these bodies of doctrines forward as "confessions" the plain intent is to formulate what is held in common by full-fledged members of the communion in question. But there is no indication that anyone is required to *believe* these doctrines rather than to *accept* them.

Wilfred Cantwell Smith argues that our currently familiar propositional sense of "believe" is a relative newcomer to religious discourse.[35] He amply documents the fact that "believe" originally meant "to hold dear" or "to love," as its German relative *belieben* still does. One of his examples involves two manuscripts of a thirteenth-century poetical composition. At a certain point, one manuscript has (in modern rendering) "to her he had love" while the other has "in her he believed." Even as late as Shakespeare's *All's Well That Ends Well*, when the king says to Bertram, "Believe not thy disdain," this is not to be understood as exhorting the hearer not to believe (in our sense) that he has disdain, but rather not to cherish, foster, or hold dear the disdain that he obviously has.[36] To be sure, the fact that "believe" prior to the sixteenth century or so didn't mean what it does currently, doesn't show that the English prior to that time lacked the current concept of propositional belief or that they didn't have other linguistic means of expressing it. But at least it shows this. When the King James translation of the Bible or the early Anglican prayer books use "believe," we cannot suppose without more ado that the word is being used in its familiar contemporary propositional sense.

I do not mean to deny, of course, that in certain quarters belief, and even firm, undoubting belief, is taken as normative for Christians. It is even sometimes taken as a mark of being "saved," and its lack as a mark of being unsaved. Perhaps unawareness of the belief-acceptance distinction is playing a role here, though even if that distinction were fully appreciated, there would, no doubt, be some who would still take the elect to be restricted to the firm believers. Nevertheless, the above survey indicates, at the very least, that it is more difficult than one might have thought to find support for such attitudes in scripture and in classic Christian creeds and confessions.

My central thesis in this paper is distinct from some other recent attempts to find an alternative to belief as a component of faith. For example, James Muyskens plumps for *hope* as the crucial propositional attitude in faith.[37] But acceptance is quite different from hope. I can hope that God will grant me what it takes to carry out tasks He gives me without accepting the proposition that He will. Indeed, what I *hope* for is typically something the reality of which I do not accept. In the usual case, I hope that Jim will keep his promise only if I neither accept nor believe the proposition that he will.[38]

Robert Audi's suggestion that propositional faith is distinguishable from propositional belief may be closer to my suggestion.[39] However, Audi's propositional faith does not seem to be identical to my acceptance. Though Audi's exposition leaves me without a clear grasp of his concept, it seems that he takes it not to be or involve any sort of act that is under voluntary control.[40]

How Recognition of Religious Acceptance Helps Resolve Difficulties

I can further elucidate, as well as recommend, my suggestions in this essay by exploring the application of the belief-acceptance distinction, in the religious sphere, to certain issues and problems.

1. An appreciation of the distinction, and of the possibilities of genuine Christian faith based on acceptance, can alleviate nagging worries about "lack of faith," where the source of the worry is a lack of belief,

the absence of any spontaneous feeling of certainty that, for example, Christ atoned for our sins. The frequency of this kind of concern is amply borne out by Christian spiritual autobiography. And if one comes to realize that a full, committed Christian life can involve acceptance of the doctrines in question, rather than belief, one may be spared much gratuitous anxiety. One can proceed more serenely and confidently with one's Christian life, while hoping and praying that one may come to believe what one now accepts.

2. Turning to more theoretical matters, I have already hinted that puzzles about whether religious faith is under voluntary control can be alleviated by the recognition that it can involve acceptance rather than belief. Such puzzles arise in connection with the idea that faith is *required* of the "believer," and that it is *meritorious*, while its absence is a demerit. But if the faith in question must contain certain propositional beliefs, and these are not within our voluntary control, how can anyone require us to have faith, and how can any merit attach to our doing so? Robert Adams wrestles earnestly with this problem and attempts to solve it by maintaining that we can be culpable, or the reverse, for items that are not under our voluntary control, provided they are items *we should repent of*.[41] This is how unbelief can be a sin and belief a virtue. But if we recognize that insofar as faith is *required* and lack of faith something for which we can be culpable, the cognitive element thereof is acceptance, which is under our voluntary control, rather than belief, the puzzle need never arise. We can give a much more straightforward account of how faith is a virtue and lack of faith a sin, without engaging in the pyrotechnics Adams feels called upon to produce. Needless to say, even if the cognitive aspect of faith is under effective voluntary control, that is not sufficient to render faith a virtue and its lack a vice. Voluntary control is only a necessary, not a sufficient condition. But it is the only one of the conditions that I am concerned with here.

3. Revisionist theologians often aver that this or that traditional Christian doctrine is "unbelievable" by people today, or at least unbelievable by those who are imbued with the modern "scientific ethos," or who take seriously the historical-critical method, or who are sufficiently reflective. This motivates these thinkers to reinterpret those doctrines in such a way as to be believable. Here is a recent example from John Shelby Spong concerning the resurrection.

> I cannot say my yes to legends that have been clearly and fancifully created.
> If I could not move my search beyond angelic messengers, empty tombs,
> and ghostlike apparitions, I could not say yes to Easter. I will not allow my

twentieth-century mind to be compromised by the literalism of another era that is not capable of being believed in a literal way today. If the resurrection of Jesus cannot be believed except by assenting to the fantastic descriptions included in the Gospels, then Christianity is doomed. For that view of the resurrection is not believable, and if that is all there is, then Christianity, which depends upon the truth and authenticity of Jesus' resurrection, also is not believable.[42]

But all this ignores the belief-acceptance distinction. Suppose these thinkers are right in taking certain fundamental Christian doctrines, as traditionally understood, to be unbelievable by contemporaries, at least those who satisfy certain widely satisfied conditions. I do not believe this to be the case, but suppose I am wrong about that. In any event, it seems clear that many Christians, especially now, do not find themselves believing in, for example, a bodily resurrection of Jesus from the dead in the distinctive sense of belief. This will not seem to require a reinterpretation of the doctrine unless the belief-acceptance distinction is ignored. For even if I don't find myself spontaneously feeling that this is what happened, and even if this is impossible for me, it is still within my power to *accept* the doctrine, at least provided I take there to be sufficient reasons to do so.[43]

4. Finally, there is a question to which the distinction gives rise, rather than a prior question on which the distinction throws light. Do belief and acceptance have different statuses vis-à-vis the need for evidence, reasons, grounds? Do judgments of rationality or irrationality, justifiability or the reverse, apply differently to them? Or is the same story to be told about the two?

In discussing this, I will not undertake to get into the complex and thorny question of the way in which, or the extent to which, sufficient grounds, evidence, or reasons are required for rational or justified religious faith. In order to compare belief and acceptance on this point, let's assume for the sake of argument that there is a significant dimension of assessment of religious faith on which sufficient reasons constitute a good-making feature, and the lack of such reasons a bad-making feature. Call this dimension "justifiability." Does this mode of assessment apply to religious belief and acceptance in the same way?

The crucial thing to note here is the distinction between a "deontological" concept of justifiability, according to which being justified is a matter of satisfying, or not violating, intellectual obligations; and an "evaluative" conception, on which being justified is a matter of one's cognitive state satisfying certain desiderata, but where notions like permission, requirement, responsibility, and the like do not come into the picture. It is because of the voluntariness issue that this makes a difference. Since acceptance is straightforwardly under voluntary control, a deontological conception of justification is unproblematically applicable. I may fail to accept a proposition I could have accepted when I ought to do so, or accept a proposition I could and should not have accepted. The deontological terms "ought" and "should" are (sometimes) applicable to acceptance. When they are, acceptances and failures to accept can be epistemically assessed in deontological terms. But since belief is not under effective voluntary control, this concept of justification is not applicable. The most we can do along these lines is to assess a belief in terms of what the believer has voluntarily done or failed to do in the past, such that these commissions or omissions have influenced the present state of belief.

With an evaluative conception of justification, on the other hand, it would seem that belief and acceptance are on all fours. Both belief that *p* and acceptance that *p* can be assessed for epistemic goodness or excellence, for example, in terms of whether one has adequate grounds for them, or whether they are based on adequate grounds.

An appreciation of the belief-acceptance distinction can open up new vistas in a variety of fields. If it is taken seriously, epistemology will be significantly transformed, since practically all recent epistemology has been hypnotically focused on belief when anything short of knowledge is discussed. Ever so many topics—justification, the internalism-externalism contrast, foundationalism, the role of coherence, the possibility of immediate justification—will have to be rethought to take into account the possibility that the applications to belief and acceptance have to be worked out separately. In this essay I have suggested that attention to the distinction will powerfully affect our understanding of the cognitive aspect of religious faith. I have mentioned only a few of the fallouts from that reexamination. I hope that others will join me in continuing the project.[44]

2

The Divine Command Ethics in
Kierkegaard's *Works of Love*

Philip L. Quinn

It is a striking feature of the ethics of love set forth in the Gospels that love is the subject of a command. In Matthew's gospel, Jesus states it in response to a question from a lawyer about which commandment of the law is the greatest. He says, "You shall love the lord your God with your whole heart, with your whole soul, and with all your mind. This is the greatest and first commandment. The second is like it: You shall love your neighbor as yourself. On these two commandments the whole law is based, and the prophets as well."[45] Mark 12:29–31 tells of Jesus giving essentially the same answer to a question by a scribe, and Luke 10:27–28 speaks of a lawyer giving this answer to a question from Jesus and being told by Jesus that he has answered correctly. In his last discourse, recorded in John's gospel, Jesus tells his followers that "the command I give you is this, that you love one another."[46] So the authors of those documents concur in thinking that Jesus expressed, or approved of others expressing, his ethics of love in the form of an ethical demand, a command that we love one another and our neighbors as ourselves.

It might be thought that this manner of expression is inessential to a Christian ethics of love of neighbor, arising merely from the fact that Jesus is portrayed as propounding the ethics of love in the course of discussion with lawyers or scribes who are concerned about his views on questions of law. Because the questions being discussed are legalistic in nature, it might be said, it is not surprising that Jesus uses or approves legalistic rhetoric involving talk of commands in the specific context of answering them. By itself, the fact that a Christian ethics of love can be put in terms of commands does not imply that it must be formulated or is best articulated in such terms. To be sure, Jesus commands love not only when addressing Pharisees who are hostile to him but also when addressing followers who are committed to him. But I think that even this consideration need not be regarded as decisive if there is no reason to believe that the particular sort of love Jesus wants people to have must, at least in the first instance, be commanded. Is there such a reason?

I think there is. To a first approximation, it is that the love of neighbor of which Jesus speaks is unnatural for humans in their present fallen condition. It does not spontaneously engage their affections, and so training, self-discipline, and, perhaps, even divine assistance are needed to make its achievement a real possibility. For most of us most of the time, love of neighbor is not an attractive goal, and, if it were optional or supererogatory, we simply would not pursue it. To get us to have such love, it must be presented to us as an obligatory love with the feel of something that represents a curb or check on our natural desires, inclinations, and predilections. In the religious tradition of Jesus and his hearers, it is taken for granted that divine commands give rise to obligations, and so an obligatory love would in that tradition naturally be represented as commanded by a divine lawgiver. It is, then, no accident that the love of neighbor the Gospels propose to us is, as Soren Kierkegaard says, a *"commanded* love."[47]

In my opinion, no Christian thinker has seen with greater clarity than he just how radical the demands of love of neighbor really are. In *Works of Love*, Kierkegaard addresses the reader in his own name, presenting, as the subtitle indicates, some Christian reflections in the form of discourses. Part One, Section II, is a discourse on Matthew 22:39, which is contained in the passage quoted above. This discourse is divided into three parts. Subsection IIA is called "You *Shall* Love"; subsection IIB "You Shall Love Your *Neighbor;*" and subsection IIC bears the title "*You* Shall Love Your Neighbor". This chapter is an exposition and critical examination of some of what Kierkegaard has to say in this discourse about the second part of the Great Commandment: You shall love your neighbor as yourself. My aim is to show that he here sets forth a view, which is for the most part defensible, of what is distinctively Christian in Christian ethics. I do not claim that what Kierkegaard calls "this Christian imperative" (40) recommends itself to those who lack Christian faith. Nor does he make such a claim. On the contrary, he insists that if a pagan is confronted with this command, it "will not only surprise him but will disturb him and be an offence to him" (41).

This chapter is divided into three parts. In the first I follow Kierkegaard in characterizing commanded Christian love of neighbor by means of some contrasts with two more familiar kinds of love, erotic love and friendship. I argue that Kierkegaard takes commanded love of neighbor to be immune from the mutability and partiality that infect other forms of love. In the second part I highlight the element of offense Kierkegaard insists is present in the claim that Christian love of neighbor has to be impartial. I consider in some detail the objection that impartial benevolence falls short of being full-fledged love. In the third part I discuss Kierkegaard's response and argue that it mitigates but does not remove the offense. Of course, this is just what one would expect in light of Kierkegaard's interest in stressing the difficulties of Christianity both in theory and practice. A brief epilogue is devoted to Kierkegaard's treatment of the suggestion that the consummation of Christian love of neighbor transcends the domain of the love commandment.

Love Neither Mutable Nor Preferential

It is a commonplace of Christian thought that there is a distinctively Christian form of love (*agape, caritas*), which stands in sharp contrast to both erotic love (*eros, amor*), and friendship (*philia, amicitia*). Early in the subsection of *Works of Love* titled "You *Shall* Love," Kierkegaard appeals to this contrast. The aim of both erotic love and friendship is to love this single human being above all others, to love this single human being in distinction from all others. According to Kierkegaard, "The object of both erotic love and friendship has therefore also the favorite's name, *the beloved, the friend,* who is loved in distinction from the rest of the world. On the other hand, the Christian teaching is to love one's neighbour, to love all mankind, all men, even enemies, and not to make exceptions, neither in favouritism nor in aversion" (36).

What is more, the Christian teaching is that love of neighbor is a duty imposed by a scriptural command. And being a duty is, Kierkegaard thinks, a necessary condition for securing love of neighbor against kinds of mutability that often destroy erotic love and friendship. As he puts the point, "*only when it is a duty to love, only then is love eternally secured against every change, eternally made free in blessed independence, eternally and happily secured against despair*" (44). When it is unpacked, this remark is, as we shall see, quite plausible.

When Kierkegaard speaks of securing love against change, he has in mind changes in the natural desires and inclinations that are constitutive of erotic love and friendship. They sometimes spontaneously change even when there is no change in the object of love or in the lover's beliefs about that object. As Kierkegaard notes, love grounded in natural inclinations can mutate into hate or jealousy. Such a love can fade, losing "its ardour, its joy, its desire, its originative power, its living freshness" (50). Robert Brown's recent book, *Analyzing Love*, confirms Kierkegaard on this point. Brown observes: "A woman's love for her husband can change into dislike even though her appraisal of his character or personality is unaltered. She can simply become bored with him for displaying the same familiar characteristics, each of which she still values but no longer wishes to observe at such close quarters."[48] Only if love of neighbor is a duty, Kierkegaard supposes, can it be properly motivated by a stable sense of duty. And only thus can it be rendered invulnerable to changes in our emotions, moods, and tastes.

When Kierkegaard speaks of making love free in blessed independence, he has in mind independence of mutable characteristics of the object of love. The dependence of erotic love and friendship on mutable characteristics of the beloved and the friend make them vulnerable to changes in their objects. If the beloved loses the traits in virtue of which she or he was erotically attractive, then erotic love without illusion dies. If the friend who was cherished for having a virtuous character turns vicious, then the friendship is not likely to survive unless one is corrupted and turns vicious too. But Christian love of neighbor is to be invulnerable to alterations in its object. Kierkegaard says

> To be sure, you can also continue to love your beloved and your friend no matter how they treat you, but you cannot truthfully continue to call them beloved and friend when they, sorry to say, have really changed. No change, however, can take your neighbour from you, for it is not your neighbour who holds you fast—it is your love which holds your neighbour fast. If your love for your neighbour remains unchanged, then your neighbour also remains unchanged just by being. (76)

If there is to be such a love that alters not where it finds alteration, it cannot be held fast by or depend on mutable features of the neighbor. According to Kierkegaard, it will have the requisite independence of such features only if it is a duty, for only then can it be motivated by a sense of duty instead of by affections or preferences that change in response to alterations in the object of love. "In this way," he says, "the 'You shall' makes love free in blessed independence; such a love stands and does not fall with variations in the object of love; it stands and falls with eternity's law, but therefore it never falls" (53). Or at least it need never fall since we may assume that, because we ought to obey eternity's law, we can always obey it.

When Kierkegaard speaks of securing love against despair, he is referring in the first instance to the unhappiness the lover feels in response to misfortunes such as the loss of the beloved or the friend. But he takes despairing unhappiness to be a symptom of the underlying state of being in despair, which is a disrelationship in one's inmost being. One can be in despair even though one's erotic loves and friendships are happy and free from misfortune. Being in despair, Kierkegaard tells us, consists in "relating oneself with infinite passion to a single individual, for with infinite passion one can relate oneself—if one is not in despair— only to the eternal" (54). In other words, one who is in despair cleaves to a finite temporal good with an infinite passion that is only properly directed to an eternal good. The only remedy for being in despair is to undergo the transformation of the eternal by investing infinite passion in obeying the commandment to love. Kierkegaard says, "Despair is to lack the eternal; despair consists in not having undergone the transformation of the eternal through duty's 'You shall.' Despair is not, therefore, the loss of the beloved—that is misfortune, pain, and suffering; but despair is the lack of the eternal" (55).

The transformation of the eternal is no cure for unhappiness. It does not remove the pain and suffering involved in the loss of the object of love. However, the command makes it a duty to love despite the risk of unhappiness and to go on loving in the face of pain and suffering brought about by loss. The courage required for not giving up on love even when severe unhappiness tempts one to despair of it can be bolstered by the thought that the command to love has a divine source. Kierkegaard asks, "Who would have this courage without the eternal; who is prepared to say this 'You shall' without the eternal, which, in the very moment when love wants to despair over its unhappiness, commands one to love?" (55). I think the answer is that without the eternal, few if any of us would be prepared to make such a demand and fewer still would have the courage to live up to it.

According to Kierkegaard, then, three things threaten to destroy our loves. There are changes in our inclinations and emotions, changes in the object of love, and unhappiness about misfortune that prompts despair of love. Such things often enough do destroy our erotic loves and friendships. Love of neighbor will not be vulnerable to the first two of them only if it is a duty and so compliance is motivated by a sense of duty independent of inclinations, emotions, and mutable characteristics of the neighbor. It will not be vulnerable to the third of them, Kierke- gaard suggests, only if it is a duty whose source is the eternal, a duty imposed, as some Christian traditions teach, by a divine command. In other words, only that love that is obedient to the divine command is immutable.

Erotic love and friendship differ from Christian love of neighbor in another important way. In the subsection of *Works of Love* called "You Shall Love Your *Neighbour*," Kierkegaard contends that erotic love and friendship are both infected with partiality because they are based on exclusive preferences. They elicit praise from poets on account of this exclusivity. Poetically understood, Kierkegaard insists, "it is good fortune, the highest good fortune, to fall in love, to find the one and only beloved; it is good fortune, almost as great, to find the one and only friend" (64). The one and only beloved or the one and only friend is the object of a passionate preference that Kierkegaard considers akin to self-love. "Just as self-love centres exclusively about this *self*—whereby it is self-love," he says, "just so does erotic love's passionate preference centre around the one and only beloved and friendship's passionate preference around the friend" (66). What is more, exclusive love cherishes features that differentiate the beloved or the friend from other people. According to Kierkegaard, "in erotic love and friendship the two love one another in virtue of differences or in virtue of likenesses which are grounded in differences (as when two friends love one another on the basis of the likeness by which they are different from other men or in which they are like each other as different from other men)" (69). Confirmation for the view that erotic love and friendship are exclusive loves comes to us on the authority of Aristotle. He restricts the highest kind of friendship to good people who are equal in virtue and holds that we must be content with only a few friends of this kind. "One cannot be a friend to many people in the sense of having friendship of the perfect type with them," he maintains, "just as one cannot be in love with many people at once (for love is a sort of excess of feeling, and it is the nature of such only to be felt towards one person); and it is not easy for many people at the same time to please the same person very greatly, or perhaps even to be good in his eyes."[49]

By contrast, Christian love of neighbor involves renunciation of self, does not play favorites, and is all-inclusive. As Kierkegaard sees it, the disagreement between the poet and the Christian is simple, sharp, and deep: "The point at issue between the poet and Christianity may be stated precisely in this way: *erotic love and friendship are preferential and the passion of preference. Christian love is self-renunciation's love* and therefore trusts in this *shall*. To exhaust these passions would make one's head swim. But the most passionate boundlessness of preference in excluding others is to love only the one and only; self-renunciation's boundlessness in giving itself is not to exclude a single one" (65). But the passion of preference is rooted in our natural inclinations and predilections. In order to counteract it or, as Kierkegaard puts it, to thrust erotic love and friendship from the throne, Christianity needs something that can win a struggle against natural inclinations. As Kierkegaard sees it, Christianity proposes for this role dutiful obedience to the divine command, this *shall*, to love God and the neighbor. Motivated by a sense of duty that goes contrary to natural inclinations, the Christian can make love of God rather than preference the middle term in love to the neighbor; only in this way can the Christian get beyond exclusive loves driven by the passion of preference. Kierkegaard says, "Only by loving God above all else can one love his neighbour in the next human being. The next human being—this [is] the next human being in the sense that the next human being is every other human being" (70). In short, only if it is mediated by the commanded love of God can the commanded love of neighbor embrace every other human being, excluding no one on preferential grounds.

Because it is to be all-inclusive, commanded Christian love of neighbor cannot rest on differences among persons or on likenesses that are grounded in differences. It demands, Kierkegaard observes, eternal equality in loving, which is just the opposite of exclusive love or preference. He explains: "Equality is just this, not to make distinctions, and eternal equality is absolutely not to make the slightest distinction, is unqualifiedly not to make the slightest distinction. Exclusive love or preference, on the other hand, means to make distinctions, passionate distinctions, unqualifiedly to make distinctions" (70).

This is a remarkable and unnatural demand. Is it even possible to love without making distinctions? And if it is possible, is such undiscriminating love desirable? Can anything that goes so much against the grain of our natural inclinations really be a human duty? Kierkegaard is well aware that questions such as these are bound to arise. He insists that the command to love one's neighbor, interpreted in this way, will be, like much else in Christianity, an offense to many. Yet, despite that, he urges us to obey it. "Only acknowledge it," he pleads, "or if it is disturbing to you to have it put in this way, I will admit that many times it has thrust me back and that I am yet very far from the illusion that I fulfill this command, which to flesh and blood is offence, and to wisdom foolishness" (71). It is, I think, worth dwelling at some length on why it is disturbing to be asked to acknowledge this command, why one is apt to be thrust back by it if one considers it in a cool hour.

Drawing Out the Offense

Members of the caring professions such as physicians, nurses, and welfare workers are expected to exercise disinterested care for their patients or clients. They have role-specific duties to act with disinterested benevolence. It might be thought that the command to love the neighbor does no more than impose on everyone, independent of special roles, the duty to exercise disinterested care for those in need of it. The story of the Good Samaritan, which Jesus tells in Luke 10:30–37 in order to illustrate love of neighbor, might be read as nothing more than a parable of action from disinterested benevolence. And if this is all the love command requires of us, there is no reason to consider it offensive or foolish.

So if we are to capture the sense in which the command to love the neighbor is to flesh and blood an offense, we must suppose there is more to such commanded love than disinterested benevolence. Robert Brown's distinction between loving care and benevolence enables us to say something about how loving care differs from disinterested care. According to Brown, a necessary feature of the sort of love involved in giving loving care is affection in the sense of tender concern. He observes that "a person can display disinterested care out of a sense of religious duty without displaying any affectionate sensitivity to the individual character of the recipient. If this special consideration is absent the relationship cannot be one of personal love; the recipient is not being singled out by the agent for attentive regard and is not being given a special favourable place in the agent's estimation."[50] Let us assume, then, that commanded love of neighbor has to be a personal love that singles out the neighbor for attentive regard and gives the neighbor a special favorable place in one's estimation. On this assumption, there is indeed something offensive about the love command. Many of those who must be embraced by a love of neighbor that is not exclusive turn out, when attentively regarded, not to deserve a favorable place in one's estimation, or so it appears judging by ordinary lights. Thus it seems as if the love command tells us to esteem some people who, we justifiably believe, deserve no such thing.

Moreover, as Brown remarks, there is reason to think it is impossible to give loving care rather than disinterested care to more than a few people. Though in principle benevolence can extend to any number of people, subject only to limits on time and energy, personal love seems bound to be more restricted in scope. Brown claims, "A relationship of affectionate care, on the other hand, is limited in its number of participants by the limitations imposed by the requirements of interest, attention, committal, and intimacy. Because we cannot be equally interested in, attentive to, committed to, and intimate with, a large number of people, we cannot enter into relationships of equally affectionate care with them.''[51]

If this is the case, presumably it would be foolish to demand that members of the caring professions give affectionate or loving care, as opposed to disinterested care, to all their patients or clients. Unless they restricted their practices, they simply could not do what was being demanded of them. For the same reason, it would appear to be foolish to require of anyone love of neighbor that calls for loving care and yet excludes no one. Hence, if we cannot sustain relationships of equally affectionate care with large numbers of people, Kierkegaard appears to be foolish in claiming that one must love one's neighbor in the next human being in the sense that the next human being is every other human being while insisting that love of neighbor involves eternal equality in loving. It seems, in other words, as though there are hard choices to be made between inclusive but disinterested benevolence and affectionate but exclusive love. And if I read him aright, Kierkegaard thinks Christianity is apt to offend because it tells us that we must not make such choices, that we are commanded instead to love both affectionately and inclusively.

There is another reason to doubt the very possibility of an eternal equality in loving that does not make the slightest distinction. We can, I suppose, love or cherish universals, multiply instantiable properties such as generosity or wisdom. To love a property would involve loving any instance of it as an exemplification of it. There is, however, room here for a distinction between particulars we love because they exemplify one or more of the universals we cherish and particulars we do not love because they exemplify none of the universals we cherish. We also claim to love particular persons who are instances of universals we cherish without loving everyone who has those qualities, and I assume that such claims are often true. But they seem puzzling if it is supposed that in loving a particular person one loves the sheer particularity of the person apart from and independent of the person's qualities. This would be like loving a bare particular if there were such things. Brown suggests what I take to be an adequate solution to the puzzle. He urges that "it is true that when the agent loves another person, and not merely some of that person's qualities, the agent is cherishing, in part, a particular complex of instantiated qualities. It is a complex, however, that is made unique for the agent and the partner by occurring at certain times and places, and by thus having an unrepeatable career or history.''[52]

We can, it seems clear, love more than one particular person by cherishing more than one such complex of qualities, contrary to what Kierkegaard suggests when, exaggerating for rhetorical purposes, he speaks of loving only the one and only. Even so, there is a distinction to be drawn between those complexes of qualities with unrepeatable careers we do cherish and those we do not, between the particular persons we love and those we do not. And, of course, we can love particular persons both because we value them as unique individuals who instantiate a complex of qualities with an unrepeatable career we cherish and because we value them as instances of universals we cherish wherever they are exemplified. But in all these cases, we love persons in virtue of and on account of qualities they possess, qualities that distinguish them from other persons.

It is far from clear that there is an alternative way of loving persons. To be sure, human persons are eternally equal in some respects; there are no distinctions among them in those respects. All human persons are rational animals, or at least they possess whatever properties define our species if there are any. But can anyone love rational animality and thereby love all its instances as exemplifications of it? All human beings are, along with many other things, particulars. But can anything be loved merely in virtue of its possessing an abstract metaphysical property such as particularity? Most if not all human persons have the characteristic humanity, whatever it may be, which, according to Kant, must always be treated as an end and never as a mere means. But can this characteristic inspire affectionate love as well as detached moral respect? When we prescind from considering properties that distinguish among human persons, it is not evident that the properties that remain, either singly or in combination, can forge or sustain the bonds of the affection ingredient in loving care. So there is reason to be skeptical about whether anyone can be the object of affectionate care in virtue of and on account of qualities he or she shares with all human persons. Kierkegaard's demand for eternal equality in loving, when construed as a call for loving care of the neighbor rather than mere disinterested benevolence, therefore does indeed seem to be foolishness, not only from the point of view of pagan wisdom but even from the perspective of sober philosophical good sense. On this interpretation of what is involved in giving loving care, Kierkegaard is right in thinking that the love command is an offense to flesh and blood.

Kierkegaard against Distinctions

Despite the apparent offense and foolishness, there seem to be actual cases of Christian love of neighbor. It may be helpful to have one before us:

The Armenian Christians are a people who have experienced centuries of suffering and know that their worship is surrounded by a cloud of martyred witnesses. A Turkish officer has raided and looted an Armenian home. He killed the aged parents and gave the daughters to the soldiers, keeping the eldest daughter for himself. Sometime later she escaped and trained as a nurse. As time passed, she found herself nursing in a ward of Turkish officers. One night, by the light of a lantern, she saw the face of this officer. He was so gravely ill that without exceptional nursing he would die. The days passed, and he recovered. One day, the doctor stood by the bed with her and said to him, "But for her devotion to you, you would be dead." He looked at her and said, "We have met before, haven't we?" "Yes," she said, "we have met before." "Why didn't you kill me?" he asked. She replied, "I am a follower of him who said 'Love your enemies.' "53

This story, to be sure, does not explicitly say that the Armenian nurse gave the Turkish officer loving care rather than mere disinterested care. In it, however, the doctor speaks of her devotion to the officer which made it possible for her to give him the exceptional care without which he would have died. Surely killing him or letting him die out of hatred would have been a perfectly natural response for her; she must have been able to mobilize extraordinary inner resources to counteract the tendency to be moved by hatred and its allies among the emotions. I think it is plausible to imagine, if only for the sake of fleshing out the story, that the sort of affectionate sensitivity involved in giving loving care was among those resources.

In the subsection of *Works of Love* titled "*You* Shall Love Your Neighbour," Kierkegaard insists that the love command is addressed to you, the reader and imagined hearer of his discourses, and so to everyone. There he connects loving one's enemies to love of neighbor by means of a polemic against making distinctions. One's enemies are among one's neighbors:

Therefore he who in truth loves his neighbour loves also his enemy. The distinction *friend* or *enemy* is a distinction in the object of love, but the object of love to one's neighbour is without distinction. One's neighbour is the absolutely unrecognisable distinction between man and man; it is eternal equality before God—enemies, too, have this equality. Men think that it is impossible for a human being to love his enemies, for enemies are hardly able to endure the sight of one another. Well, then, shut your eyes—and your enemy looks just like your neighbour. Shut your eyes and remember the command that *you* shall love; then you are to love—your enemy? No. Then love your neighbour, for you cannot see that he is your enemy. (79)

But the enemy provides only a special case of a general truth. It is true, according to Kierkegaard, that "one sees his neighbour only with closed

eyes or by looking *away from* all distinctions" (79). Yet the failure to
mark distinctions among persons does not render love to one's neighbor
blind or evasive; it is not a defective love. On the contrary, it is,
Kierkegaard tells us, "precisely because one's neighbour has none of the
excellences which the beloved, a friend, a cultured person, an admired
one, and a rare and extraordinary one have in high degree—for that very
reason love to one's neighbour has all the perfections which love to a
beloved one, a friend, a cultured person, an admired one, a rare and
extraordinary one, does not have" (77). So it is supposed to be a virtue,
or even a perfection, in love of neighbor that it shuts its eyes to, or averts
them from, excellences in the object of love other kinds of love cherish.
This is, at the very least, a conterintuitive supposition. Far from removing
the apparent offense attached to the love command when he insists that
it is addressed to us, Kierkegaard acts to sharpen and spotlight it.

But he also gives us something to mitigate it. As he develops the
seemingly paradoxical metaphor of seeing with closed eyes, he suggests
that something positive may become visible when but only when ordinary faculties of discernment are switched off. Closing one's eyes to
distinctions among persons may enable one to envisage something in
them hidden from ordinary sight, something to be discerned only with
divine help. Kierkegaard says, "When one walks with God, he no doubt
walks free from danger, but one is also constrained to see and to see in a
unique way. When you walk in company with God you need to see only
one single person in misery, and you will not be able to escape what
Christianity will have you understand, human likeness" (87).

What does this unique way of seeing reveal in the person in misery? It
might be described in scriptural language as the image of God in
that person, for Christianity teaches that all human persons without
distinction bear within them that image. For Kierkegaard it is a question
of seeing every other human person as a neighbor, perceiving neighbor
as a mark of each human person one encounters. This discernment
requires both special effort and special spiritual lighting conditions.
Kierkegaard offers us this striking analogy: "Take many sheets of paper
and write something different on each one—then they do not resemble
each other. But then take again every single sheet; do not let yourself be
confused by the differentiating inscriptions; hold each one up to the light
and you see the same watermark on them all. Thus is neighbour the
common mark, but you see it only by help of the light of the eternal
when it shines through distinction" (97). But the image of God, who is
perfectly good, is presumably a mark that renders all who bear it lovable.
If one can discern it in another, one can give the other loving care in

virtue of and on account of the other's possession of it. Thus, we may imagine that the Armenian nurse of our example was able to give her enemy, the Turkish officer, loving care because she saw in him, by means of the light of the eternal, the mark of neighbor, the image of God.

Kierkegaard sums up much of what he has to say about seeing with eyes closed or averted in the form of a brilliant simile. Looking at the ordinary world of differences and distinctions is like looking at a play, only the plot is vastly more complicated. He continues:

> It is like a play. But when the curtain falls, the one who played the king, and the one who played the beggar, and all the others—they are all quite alike, all one and the same: actors. And when in death the curtain falls on the stage of actuality (for it is a confused use of language if one speaks about the curtain being rolled up on the stage of the eternal at the time of death, because the eternal is no stage—it is truth), then they also are all one; they are human beings. All are that which they essentially were, something we did not see because of the difference we see; they are human beings. (95)

Moreover there is an equality within life that corresponds to the equality of death. It does not appear openly on the stage of life, but it can be glimpsed through life's differences by means of obedience to the love command. "Yet if one were in truth to love his neighbour," Kierkegaard tells us, "he would be reminded every moment that the differences are a disguise" (96). And just as the audience of a play can see through the disguises of the actors, so also Christians are meant to see through the disguises of differences. According to Kierkegaard, Christianity "wills that differences shall hang loosely about the individual, loosely as the cloak the king casts off in order to show who he is, loosely as the ragged costume in which a supernatural being has disguised itself" (96). Loosely hanging garments are transparent to an inner illumination. "When distinctions hang loosely in this way," Kierkegaard affirms, "then there steadily shines in every individual that essential other person, that which is common to all men, the eternal likeness, the equality" (96). He calls what is to be seen through both the king's magnificent raiment and the beggar's wretched rags "inner glory, the equality of glory" (97). According to Kierkegaard, then, there is in each human person an inner glory that is invisible to the eye focused exclusively on distinctions and differences but visible to the eye that penetrates these disguises with the aid of eternity's light. It is this glory that makes each human person lovable quite apart from any distinguishing excellences; this is the mark of neighbor that renders everyone worthy of loving care no matter what their other qualities may be.

Following Kierkegaard, we may speak of giving care as performing works of love. In obedience to the command, one may have to perform works of love for someone for whom one feels no affection because one can see nothing lovable in that person. In such a case one is to give care from a sense of duty, but such care is not an expression of love. As Kierkegaard reminds us, "in truth, because one makes charitable contributions, because he visits the widow and clothes the naked—his love is not necessarily demonstrated or made recognizable by such deeds, for one can perform works of love in an unloving, yes, even in a self-loving way, and when this is so, the works of love are nevertheless not the work of love" (30). But if Kierkegaard is right about there being an inner glory in each of us, loving care can be given to anyone, absolutely anyone, out of affection for it if one can but see it. When this happens, works of love are the fruits of love; they are then the work of love because they manifest love.

It must be emphasized, however, that even if Kierkegaard is right about there being an inner glory in each of us, many will still be thrust back by the command to love the neighbor. Some will think it foolish to look for the image of God in all those they encounter; others are unlikely to see it no matter how hard they look. Yet others will write off ostensible perceptions of the image of God as illusions, fostered by religious sentimentality. It must also be admitted that eternity's light shines dimly and fitfully at best in the lives of many ordinary Christians. All too often they can see nothing of the image of God in their enemies and in those who lack the qualities they cherish in friends and lovers. Frequently enough, even for Christians, the differences that preoccupy ordinary affections remain opaque to any common mark of glory that lies behind them.

I myself find in these sad facts about the human condition a strong reason for thinking that Christian love of neighbor must, at least in the first instance, be a commanded love. In the presence of the command, a Christian can perform works of love for a particular person from a sense of duty even when it is far from apparent that there is anything lovable about that person. Without the command, there would be no such incentive for even trying to love those who do not appear to be lovable. Christians are, I take it, expected to be confident that there is something lovable about each human person, even if they do not see what it is, because God loves all his human creatures. But perhaps only those who are well advanced in the practice of works of love should hope to be blessed with a growth in the brightness of eternity's light that will enable them to see steadily what makes some of their neighbors worthy of love.

If this is so, only those who first perform works of love because they are commanded should hope eventually to be able to give tender care to all those to whom the command tells them to direct love because they have come to see in their neighbors an inner glory that evokes tender affection. In other words, Christians may hope to perfect their love of their less attractive neighbors to the point at which they practice works of love on account of a lovable glory they discern in those neighbors only if they begin by practicing such works of love for duty's sake in response to the divine command. On this view, dutiful obedience to the divine command is an essential part of training in Christianity. It almost goes without saying that very many Christians are destined to remain in training throughout their earthly lives.

One concession must be made to sober realism. It is clear that none of us can give equally loving care to everyone except by giving no loving care to anyone. Even Mother Teresa has given loving care to only a small fraction of the earth's present population. But I think a Christian must be prepared to perform works of love for anyone, motivated solely by desire to obey the divine command if nothing in the neighbor spontaneously engages the affections. Saintly exemplars such as Mother Teresa warn us that we are sinfully apt to underestimate the number of people for whom we could, if we would, perform such works of love. I think they also show us that we might, if we would but try, find something glorious in anyone and as a result might come to perform works of love not merely out of obedience to the divine command but also in affectionate response to the glory perceived in the one for whom the works are performed. This, I take it, would be the perfection of Christian love for the neighbor.

Epilogue: Love's Consummation

Should ordinary Christians expect to achieve such perfection in their earthly lives? Should they count on attaining a state in which they reliably perform works of love not from obedience but solely in affectionate response to the image of God perceived in their neighbors? Kierkegaard is skeptical about affirmative answers to such questions, and so am I.

At the beginning of the conclusion to *Works of Love*, he introduces the apostle John, who says: "Beloved, let us love one another."[54] He remarks that "you do not hear in these words the rigorousness of duty; the apostle does not say, 'You *shall* love one another'" (344). But Kierkegaard insists that the command to love, which is eternity's law, is not altered in the slightest way, least of all by an apostle. To be sure, the apostle speaks so mildly that it is almost as if it had been forgotten that love is the commandment. "If, however, you forget that it is the apostle of love who speaks, then you misunderstand him," Kierkegaard claims, "for such words are not the beginning of the discourse on love but are the consummation of love" (345). He warns us, "Therefore we do not dare talk this way. That which is truth in the mouth of the veteran, perfected apostle could in the mouth of a beginner easily be flirtation whereby he would seek to leave the commandment's school much too soon and escape the *school-yoke*" (345). Except for the greatest saints, all Christians are, I think, included in the "we" who dare not make the apostle's words our own.

The reason ordinary Christians would go astray by trying to escape the school-yoke of the love command is simple. In their lives, eternity does not cast its light on everyone at all times. They cannot rest assured that all those for whom they should perform works of love will appear lovable to them and engage their affections; they may never discern the inner glory in their worst enemies or the wretched of the earth. Nor can they be confident that their perception of the image of God in others will be continuous rather than intermittent, and so they cannot rely on this perception being present on every occasion when it is needed to motivate works of love performed for those in whom they sometimes see the inner glory. Moreover, the image of God is often too faintly perceived to be motivationally sufficient for those works of love that demand great sacrifice. So ordinary Christians need to be able to trust to the "Thou *shall*" of the command for backup motivation. They will have to appeal to the motive of duty on many occasions as a substitute for or a supplement to the motives provided by perceived inner glory. As I see it, there is cause for melancholy in the fact that most of us cannot count on getting beyond the elementary classes in the love command's school during our earthly lives.[55]

Part II
Freedom

3

Free Agency and Materialism

J. A. Cover and John O'Leary-Hawthorne

Famously, Kant insisted that, given that the natural order is deterministic, we must conceive of free agents as somehow standing outside that order. The determinism that Kant had in mind is familiar enough; it is one according to which the laws of nature and the past together render impossible all but one subsequent course of events. Our contemporary picture of the natural order is not as a deterministic order in this sense. So if this sort of determinism provides the only legitimate reason for placing agents outside the natural order, then naturalism about free agents is in very good shape.

Yet there is a different sort of determinism associated with naturalism that, while very much alive today, has not found its way into discussions of human freedom. It is a sort of determinism according to which the microphysical world determines the distribution of the higher level properties of material beings, adumbrated in various popular supervenience theses. Given this sort of determinism in the natural order, must we again conceive of genuinely free agents as somehow standing outside that order? We shall be addressing that question in this chapter.

Three Tenets of Mind/Body Materialism

Let us begin with three assumptions that are typically part of any materialist worldview that is not also eliminativist about thinkers and their mental lives.

Assumption 1: People are wholly material beings.

That is to say, human persons have no immaterial parts. Whenever any human person says or thinks "I think," that person refers to a material being.

> Assumption 2: Alien worlds aside, mental states supervene on microphysical states.[56]

That is to say, necessarily, if the distribution of microphysical properties at two possible worlds is exactly the same, then the distribution of psychological properties at those worlds will be exactly the same. The supervenience thesis of Assumption 2 should be distinguished from some stronger theses, such as

> 2A. The mental states of an individual supervene on the microphysical states of that individual, and

> 2B. The global distribution of mental states at a time supervene on the global distribution of microphysical states at that time.

Recent discussions of mental content have urged the externalist lessons that (i) owing to the fact that environment partially constitutes content, 2A is false, and (ii) owing to the fact that history partially constitutes content, 2B is false.[57] Thus, for example, there are possible worlds exactly like the actual world now but where a different individual is the referent of "Napoleon," and thus where a different *de re* proposition (hence a different belief) is expressed by "Napoleon was a man."

While supervenience theses 2A and 2B may be false, there may well be true supervenience theses, akin to them, that are restricted to a certain domain of psychological properties. For example, if there is such a category as "narrow content," then a supervenience thesis in the style of 2A restricted to narrow contents may well be acceptable.

Return again to Assumption 2. Why the qualification about "alien worlds"? Even most hard-nosed materialists will concede that there is a logically possible world that duplicates all the physical properties of this one but where there are extra immaterial entities—angels or spooks—thrown in. Assuming there are no angels or spooks at the actual world, the physical properties of that world will duplicate those of our own, but the mental properties will not. An unrestrained supervenience thesis according to which physical similarity between worlds guarantees psychological similarity is thus too strong: so-called "alien worlds," with fundamental ingredients that do not figure at the actual world, will have to be excluded insofar as one claims that physical similarity guarantees psychological similarity.[58]

Our third assumption offers another restricted supervenience thesis in the style of 2A:

> Assumption 3: Immaterial beings aside, the property of *an agent's making a free decision at t* supervenes upon the intrinsic microphysical history of an agent up to *t*.[59]

That is to say, if there are two possible material beings that are duplicates with respect to intrinsic microphysical history up to *t*, then both or neither makes a free decision at *t*. Now it must be granted that the *content* of an agent's free decision may not supervene on the intrinsic microphysical history of that agent. (The *de re* content of an agent's decision, say, "to study the life of Napoleon," will not supervene on the agent's current microphysical structure.) Nevertheless, Assumption 3 seems to us a rather plausible view to take for anyone accepting Assumption 2. For if the mental globally supervenes on the microphysical, then Assumption 3 could fail for only one of two reasons: (a) because the microphysical future is partially constitutive of whether one makes a free decision, or (b) because the current microphysical environment outside of the agent is partially constitutive of whether one makes a free decision. Option (a) seems outright implausible. Option (b) seems unlikely as well, once one remembers that freely making a decision to do *x* doesn't entail that one is able to do *x* (though, of course, it may well entail being able to decide not to do *x*). One can freely decide to leave the room even though one is not free to leave the room; one can freely come to the decision to pull the trigger even if the trigger is stuck or locked.

Now, Assumptions 1–3, even if accepted, still leave open a number of questions concerning the metaphysics of mind. Among them are

> (i) Is token dualism true? Are token mental events and states identical with or distinct from (though supervenient upon) complex microphysical states and events?

> (ii) Is property dualism true? Are mental properties identical with complex (presumably, hugely gerrymandered) microphysical properties or distinct from (though supervenient upon) complex microphysical states and events?

Our concern here is not to answer these questions, but instead to ask: How well do Assumptions 1–3 cohere with our ordinary conception of freedom and agency, coupled with our commonsense belief that we are agents who are sometimes free? Note that Assumptions 1–3 do not entail determinism at the microphysical level. Thus, even if our ordinary conception of freedom is incompatible with the thesis that our actions are determined by the past and the laws of nature, it does not immediately follow that our ordinary conception of freedom sorts ill with Assumptions 1–3.

Assumptions 1 and 2 are, by our lights, obligatory for any materialist about the mind. It is unclear whether "token monism" and "property monism" are also obligatory. We don't want to pin too much on the materialist here; we recognize that some calling themselves materialists will balk at having property monism pinned on them. So we shall require only that the materialist be committed to Assumptions 1 and 2. We have suggested, however, that anyone subscribing to Assumptions 1 and 2 will also inevitably find Assumption 3 compelling. So we shall also presume that the materialist about the mind will be prepared to endorse 3. The main question of this chapter may thus be posed in the following way: What are the costs of wedding our ordinary conception of freedom with materialism about the mind? Is materialism about the mind compatible with our ordinary conception of freedom?

Before proceeding directly with these questions, it will be helpful to say a bit more about our ordinary conception of freedom.

Robust and Deflationary Accounts of Freedom

Let's distinguish robust from deflationary accounts of freedom. The robust theorist argues that there is a phenomenon out there in the world meeting the contours of our ordinary conception of freedom. The deflationary theorist argues that while there is something in the world deserving the titles "freedom" and "agency," nevertheless significant bits of the picture surrounding ordinary thought and talk about freedom and agency in fact have no correlate in the world, and thus are either to be dropped altogether from our best theory or else to be somehow accommodated but recognized for what they are. (There is also the eliminativist about freedom—who argues that ordinary ascriptions of freedom and agency are simply false or else truthvalueless.)

Standard compatibilist accounts of freedom seem deflationary at best. Not all compatibilists will agree. They may insist that their compatibilism does full justice to our ordinary conception of freedom—insisting, for example, that all it means to be free in the ordinary sense is for one's actions to be the causal upshot of one's beliefs and desires (it being neither here nor there where one's beliefs and desires come from). A full treatment of this compatibilist claim to do justice to our ordinary conception of freedom is beyond the scope of this paper.[60] It will suffice for now simply to declare our own orientation—that any such claim on behalf of compatibilism is at best poor anthropology. There are real phenomena, such as the following, which need to be explained: When ordinary people come to consciously recognize and understand that some action is contingent upon circumstances in an agent's past that are beyond that agent's control, they quickly lose a propensity to impute moral responsibility to the agent for that action. We can readily explain this fact by supposing that ordinary people have a conception of freedom, agency, and moral responsibility according to which an action by an agent is free and accountable only if that action is not fully determined by circumstances, past or present, that are beyond the agent's control. Similarly, we believe that the best explanation for why so many philosophy students find compatibilism *prima facie* implausible is that they carry with them a workaday conception of freedom that cannot be done full justice by the compatibilist account.

It is somewhat easier to be sympathetic with standard compatibilist accounts if they are offered as explicitly deflationary theories. There is nothing incoherent in the nature of a claim to the effect that ascriptions of choice are often true even though certain philosophical pictures accompanying such ascriptions are confused. By way of analogy, it may well be argued that certain conceptions that we ordinarily have of time are strictly speaking wrongheaded and yet allow that there is nevertheless a phenomenon deserving the title "time." (One way of fleshing out a semantics along these lines is to say, with David Lewis, that a near-realization of folk theory about some subject matter may provide the denotation of the relevant folk predicates even though there is no perfect realizer of folk theory concerning that subject matter.[61]) Clearly, deflationary accounts of freedom are compatible with the materialist theory of mind. Our concern in this chapter is to inquire whether a robust account of freedom is so compatible, and if so, at what cost materialism is brought alongside robust freedom.

What will a robust conception of freedom look like? So-called agency theories attempt to provide the *bare bones* of a metaphysical story concerning robust freedom and moral responsibility. Here, in short, is what agency theory tells us:

(i) Among the things that exist, there are *agents*.

(ii) There is a fundamental relation between agents and actions—call it *agent causation*—such that by standing in that relation to actions, agents count as performing those actions freely and count as being accountable for those actions.

Some have said that agency theory is outright incoherent, since it aims to find a logically impossible *via media* between statistically random actions (i.e., actions rendered less than inevitable by the past course of events and the laws of nature) and actions determined by the past and the laws of nature. We don't see the incoherence. There is nothing outright contradictory about the following claim: There is some differentium R such that the class of undetermined actions divides into those that are morally accountable and those that aren't, according to whether they have or lack R respectively. Perhaps it is supposed to be self-evident that if any undetermined event is morally accountable, every undetermined event is; or perhaps it is supposed to be self-evident that no undetermined event is one for which anyone could be morally responsible. But neither of these is self-evident. So agency theory is not outright incoherent.

Agency theory has at least two virtues relative to the aim of doing justice to our ordinary conception of freedom. First, agent causation, if true, offers the real possibility of *doing otherwise*. Consistent with the claim that agent *s* stands in *R* to action *a*, one can insist that *a* is not determined by past events or laws of nature; *s* could do otherwise than *a*. The second virtue addresses itself to the belief that it is *we* who act properly or blameworthily, and, moreover, that this is not simply a matter of there being certain properties we happen to be carrying around, but rather that some action springs from our being, so to speak—that the action in some unnegotiable sense comes from us.[62] In at least these two ways, then, it might be felt that agency theory does full justice to our ordinary conception of freedom, and that anything less would be tantamount to a deflationary view.

It is worth noting that someone might in effect offer a version of agency theory preserving one but not both of these virtues. Consider Leibniz, for example. According to Leibniz, one's actions flow from one's individual essence.[63] Thus, in a very deep and unequivocal sense, one's actions express who *one* is. Indeed, actions flowing from one's individual essence are certainly not contingent upon circumstances beyond one's control. For an action to be so contingent requires that there be possible worlds where the circumstances are different and where, as a result, one does something different. But if some trait or disposition or action were necessitated by one's individual essence, then quite clearly, that trait or disposition or action would not be so contingent. By capturing the second virtue of agency theory, Leibniz thus preserves something quite intuitive. If I act badly in some way, then on the Leibnizian conception, I cannot very well "put that down" to bad upbringing or to some purely circumstantial or "extrinsic" facts, since the action itself reflects my very essence—who I am. It is not as if, had *my* upbringing being different, I would have been a better person. (It is important, further, to Leibniz, that the action stem from my individual essence and not my essence *qua* human being, since otherwise that action would be an expression of humanity in general rather than who I am in particular.) Clearly, this conception of freedom, while preserving the second virtue, goes rather a short distance toward preserving the first (nor do the various Leibnizian maneuvers around the notion of inclining without necessitating go very far here). We shall be focusing here on a fully robust conception of freedom, one that aims to preserve both strands, acknowledging that there may be middle ground (e.g., Leibniz) between that fully robust conception and familiar deflationary views.

The Mystery of Agent Causation

If we can suppose that agency theory goes some distance toward capturing a bare-bones story about our ordinary conception of freedom, we cannot pretend that the concept of agent causation approaches anything like a clear and distinct idea. Agency theory is radically underdeveloped and seems likely to remain so. The point can be best illustrated, in the present context, by examining the most recent attempt to develop a theory of agent causation, found in Randolph Clarke's "Toward a Credible Agent-Causal Account of Free Will."[64] Clarke makes two basic moves in attempting to render agent causation more palatable. The first—which we applaud—is to suggest that while facts about an agent's prior reasons for action will not be determining causes in cases of agent causation, they can nevertheless properly be counted as causally relevant to the freely produced action. The second basic move is to offer the following story about the agent-causal relation:

> What remains is to say just what this relation is. The prevailing tendency among agent causalists and their critics alike on this point has been to stress how different agent causation is from event causation and indeed how 'mysterious' the former is. However, the proper line here, I believe, is to maintain that agent causation, if there is such a thing, is (or involves) exactly the same relation as event causation. The only difference between the

two kinds of causation concerns the types of entities related, not the relation. (197)

Clarke then goes on to recommend that we take

> the causal relation to be among the basic constituents of the universe. Causation may be held to be a real relation between particulars, one that, although analyzable, is not reducible to noncausal and non-nomological properties and relations. . . .
>
> One type of realist account of event causation can be sketched, in broad strokes as follows. An event (particular) causes another just in case the relation of causation obtains between them. Two events can be so related only if they possess (or are constituted by) properties that are in turn related under a law of nature. Ultimately, then, causal relations are grounded in laws of nature, which consist of second-order relations among universals.
>
> Such an account resembles that favored by Tooley for event (or, as he would have it, state-of-affairs) causation. Tooley maintains that the relations involved in this sort of account—causation, as well as the higher-order relations among universals—can be adequately specified, without reduction, by a set of postulates indicating the roles of these relations within the domain of properties and states of affairs. If he is correct about this, then we have an analysis of the causal relation that can be employed in an account of agent causation. An agent causalist can say that it is the relation thus analyzed that obtains between a person and her action when she acts with free will; it is the very relation that, within the domain of properties and events or states of affairs, occupies the specified role.
>
> Moreover, an account that runs parallel, at a certain level of description, to that suggested for event causation would seem to be available for agent causation. An agent may be held to cause a particular action (more precisely, an event of acting on a certain ordering of reasons) just in case the relation of causation obtains between these two particulars. And an agent can be said to be so related to one of her actions only if these two particulars exemplify certain properties. Perhaps the only agents who cause things are those who have the property of being capable of reflective practical reasoning, and perhaps such an agent directly causes only those events that constitute her acting for reasons. There might, in that case, be a law of nature to the effect that any individual who acts with such a capacity acts with free will.
>
> Natural law, then, may subsume all free action without undermining the freedom with which human beings act. On this sort of account, the agent causation on which free will is said to depend is seen as thoroughly natural. (197–98)

To what extent does this story provide us with an intelligible naturalistic account of agent causation? Is our understanding of agent causation rendered satisfactory by seeing the agent-causal relation as the familiar causal relation with an abnormal relatum, and treating that relation as irreducible? It is worth listing four residual and persistent difficulties of this picture, some of which Clarke is aware of.

(1) Clarke concedes that we have no idea of what it would be like to recognize the agent-causal relation as obtaining: "There is," he says, "no observational evidence that could tell us whether our world is an indeterministic world with agent causation or without it" (199). So our grasp of the truth conditions of agent-causal ascriptions must radically transcend any grasp of what it would be like, even in principle, to recognize agent causation as obtaining. (Some have recommended that at least in the first person we know perfectly well how to recognize agent causation—that the agent-causal relation is manifest to us from the first person in the ordinary context of deliberating and acting on that deliberation. Clarke rejects this in passing, and indeed there are good reasons for rejecting it. In particular, there is excellent reason to think that robust freedom is not always manifested in ordinary deliberation, especially where the deliberation brings to light overwhelming reasons in favor of one action over any other.[65])

(2) Clarke claims that agent causation "would not improve our ability to predict and explain human behavior," adding that, "If prediction and explanation are paradigmatic of scientific understanding, it appears that agent causation neither contributes to nor detracts from such understanding" (199). Why then does Clarke think we ought to believe in robust freedom of an agent-causal sort? Because he thinks that this is presupposed by our ascriptions of moral responsibility to one another. That may well be. But if he is right that the agent-causal picture has no place in the project of gaining a "scientific understanding" of the world, it is not surprising that its status continues to be—and will remain—problematic.

(3) A crucial issue that Clarke does not address—crucial, in particular, given his tentative suggestion that agent causation and event causation alike are grounded in causal laws—concerns the purported connection between agent causation and being able to do otherwise. Let us grant that the causal relation sometimes obtains between agents and events rather than only between events. What would prevent God from issuing the following decree?

If agent *S* exists at time *t* and has motives m₁, m₂ and m₃, then the causal relation will obtain between *S* and action *a*.

If agent causation is the familiar causal relation, why should God be any less able to decree when and where some agent will stand in the causal relation to actions than He is able to decree when and where events will stand in the causal relation to one another? And if, as seems plausible, God can so decree that this familar causal relation hold, it would hardly appear that "agent causation" entails freedom to do otherwise, and so it would hardly seem that agent causation entails robust freedom. (God's decrees might be more general than the one just expressed. They might be of the form "When agents are in states *x, y, z*, they will stand in the causal relation to actions of type *F.*")

Note that on the present account, we have not secured freedom even in the weak sense of one's actions being undetermined by event-event causal laws. For, according to the story, there is no reason *a priori* why an action might not be *overdetermined*. If the agent-causal relation is the familiar causal relation, why shouldn't some action be overdetermined by a causally sufficient event and some agent, both standing in the causal relation to that action, just as two causally sufficient events can stand in the causal relation to an action? (It may be that Clarke himself doesn't care so much about being able to do otherwise. In a footnote he writes, "I see no problem in saying that, on the agent causal account, the agent, together with her having certain reasons, jointly deterministically cause her acting on those reasons" (202). But this removes at least one main sort of motivation for agency theory. After all, the incompatibilist will now say, "Suppose one has no choice about agent-causal laws. And suppose an agent has no choice about the reasons in her possession for acting. If some agent-causal laws together with those reasons entail her doing *a*, then whatever the relation between an agent and *a*, it will not be up to that agent whether or not to do *a*." Perhaps Clarke has a more Leibnizian compromise in mind, of the sort we sketched earlier.)

(4) Consider Clarke's suggestion, quoted earlier, that "There might be a law of nature to the effect that any individual who acts with such a capacity acts with free will" (198), where the capacity is that of practical and reflective reasoning. Now on most accounts, including Tooley's, laws of nature are contingent. Where exactly is contingency seen to enter into the present account? The idea might be that it is a contingent fact that when a practical reasoner stands in the causal relation to an action, that constitutes free will. But this will once again leave the concept of free will mysterious. For if it is only nomologically necessary that agent causation be associated with free will, then it is not metaphysically necessary that if the causal relation obtains between an agent and an action, the agent performs the action freely. In that case we should still

want to know what freedom *consists in*. (Does it remain open, for example, that there are possible worlds wherein exist laws of nature to the effect that whenever there is a certain sort of event causation, there is freedom?)

A different way of installing contingency is to make it a contingent fact that when an agent with such-and-such a capacity performs an action, the causal relation obtains between the agent and the action. If this is contingent, is there then a possible world where (say) the causal relation holds between an electron and certain events, or a possible world where the causal relation holds between sleeping people and certain events?

What these questions help to bring out is this: It is simply not clear to human minds why the obtaining of the familiar causal relation between a thing and an event should constitute free will; and this is because the human mind recognizes no combination of ordinary explanatory and causal notions that is *a priori* sufficient for freedom, agency, and moral responsibility. Now, it might be a brute speculation that, necessarily, when the causal relation holds between a thing and an event, the thing freely brings about that event. But this proposal will remain just that—a brute modal speculation. (There are analogies from other domains. We might offer the brute speculation that anything with a certain physical structure will have qualia of a certain sort. But such speculation will be inevitably dissatisfying to the human mind because there will be neither empirical nor *a priori* resources for providing a compelling story as to why there couldn't be that physical structure without qualia. The is-ought gap, brought out by Moore's famous Open Question Argument, might also offer a relevant analogy here.)

None of this is meant to show that agent causation is incoherent. It simply makes vivid why agent causation theory will seem unsatisfying. We can, on the one hand, commence by means of a certain reference fixer: there is a special relation R holding between things and actions that make things morally responsible for that action. Call the relation agent causation. (This is roughly van Inwagen's strategy.[66]) Beginning in that way, the problem is then to spell out agency theory by integrating R with other properties and relations of which we have independent grasp via segments of folk theory or science or *a priori* metaphysics. This has remained very hard to do. It has become increasingly clear that no putative sufficient conditions for free agency constructed out of causal, structural, and explanatory concepts will emerge as *a priori* compelling; and in the absence of compelling *a priori* links, it is hard to see how this gap can be bridged by empirical investigation, seeing how elusive agent causation is to empirical observation. On the other hand, we can straight-away fill out agency theory by identifying agent causation with some familiar relation or relations from science or folk theory or metaphysics. This is Clarke's strategy. The difficulty then comes in providing oneself with compelling reasons for thinking that the story, thus filled out, tells one what is necessary and sufficient for moral responsibility. And added to each of these respective difficulties is the apparent vacuity of agent causation with respect to recognition conditions and the project of pre-diction.

So agent causation, if there is such a phenomenon, is not one that we understand well; nor, especially, does it even seem to be a phenomenon that the "natural light" of human beings is capable of understanding very well. Now our present question concerns the compatibility of a robust conception of freedom with a materialist theory of the mind. In attempt-ing to answer this question, one shall, as in any other context, be inevitably hampered by the paucity of our conception of robust freedom. If in the sequel we encounter respects in which a materialist theory of mind is not very well suited to a robust conception of freedom, we cannot pretend that a dualist theory of mind magically renders agent causation fully intelligible or magically provides us with the possibility of a well-developed story about agent causation. The point is worth emphasizing: robust freedom will remain somewhat elusive whether or not we embrace dualism about the mind.

What follows is a sort of progress report on our own efforts to make good on the hunch that agency theory, impoverished as it may be, provides its proponents with considerable reason to resist a materialist theory of mind. It thus provides some reason to question the claim of those like Clarke that agency theory is compatible with a fully naturalistic picture of human agents.

An Outline of Materialist Agency Theory

Let us make a start at fleshing out a materialist agency theory and certain crucial decisions the materialist must make. We'll do this by considering an apparent threat to the supervenience doctrine expressed in Assumption 3. Begin with an inferential principle ("Principle ß") advanced by van Inwagen in his elaboration and defense of a robust conception of freedom:

Np and N(if p, then q) entails Nq

(where "Np" means "p and no one ever had a choice about p").[67] This principle underwrites the common intuition that freedom is incompatible with determinism. For none of us have a choice about the laws of nature and none of us have a choice about the distant past. Coupled with Principle ß, those platitudes entail that, if determinism is true, none of us have a choice about what we do.[68] We shall be assuming that any robust conception of freedom will subscribe to something like that principle.

It is tempting to suppose that we can use Principle ß to show that the sort of determinism noted in the introduction, at work in the purported supervenience of the mental on the microphysical, can also be shown to be incompatible with free will robustly conceived. Let us pursue this thought, beginning with the supposition that

> If we are ever free, then the property of *an agent's making a free decision at t* supervenes upon the intrinsic microphysical history of an agent up to *t* (from Assumption 3).

And let us add the following thesis:

> T1: No one has a choice about what supervenes on what.

T1 is rather analogous to the view that people have no choice about the laws of nature. But notice that T1 is even more compelling than this latter thesis: since supervenience—as we are understanding the term in its normal usage—is a modal relation of metaphysical necessity, it is very strange to suppose that people have a choice about what metaphysically necessitates what.[69] (Indeed, few think that even God has a choice about that sort of thing.) Meanwhile, anything less full blooded than the claim that the microphysical necessitates the mental would fall short of materialism about the mind. So T1 is extremely compelling.

Suppose now that we add another thesis:

> T2: People don't have a choice about any of their microphysical details.

Surely people don't have a choice about the exact spatial relations among electrons and other microphysical particles making up their microstates. And it seems clear that this thesis, in conjunction with Principle ß and thesis T1, will entail that, if an agent's making a free decision at *t* supervenes upon the intrinsic microphysical history of an agent up to *t*, then we are never free. (Note we are not assuming deterministic physical laws here.)

What is one to say in the light of this argument? One could deny that people are free. Or, one could deny Principle ß and affirm some deflationary view of what it takes to be free. Or, one could give up one or another of Assumption 3, T1, or T2. Since we are interested in the consequences of ascribing robust freedom to people, the first two options—of denying we are ever free and denying Principle ß to adopt a deflationary view—are of no interest in this context. Now T1 seems unchallengeable; and giving up Assumption 3 is tantamount to giving up a materialist theory of mind. Thus, if one is to try to reconcile robust freedom with a materialist theory of mind, one will have to give up T2, affirming that people do indeed have a choice about their microphysical history.

We can go further. Suppose, by hypothesis, that one freely makes a decision at t and that Assumption 3 holds. What sort of control of one's microphysical history will this require? It will not be good enough to have control over one's microphysical history after t. For if one does not have control over one's microphysical history up to t, and if one's decision supervenes on one's microphysical history up to t, then Principle ß tells us that one's decision at t is not free. Given that we have no choice about the past, we cannot say that by virtue of exercising a choice at t, one exercises control over one's microphysical history prior to t.[70] So, if we wish to affirm robust freedom and retain Assumption 3, we will be forced to say that if some agent makes a free decision at t, then it will be up to that agent what microphysical states he is in at t. That is, one will have at a time "top-down" agent-causal control over one's microphysical states at that time.

Suppose we go with this top-down causal picture and see where it takes us. On behalf of the materialist, let us run the following line. Agents are material beings. Facts about whether an agent makes a decision at t supervene on the agent's microphysical structure at t. Agents are sometimes free. Insofar as an agent is free at t, it is up to an agent what microphysical states he is in at t. And insofar as "up to" involves agent causation, the agent will thus have the ability to agent cause some of his own microphysical facts, even though these agent-causal facts at t supervene on the microphyscial history of the agent up to and including that time.

Is there any logical incompatibility between "agent causation supervenes on microphysics" and "an agent is causally responsible for some of the microphysical facts forming the subvenient base for that very causal responsibility"? There is certainly no inconsistency in the following triad: a family A supervenes on family B, family B doesn't supervene on

A, and yet some member of A is causally relevant to some member of B. Supervenience does not straightforwardly entail anything about causality. That is, the modal determination of family A by B doesn't straightforwardly mean that there is no causal determination of some member of B by some member of A. (Here is a simple example, departing perhaps from the sort of supervenience (of nonoverlapping families) most commonly discussed in the literature, but still in keeping with the letter of the requirements for supervenience. Suppose e_1 causes e_2. The family $\{e_2\}$ supervenes on the family $\{e_1, e_2\}$ and not vice versa; and yet a member of the former family causes a member of the latter family.) So there is no cheap and easy way to show that agent a's causing microstate m is incompatibile with the supervenience of "a's causing m" on a set of microphysical facts that includes m.

We can, in this context, get clearer about the sense in which a materialist will affirm that his microphysical states are up to him. Consider the proposition P expressing a precise specification of all one's microphysical states at t. One might now think: "It is not up to me whether or not I enjoy that precise arrangement of microphysical states. For I certainly don't have control over, say, the exact location of each of my microparticles. I can now import Principle ß and Assumption 3. Suppose I make a decision at t. It is not up to me whether or not P. And it is not up to me whether or not supervenience relations of sort R hold. P and R obtain and together entail my decision at t. So my decision at t is not up to me." But consider now an analogous argument. Suppose that my arm takes some precise trajectory T. It might be argued that I don't have control over whether my arm takes exactly that trajectory. And my arm moving supervenes on T. Thus, I don't have control over my arm's moving (by Principle ß). But presumably I do; something has gone wrong.

What needs further clarification on behalf of the materialist is the sense of "up to me" that may be reckoned operative here. As van Inwagen implies, so long it is up to me whether my arm moves at all, I do indeed have a choice about that trajectory T.[71] That trajectory is up to me in this sense: T can be avoided by *avoiding arm-moving altogether*. (What is not up to me is whether, *given* that my arm moves, it takes trajectory T.) Analogously, so long as it is in my power to bring it about at t that P is *false* (so long as I can avoid decision making altogether at t), then even though I don't, as it were, have control over all the exact microphysical details of my state at t, I will be such that it is up to me at t whether or not P; my decision is up to me.

Let us suppose, then, that we cannot exhibit any logical incompatibility between "agent causation supervenes on microphysics" and "an agent is causally responsible for microphysical facts at the subvenient base for that very causal responsibility." Having nevertheless gone a short distance toward fleshing out a view on behalf of the materialist agency theorist, it is worth acknowledging some of the decision points that such a theorist will face along the philosophical decision tree. Two such decision points can be framed in the form of questions the materialist must answer.

First: "What do we say about the relation of agent causation to microphysical laws?" We note two main options here.

1. The materialist could say that the normal operation of microphysical laws is disrupted by downward causation. One who embraces this picture might envisage the following sort of scenario:

> The following sequence of microevents occurs: m_1 and m_2 are followed by m_4 and m_5. At the time at which m_4 and m_5 occur, an agent causes m_5. In the world in which this sequence occurs, it is a microphysical law that if m_1 and m_2 occur, then m_3 and m_4 will follow (though the actual sequence in the present instance does not accord with this law). It is a true supervenience principle that if m_4 and m_5 obtain at some time, then an agent causes m_5 at that time.

Is this coherent? That depends in part upon whether there being a law that Fs cause Gs entails there being a universal regularity of Fs being followed by Gs. Clearly, the sort of materialist agency theory just now sketched must bring with it a considerably different picture of laws of nature, a picture allowing for local breakdowns of normal laws for microphysical particles when those particles are caught up in complex systems of a special sort. (Note that this picture might even allow that the laws of nature be deterministic, since freedom is secured by allowing for the possibility that, so to speak, the laws of nature be broken.)

2. Alternatively, the materialist can say that normal microphysical laws are not disrupted, that agent-causal facts are additional causal facts that do not interfere with microphysical laws. (Note that since this picture will not tolerate an agent's breaking the laws of nature, the laws of nature had better be statistical and not deterministic. Were they deterministic, then given their unbreakability and given that we have no choice about the distant past, Principle ß would make trouble for any claim of freedom for our decisions.)

The picture adumbrated by option 1 has been entertained in a recent paper by Tim O'Connor.[72] He notes that if we take option 1 seriously, we can envisage getting empirical evidence for top-down causality. The proponent of option 2, meanwhile, while having a much harder time telling a story about how to garner scientific evidence for top-down causality, will have the advantage of less conceptual strain.

We turn now to a *second* important decision point: "What exactly should be said about the relation between the willing, the micro-events, and the agent?" We know the materialist will be committed to the supervenience of willing-facts upon microfacts. But there are a number of options consistent with that supervenience thesis:

(a) We can say that a willing is token identical with a complex microphysical event, and that agent causation relates the agent to that complex event directly.

(b) We can say that a willing is token distinct from micro-events, though supervenient on them, and that the agent causes the willing, which in turn causally influences the micro-level.

(c) We can say that a willing is token distinct from micro-events, though supervenient on them, and that the agent causes some complex micro-event that in turn causes the willing.

It might be thought that there is an epiphemonal alternative, according to which the agent causes a willing (that is token-distinct from microphysical phenomena), but exerts no influence whatever on micro-events (whether directly or indirectly). But this option is not available for anyone who endorses Principle ß. If your willing supervenes on microphenomena then, if Principle ß is correct, it had better be up to you what microphysical states you are in (for otherwise, we can deduce that your willing is unfree).

So the materialist agency theorist is left with (a), (b), and (c) as ways of relating the willing, the agent, and the micro-level. Note that in cases (a) and (b), the willing is proximal to the agent, whereas in (c), it is distal. Surely this third option is less plausible by far. Case (c) is a theory of agency according to which the fundamental agent-causal relation is between an agent and *nonmental events*. We find this picture too far removed from our normal intuitions about agency. In part, at least, one should have thought that deciding is a basic action: one doesn't decide by doing something else.[73] Hereafter, we'll be concerned with the merits of (a) and (b), leaving aside (c) as relatively undeserving of attention. For ease of reference, we can call option (a) Token-Reductive Materialism, and option (b) Token-Emergent Materialism.

That completes enough of our story about what materialist agency theory might look like. We now switch to a more polemical mode: our aim is to indicate why on balance an immaterialist agency theory appears more rational than a materialist one. In this connection, it is (again) no use pointing to costs that must be paid by any agency theory, whether of a materialist or immaterialist stripe. As we have said, any agency theory is likely to remain elusive with regard to details. Similarly, any agency theory may well have to reject what Lewis dubs "the explanatory adequacy of physics," according to which "there is some unified body of scientific theories, of the sort we now accept, which together provide a true and exhaustive account of all physical phenomena."[74] Shy of projecting that agency theory is to become part of natural science (a dim prospect, we conjecture), the agency theorist cannot accept the complete explanatory adequacy of natural science. (And at any rate, it certainly does not seem that an explanatory theory in which agency theory is central would be a scientific theory "of the sort we now accept."[75]) Considerations of this latter sort, if correct, provide no reason for preferring a nonmaterialist agency theory over a materialist agency theory. What we need to do is identify the special costs incurred by materialist agency theory that are not incurred by a dualist agency theory.

We shall discuss, in turn, the two central ideas of materialist agency theory—first, the supervenience thesis adumbrated by Assumption 3, and second the thesis that the agent is a material being.[76]

Costs of Combining the Supervenience Thesis with Agency Theory

We begin with two general difficulties for the materialist agency theory as sketched. A first point to acknowledge is that the materialist agency theorist offers a picture that is at best strained, in the following respect. We are invited, on the one hand, to imagine that certain microphysical P-facts metaphysically determine (thanks to supervenience) distinctively mental agent-theoretic M-facts, while yet (on the other hand) admitting that certain agent-theoretic M-facts are causally relevant to some of those very microphysical P-facts upon which they supervene. By our lights, this combination of theses will strike any reader who fully absorbs them as intuitively odd, odd in *something like* the way that talk of self-causation is odd. It would be nice to articulate what is odd about this combination in terms of one or more intuitively compelling principles that must be violated by this version of agency theory. The best we can offer here is the following principle (we invite readers to see if they can do better):

No state of affairs x can metaphysically necessitate some state of affairs y if y is causally relevant to the obtaining of x.[77]

Suppose that facts about agency supervene on microphysical facts and not vice versa. It will then be hard to deny that there is a minimally sufficient supervenience base that necessitates the agent-causal facts one level up. By the above principle, there can be no agent-causal explanation for the obtaining of that subvenient base. So if the principle is correct, materialist agency theory cannot be sustained, since it precisely does claim that the microphysical base necessitates agent-causal states of affairs that causally explain that base itself.

Is the above principle true? While it falls short of anything like self-evident, we find it compelling. By our lights, the fact that materialist agency theory needs to reject the principle must be reckoned a cost of the theory.

A second cost to acknowledge is the following. Metaphysicians often find attractive the idea that supervenient facts are nothing over and above the facts that they supervene upon. In David Armstrong's characterization (in conversation), supervenient entities are "an ontological free lunch." Now, clearly, our materialist agency theorist cannot buy into this picture. On his account, agent causation is one of the "joints of nature," hardly assimilable to some purely microphysical relation or some gerrymandered disjunction of them. Nor could the picture of downward causation be readily sustained if the M-facts of agency were "nothing over and above" the P-facts of microphysics. What the agency theorist needs is some sort of "emergentism" according to which, though agent-theoretic M-facts supervene on the microlevel, they are in some important sense "something over and above" the microphysical P-facts. He will thus postulate some sort of necessary connections (or, in an alternative lingo, "internal relations") between distinct existences— between facts that are both conceptually and genuinely distinct.[78]

Now clearly this internal relation is nothing like an analytic one. It is surely *conceivable* that there be a possible world whose microphysical structure is just like this one, with the same statistical laws of nature in operation and where there is no agent-causation that brings about some arm movement that at this world is freely brought about by a person in an agent-causal manner.[79] At that world, the arm movement is an undetermined event that is not caught up in that agent-causal relation.

While conceivable, the materialist agency theorist cannot allow that this scenario is possible. Nor can this internal relation be merely nomological, since nomological connections are weaker than necessary connections. In short, it looks as if materialist agency theory presents us with a particularly puzzling brute necessary connection between distinct existences.

If it is an advantage of a theory to minimize obscure necessary connections between distinct existences, then it will be an advantage for the proponent of robust freedom to avoid materialism about the mind. Of course, it would be no improvement to say that agents are immaterial and then go on to claim that agent-causal facts supervene on quasi-structural ectoplasmic properties. One would be left once again with obscure necessary connections between distinct existences. The difficulty can be avoided only by an agency theory that makes agent-causal facts nonsupervenient.

So much for general costs of the supervenience thesis. As we said earlier, it can be combined with token monism or token dualism. We outline below the costs of each particular combination.

A Special Cost of Token-reductive Materialism

Suppose some neural event is a willing. Is it essentially a willing? Many token identity theorists talk as if neural events only enjoy mental descriptions contingently. If that is so, a special worry seems to confront the materialist who believes in robust freedom. For it is arguable that events are capable of entering into the fundamental causal relations by virtue of their intrinsic, essential natures and not their accidental, purely circumstantial properties.[80] If agent causation is a fundamental causal relation, and being a willing is a merely contingent feature of an event, then it does not seem that events enter into the agent-causal relation by virtue of their being willings. But then it is hard to see why an event that is not a willing couldn't enter into that relation. This conflicts with the fairly compelling intuition that agent causation, if there is such a thing, is restricted to willings; it is by virtue of their being *willings* that those events are fit relata for agent causation.

One might insist that being a willing is a contingent, relational (circumstantial) property of an event, and preserve the claim that *necessarily agent causation produces willings* by reckoning it analytic: "being a willing," on this account, would just be understood to mean "being an event that is the proximal effect of agent causation." But on this proposal, one does not genuinely *explain* the suitability of an event for being the proximal effect of agent causation by saying that it was a willing.

Consider any event kind K and assume events of that kind get caught up in fundamental causal transactions. There will then be truths to the effect that events of kind K get caught up in certain sorts of fundamental causal transactions but not others. Call truths of this sort the "fundamental causal truths about Ks." We're supposing that there are fundamental causal truths about willings. If we invoke the causal-explanatory premise that a perspicuous explanation of fundamental causal truths about Ks will proceed by invoking intrinsic, nonrelational properties of Ks, then on our materialist's relational treatment of being a willing, we arrive at the conclusion that one cannot explain the fundamental causal truths about willings by appealing, in part, to their status as willings. But this conflicts with our initial conjecture that it is by virtue of their status as willings that certain events are fit relata for agent causation.

Whether or not the property of being a willing is essential to an event, it is worth underscoring the fact that nearly all philosophers of a naturalistic bent assume that the preferred description for a mental event vis-à-vis the project of deep explanation is as a neural event of a certain sort. Thus, for example, Donald Davidson's anomalous monism insists that mental events need to be redescribed neurally if they are going to become fully intelligible *qua* events in the natural causal order.[81] There is good reason for this. It is very plausible to think that the natural kinds to which neural events belong are neural kinds, and moreover that deep explanation of events will proceed by considering events *qua* the natural kinds to which they belong. But if agent causation holds between agents and neural events, we shall have something like the flip side of anomalous monism. Agency theorists of a materialistic bent will have to maintain that the special agent-causal relation holds between material things and a particular sort of neural event when those material things and neural events are redescribed in terms of the categories of moral psychology. (And, if by the lights of token identity theory the neural events that are in fact willings don't form their own natural kind, it would seem odd at best to postulate a unique (agent-) causal relation that's restricted to an event-type that is not a natural kind among events.)

A Special Cost of Token-emergent Materialism

Token-emergent materialism claims that there is a mental event—a willing—that is distinct from any microphysical event and that an agent influences its microphysical states by agent-causing a willing, which in turn causally influences how microphysical states are distributed. A cost here, as we see it, is the violation of a moderately compelling Humean thesis about causation. The thesis is the following:

> No causal relation obtaining between a member of a family of events A and some member of a distinct family of events B is necessitated by the existence of A.

Token-emergent materialism violates this principle in the following way. It tells us that some family of microphysical events is sufficient for the existence of some willing distinct from the microphysical events and sufficient for that willing's being causally related to one or more of those microphysical events. So it appears that in order to combine supervenience with downward causation of microphysical phenomena by willings, a staunchly anti-Humean position on causation must be defended. Again, while we have identified this as indeed a cost, nevertheless—like all those commitments of the supervenience thesis that we have identified as costs—it is imaginable that someone would deny this, or believe it a cost worth paying.

Costs of the Thesis That Agents Are Material

We end with several reasons for worrying about treating the agent that enters into agent causation as a material object. These will provide at least some reasons for an agency theorist's believing that the agent is immaterial.

In answer to the question "What physical object is the agent?," we have been thinking that persons, according to a materialist agency theorist, are physical organisms, and that such organisms are the agent-causes of their decisions. Earlier we took seriously the idea that the fundamental causal powers of an event are determined by its intrinsic, essential properties.[82] Consider now the following, closely related, thesis—which also strikes us as true:

> The fundamental causal powers of a thing aren't determined wholly or partly by properties that are extrinsic to it.

Applying this principle now to agency theory, we can infer that the causal power of a thing to produce decisions doesn't depend upon its environment; if two things are intrinsically qualitatively identical, then either none or both are agent-causes of decisions. But this truth seems jeopardized by materialist agency theory. In the actual world, Jan agent-causes his decision to stop daydreaming about climbing big mountains and to work on philosophy instead. Suppose the agency theorist identifies Jan with the salient physical organism. Consider now world W where the decision is made by a brain in a vat instrinsically identical with the one Jan enjoys in this world, surrounded by 145 pounds of organism-stuff. In the actual world, the brain does not agent-cause the decision, but in the brain-in-vat world, it does. We have violated the principle. Thus the materialist agency theorist will have to either give up the principle or claim that even in the actual world, agents are brains and not physical organisms.

The second option strikes us as *prima facie* more plausible, though it is still troubling: there is an undeniable strain to claiming that strictly speaking moral predicates of praise and blame apply to brains. Moreover, further trouble looms ahead. Shall we say all or some proper part of the brain is the agent? Suppose that we are materialists and on some occasion identify the right hemisphere of an individual as most intimately involved in some decision that is agent-caused. Consider now a right-hemisphere-in-vat world. . . .

Even ignoring the compelling nature of the above principle, this latest difficulty highlights a certain awkwardness in the task of saying what physical object does the agent-causing. The organism? The *whole* organism, feet and arms and all, or some proper part of it? The brain, perhaps; or perhaps one hemisphere, or some smaller part. Sometimes this hemisphere, sometimes that. The whole business looks to emerge as arbitrary, in a way that no facts-of-the-matter are.[83]

Few thoroughgoing naturalists would shy away from allowing that, at the end of the day, there must be some principled way of marking off what physical object as a matter of fact does the deciding. This said, it is worth noting that one of the most attractive conceptions of material things is one according to which the really fundamental relations holding between material things hold between the microphysical particles, at the deepest level of physical theory. Whatever agents may be, it will strike many of us as both odd and a surprising concession to have very large material beings enter into the fundamental explanation of many microphysical events.

A while back, H. Feigl and then J. J. C. Smart worried about nomological danglers: they could not bring themselves to believe that physics had all its fundamental laws holding among tiny particles save for a few special laws holding between large complexes of millions of particles and conscious states. Their conclusion, or anyway Smart's, was that "man is a vast arrangment of physical particles and that there are not, over and above this, sensations or states of consciousness." If we are to accede in the claim that man is a vast arrangement of particles, there is considerable pressure to hold that the microlevel is metaphysically prior in order of explanation. We want to leave fundamental physical explanation all at the level of the microparticles, where deep physical explanations of physical things ultimately belong.

Is there any advantage for dualistic over materialistic agency theory here? Well, dualism allows one to stick with the idea that the fundamental material processes are at the microphysical level. That is to say, all fundamental transactions between wholly material things are at the microphysical level. It also allows one to stick with the intuition that the fundamental explanations for such transactions proceed by appeal to laws of nature. We've already seen how difficult it is for robust freedom to be grounded by laws of nature. If one wants robust freedom and also thinks of purely natural processes as grounded by laws of nature, then one had better place agents outside the natural world. In short, it seems to us that dualism affords the proponent of robust freedom the prospect of a more orderly and unified conception of the material world, of material things. Relatedly, the immaterialist is not forced to graft a radical difference in kind onto what appears to be a mere difference in degree. If it is acknowledged that agent causing is, as it seems, a radically unique kind of making or bringing about relation, the materialist agency theorist must acknowledge that there is such a relation out in the world that crops up in certain physical organisms. These organisms differ from other organisms, trailing off in degree from chimps to bunnies to lizards and on down. The materialist must say that the difference in degree between the organisms that are our bodies and those of, say, monkeys, produces a radical difference in kind. It must surely be a point in favor of the immaterialist that a difference in kind, when it comes to unique causation and agency (and the moral responsibility brought with it) is marked by an ontological difference between things capable of entering into such causation and things incapable of entering into it.

Finally, to return to an earlier point, agent causation is a genuinely mysterious sort of phenomenon. If it occurs at all, one might reasonably expect it to emanate from a very mysterious sort of thing. And one might reckon organisms or brains scarcely mysterious enough: souls, substantial forms, and entelechies seem eminently suited to that role.[84]

Conclusion

We have found nothing outright incoherent about materialist agency theory. If the materialist accepts, for example, that for certain deep explanatory purposes, the flip side of anomalous monism should be accepted, doesn't mind saying that there are deep explanations of microphysical events that are provided by certain hulking large material objects, isn't especially attracted to a simple and unified conception of material beings, doesn't mind saying that the agent-causal relation is constituted in part by facts extrinsic to the relata, and so on, then he will find the marriage of agency theory to materialism relatively untroubling—certainly little more troubling than agency theory is in its own right. What we have aimed to do is alert agency theorists to the costs of embracing materialism, and leave them to decide whether these costs— ones rather less heavy than embracing contradictions or denying positively self-evident principles—are prices worth paying.[85] While we shan't pretend that the cumulative weight of the points we've raised against materialist agency theory are overwhelming, perhaps it will at least be clearer why we found ourselves with the belief that there are connections of interest and importance between freedom and materialism.[86]

4

Libertarian Freedom and the Principle of Alternative Possibilities

Eleonore Stump

Introduction

In two recent papers, David Widerker argues against attempts to show that a proponent of libertarian free will and moral responsibility need not accept the principle of alternative possibilities (PAP).[87] PAP has many different formulations, but they are all based on this sort of claim:

> PAP. A person is morally responsible for doing an action A (or has free will with respect to an action A) only if he could have done otherwise than A (or could have failed to do A).[88]

A standard strategy for showing that PAP isn't true is what has come to be known as a Frankfurt-style counterexample.[89] In a Frankfurt-style counterexample, a person P does an action A in circumstances that incline most people to conclude that P is doing A freely, but the circumstances involve some mechanism that would have operated to bring it about that P did A if P had not done A of his own accord. In the actual sequence of events presented in the counterexample, the mechanism does *not* operate, and P does do A of his own accord. So the counterexample is designed to make us think that P does A freely in the actual sequence of events although it is not the case that P could have done otherwise than A.[90] Frankfurt-style counterexamples can be constructed either for bodily actions such as leaving a room or for mental actions such as deciding to leave a room. One way Widerker challenges Frankfurt-style counterexamples for mental acts is by focusing on a recent argument of John Martin Fischer's.[91] Here is Fischer's Frankfurt-style counterexample (FFC):

> FFC. Black is a nefarious neurosurgeon. In performing an operation on Jones to remove a brain tumor, Black inserts a mechanism into Jones' brain which enables Black to monitor and control Jones' activities. Jones, meanwhile, knows nothing of this. Black exercises his control through a computer which he has programmed so that, among other things, it monitors Jones' voting behavior. If Jones shows an inclination to decide to vote for Carter, then the computer through the mechanism in Jones's brain intervenes to assure that he actually decides to vote for Reagan and does so vote. But if Jones decides on his own to vote for Reagan, the computer does nothing but continues to monitor—without affecting—the goings-on in Jones' head. Suppose that [in these circumstances] Jones decides to vote for Reagan on his own, just as he would have if Black had not inserted the mechanism into his head.[92]

Fischer argues that in this situation Jones is morally responsible for choosing to vote for Reagan, even though he could not have done otherwise. Fischer goes on to claim that

> F. Nothing about [this] . . . example *requires* the actual sequence issuing in the decision and action to proceed in a deterministic way.

And he says, "if it proceeds in a non-deterministic way that satisfied the libertarian, then Jones can be held responsible, even though he could not have done otherwise."[93] Widerker, however, thinks that F is false.

Libertarians, Widerker says, maintain that

> L. A decision is free only if [1] "the decision [is] not . . . causally determined, and . . . [2] the agent could have avoided making it."[94]

L2 is, of course, the point of contention between Widerker and Fischer; Widerker claims and Fischer denies that PAP is true with regard to mental acts such as decisions. Consequently, Widerker would be begging the question against Fischer if he argued that FFC didn't apply to libertarianism because in that example the putatively free agent in fact violated L2. Widerker's rejection of F, therefore, must focus on whether the putatively free agent in FFC violates

> L1. A decision is free only if it isn't causally determined.

On Fischer's view, nothing in FFC compels us to suppose that the agent is causally determined with respect to deciding to vote for Reagan; and so, on Fischer's view, a version of libertarianism that maintains L1 is compatible with FFC. That is why Fischer thinks F is true and Frankfurt-style counterexamples such as FFC constitute an argument for a rejection of PAP, even for libertarians. But Widerker thinks that no Frankfurt-style counterexamples will be compatible with L1. Since, on Widerker's view, the agent who is putatively free in Frankfurt-style counterexamples is in fact causally determined with respect to his action, the agent will not count as free in the sense libertarians recognize. And so, Widerker thinks, Frankfurt-style counterexamples don't in fact show—at least, don't show libertarians—that agents can be free or morally responsible with regard to mental acts when they can't do otherwise, or that PAP isn't true with regard to mental acts.

Widerker's Argument

Why does Widerker think that no Frankfurt-style counterexamples will be compatible with L1? Why does he think that putatively free actions in Frankfurt-style counterexamples are causally determined? On his view, FFC rests on the presupposition that

> P1. Jones's showing an inclination to decide to vote for Carter is (in the circumstances) a causally necessary condition of his deciding to vote for Carter.[95]

If P1 weren't true, then Jones would after all have had it in his power to decide to vote for Carter. Fischer thinks that it isn't in Jones's power to decide to vote for Carter because he thinks that Jones can't decide to vote for Carter without previously showing an inclination for that decision. And whenever Jones shows such an inclination, the neurosurgeon's mechanism operates to bring it about that Jones decides to vote for Reagan. If Jones could suddenly decide to vote for Carter without having shown any inclination for that decision, the neurosurgeon's mechanism couldn't operate in time; and in that case, contrary to FFC, Jones would have it in his power to decide to vote for Carter. So FFC must presuppose P1 or something very similar.

But if P1 is true, Widerker says, then so is

> P2. Jones's not showing an inclination to decide to vote for Carter is (in the circumstances) causally sufficient for his not deciding to vote for Carter.[96]

So, since in FFC Jones showed no inclination to decide to vote for Carter, Jones's not deciding to vote for Carter was causally determined, Widerker argues. In FFC there are only two possibilities for the agent— voting for Carter or voting for Reagan; consequently, if Jones's not deciding to vote for Carter is causally determined, so is his decision to vote for Reagan. In that case, Jones's decision doesn't meet the condition in L1. Therefore, F is false. And if F is false, Frankfurt-style counterexamples don't after all constitute an argument against PAP as far as libertarians are concerned.

Widerker's argument against Fischer has intuitive appeal. Many libertarians, and others as well, do suppose that a person can choose to do A without having previously had an inclination to choose to do A. In fact, many people tend to think a person can choose to do A after having previously had only inclinations to do not-A. Consider, for example, the criminal who is strongly inclined to lie to the police and who instead finds himself, to his horror, spontaneously and of his own accord confessing to them. Or consider the dieter who was strongly inclined not to eat anything but vegetables at the cocktail party but who finds himself willingly eating the potato chips. It seems to many people that the act in question (confessing to the police or eating potato chips at the party) is freely chosen but without any previous inclination for that choice— rather with a previous inclination opposed to such a choice. Moreover, those libertarians with a commitment to L1 will in particular reject claims such as P1 and P2 as false: an inclination to decide to do A isn't a causally necessary condition for a decision to do A, and the absence of an inclination to decide to do A isn't causally sufficient for a decision not to do A.

Insofar as FFC presupposes P1 and P2, then FFC will not be effective against its intended opponents. In particular, it won't constitute an argument against those libertarians who reject P1 and P2. But all Frankfurt-style counterexamples (at least as regards mental acts) will share such features of FFC, Widerker thinks, because there has to be some antecedent condition that is correlated with the mental act at issue and that can signal the neuroscope (or whatever fictional device the example posits) whether or not to initiate the coercive mechanism. All Frankfurt-style counterexamples will therefore apparently require some analogue to P1 and P2. Consequently, Widerker thinks, Frankfurt-style counterexamples cannot do the job for which they were designed: they cannot show that PAP isn't true. At any rate, they cannot show this without begging the question against libertarians, since they must presuppose the denial of L1, which is constitutive of libertarianism.

Does Widerker's argument against Frankfurt-style counterexamples succeed? I don't think it does.[97]

Friendly Amendment to Fischer's Account

As I will argue, not all libertarians share a commitment to L1, and so not all libertarians would be moved by Widerker's reasons for rejecting FFC. Aquinas, for example, supposes that all acts of will are preceded by acts of intellect of some sort, which play a causal role in volition. But before looking at L1 directly, it is worth asking whether Frankfurt-style counterexamples for mental acts such as deciding *require* supposing that such a mental act is causally dependent on some antecedent mental state, such as Fischer's inclinations. I think the answer is "no." It seems to me possible to construct a Frankfurt-style counterexample for a mental act D of deciding without supposing that the fictional neuroscope of the counterexample detects a mental state or act that is antecedent to D.[98]

To see how to construct such a counterexample, it is helpful to notice that Fischer's evil neurosurgeon uses fairly clumsy neuroscientific technology, since his neuroscope is sensitive just to mental phenomena such as inclinations. So suppose that we replace Fischer's neurosurgeon Black with a more sophisticated neurosurgeon Grey, who uses a neuroscope sensitive to neural firings. Grey ascertains that every time Jones decides to do any of a certain range of actions—say, voting for Republican candidates—the decision to do so regularly correlates with the completion of a sequence of neural firings in Jones's brain that always includes, near its beginning, the firing of neurons a, b, c (call this "neural sequence 1").[99] On the other hand, Jones's deciding to vote for Democratic candidates is correlated with the completion of a different neural sequence that always includes, near its beginning, the firings of neurons x, y, z, none of which is the same as those in neural sequence 1 (call this "neural sequence 2"). For simplicity's sake, suppose that neither neural sequence 1 nor neural sequence 2 is also correlated with any further set of mental acts.[100]

Then Grey can tune his neuroscope accordingly. Whenever the neuroscope detects the firing of x, y, and z, the initial neurons of neural sequence 2, which is correlated with Jones's decisions to vote for Democrats, the neuroscope immediately disrupts the neural sequence, so that it isn't brought to completion, and activates the coercive neurological mechanism which brings it about that Jones decides to vote for Republicans.[101] But if the neuroscope detects the firing of a, b, and c, the initial neurons in neural sequence 1, which is correlated with decisions to vote for Republicans, then the neuroscope does not interrupt that neural sequence. It doesn't activate the coercive neurological mechanism, and neural sequence 1 continues, culminating, at least sometimes, in Jones's deciding of his own accord to vote for Reagan.

I have now revised FFC so as to omit all mention of inclinations. I'll call the revised counterexample RCE.

It should be clear that we need not espouse any type-type identity theories to tell the story in RCE, although type-type identity theories are compatible with RCE. RCE doesn't presuppose even token-token identity theories, although it is compatible with them also. It requires only that there be *some* correlation between neural sequences and mental states.

By saying that mental states are correlated with neural sequences, I mean to make only a vague association between mental states and neural sequences, compatible with various different theories of relations between mind and brain. Those who think that the mental is identical to the physical can suppose that the decidings and the neural sequences are correlated because the decidings are the neural sequences. Nonreductive materialists can take the correlation as some version of emergence or supervenience. Cartesian dualists might interpret the correlation as caus-ally connected states of body and soul. RCE is, therefore, also compati-ble with some dualist theories of mind, namely, those that don't suppose mental acts are isolated in the soul, altogether unconnected to neural states. (In my view, Aquinas's account of the soul is a dualism of the sort compatible with RCE, except that Aquinas thinks in terms of bodily states in general, not neural states.[102])

Furthermore, the correlation in question need not even be law-like. All Grey's neuroscope needs in order to operate is a current correlation in Jones between the decisions to vote in certain ways and the neural sequences described. But this correlation need not hold across human beings; it need not even hold throughout Jones's lifetime, as long as it characterizes him in the period in which Grey is investigating and manipulating him.

The neurological fantasy story in RCE is, therefore, compatible with all current theories of mind except the most extreme versions of Cartesian substance dualism. On an extreme version of Cartesian dualism—which Descartes himself may have held—thinking of any sort (including decid-ing) goes on only in the immaterial soul and isn't mirrored by or correlated with brain processes.[103] On any theory of the mind that sees a stronger tie between mind and brain than extreme Cartesian dualism, there will be some sort of correlation (correlation up to and including identity) between mental processes and brain processes, and that is all RCE needs.

The falsity of P1 and P2 is irrelevant to RCE since it makes no mention of inclinations.[104] In RCE the neurosurgeon's neuroscope responds not to inclinations preceding a decision but to patterns of neural firing correlated with the decision itself. Now RCE is a Frankfurt-style counterexample to PAP.[105] Will RCE, therefore, evade Widerker's arguments?

Frankfurt-style Counterexamples Defended

To answer this question, we have to consider the notion of libertarian free will operative in Widerker's discussion. Widerker's argument focuses on the fact that Fischer's FFC is expressed in terms of inclination, and so RCE, which makes no mention of inclinations, escapes Widerker's argument as he devised it against FFC. But Widerker argues as he does against P1 and P2 because he is convinced that libertarians are committed to L1, the claim that a decision is free only if it is not causally determined.

Now in RCE, the decision to vote for Reagan is still causally determined—not in the sense it was in FFC, in which (as Widerker argues) preceding inclinations are causally necessary for particular decisions, but in a more complicated way. Whatever exactly we take the relation between mental and neural states to be, one mental state is correlated with an entire neural sequence. And the neural sequence consists in a chain of neural firings, in which the firing of one set of neurons causes the firing of other sets. The whole neural sequence of firings, then, is the causal outcome of the chain of causal interactions among the individual neurons constituting the sequence. So because of the correlation between a neural sequence and, say, the mental state of deciding to vote for Reagan, the latter is determined by the chain of causal interactions among the neurons of the sequence. If the mental state is identical to the neural state, or if mental states are states of soul that are causally produced in the soul by the brain, then the mental state is causally produced by the preceding neural states in the sequence. If the mental state is a state of soul that is merely correlated with neural states, without being identical to a neural state or directly caused by it, then the mental state is determined by the causal interactions of the neurons in some more complicated way—for example, in the way some emergentists or supervenience theorists suppose mental states to be a function of neural states.

RCE, then, doesn't presuppose P1 and P2, but it does nonetheless

violate L1 in virtue of supposing that a mental act such as deciding is
determined, in one way or another, by underlying neural processes.
Does this result show that RCE also fails as a candidate for a Frankfurt-
style counterexample to PAP, because it, too, begs the question against
libertarians by presupposing the denial of L1, which is constitutive of
libertarianism?

   Although it might look as if we should answer in the affirmative here,
the correct answer in my view is "no." The reason RCE seems to beg
the question against libertarianism lies not in RCE but in Widerker's
formulation of libertarianism. On L1, only those mental acts that are not
so much as correlated with patterns of neural firings can count as morally
responsible or free. But then libertarianism could be held only by
extreme Cartesian dualists. Clearly, there are committed libertarians who
reject any form of Cartesian dualism. Thomas Aquinas is one such
libertarian; among contemporary philosophers, Peter van Inwagen is
another. So I am inclined to think that Widerker has formulated the
conditions for libertarianism too strongly. To avoid making libertarianism
a theory only extreme Cartesian dualists can hold, L1 needs to be
revised. Libertarians do need to rule out as nonfree mental or bodily acts
that are causally determined to be what they are *by something outside the
agent.* The claim that a free act is the outcome of a causal chain that
originates in some cause external to the agent *is* incompatible with
libertarian free will. But the mere claim that a free act is the outcome of
any causal chain at all is not.

   A more reasonable version of L1, therefore, would count a decision
free only if it meets this condition:

   L1'. A decision is free only if it is not the outcome of a causal chain that
   originates in a cause outside the agent.

Of course, L1' is not *sufficient* for libertarian freedom. Aquinas, for
example, thinks that the essence of freedom is that the agent's own
mental faculties, her intellect and will, are the ultimate source of any free
act, and not something outside the agent. But L1' captures what Aquinas
takes to be a *necessary* condition for freedom, namely, that a free action
(mental or bodily) not be caused by something external to the agent.[106]
On this way of thinking about L, the issue between Fischer, who
takes libertarianism with regard to mental acts to be compatible with
Frankfurt-style counterexamples and the rejection of PAP, and Widerker,
who doesn't, is this: are the actions meeting condition L1' just those
actions where the agent could have done otherwise? And here Frankfurt-

style counterexamples, such as RCE, seem to me decisive. RCE is compatible with supposing that nothing outside the agent causally determines the mental act in question; and yet in RCE the agent could not have acted otherwise than he did.

An Objection

At this point someone may object. If we bring contemporary theories of the nature of the mind into the discussion of free will, the objector will argue, then (unless we accept extreme Cartesian dualism) it will not be possible for RCE to be compatible with the requirement of L1'. Contemporary theories of the mind other than extreme Cartesian dualism correlate mental and neural states. But, the objector will maintain,

> O. There are no uncaused neural events, and the chain of causation will eventually be traceable to something outside the agent.

So if mental states are determined by neural states, they will also be determined, more remotely, by causes outside the agent, contrary to the stipulation in L1'.

The objector will perhaps meet little opposition regarding his claim that all neural events are caused. Is he also right in supposing that, therefore, the chain of causation will lead outside the agent? Are all brain processes causally determined, ultimately, by something outside the agent?

This is a difficult and complicated question that carries considerable philosophical freight. The first thing to see about it is that it certainly isn't answerable by appeal to neurobiology. We are very far from having a complete or even reasonably adequate neuroscience. It is fitting that the third edition of the widely used textbook *Principles of Neural Science* has a photograph of the Rosetta stone as its frontispiece.[107] We still lack the Rosetta stone for neurobiology, in the sense that we don't understand even the general principles by which the brain produces or contributes to cognitive function, as we do understand at least the general genetic principles that underlie biological inheritance and differentiation. Even for visual perception, where we know a considerable amount about how things outside the perceiver affect the brain, we are far from having a clear idea of the causal relations leading from a visually presented object to the neural states that constitute or are correlated with visual recognition of the object. But what we currently know of such processes strongly suggests that the neural states in question are underdetermined by the impact of the perceived object on the perceiver. As one pair of neuropsychologists put it, "although the kind of information sent to a [neural] network restricts what it can do, the input alone does not determine what a network computes."[108] As matters now stand, then, neuroscience alone won't tell us whether the objector is right or not, although what evidence we have undermines rather than supports his position. The objector, therefore, can't point to results in neuroscience to demonstrate his claim that all brain processes are ultimately causally determined by something outside the agent.

We might suppose that science in general shows that any neural event must be caused by something outside the agent, because all events are part of an extensive set of causal chains that lead back to the Big Bang, so that a perfect knowledge of natural laws and conditions at the time of the Big Bang would enable a person to predict everything that came thereafter. But the growth of interest in chaos theory has made this form of determinism unpopular. In a recent article, Stephen Jay Gould, for example, associates this view with eighteenth-century optimism and rejects it with this dismissive remark: "The nature of universal complexity shatters this chimerical dream."[109]

What chaos theory undermines is just our ability to predict or explain the causal chains of events found in nature. So we might suppose that even if deterministic causal series aren't always predictable, they nonetheless exist. Although it might, therefore, be true that we couldn't predict the causal series that link the world outside a human body with events in the brain of that body, we might think, there still are such causal chains, and they determine what happens in the brain. Otherwise, it would seem, brain events would be insulated from the physical interactions of the surrounding extrabodily environment, and the causal nexus of brain events would be incomplete and perplexingly truncated. So, on this view, the events at the time of the Big Bang are the start of causal chains that eventually lead in a deterministic way (or a probabilistic way, to account for the indeterminacy introduced by quantum mechanics) to all subsequent events, including brain events, even if those subsequent events aren't knowable or predictable at the time of the Big Bang.

This way of looking at things, which will perhaps seem obviously right to many people, rests not so much on scientific results as on philosophical convictions that include both reductionism and determinism. It assumes that all events, including biological events and events at the macroscopic level, are reducible to causal interactions at the microstructural level; and it supposes that (apart from quantum indeterminacy) there is a complete causal story to be told about everything that happens, that there is no genuine contingency or chance in nature. What we call chance is only a matter of our ignorance, stemming from our inability to comprehend all the forces operating on complicated sets of initial conditions and our consequent inability to predict the outcome of a particular event or series of events.

Although reductionism comes in many forms, its different forms share a common attitude: all the sciences are reducible to physics, and scientific explanation will be ultimately formulable solely in terms of the microstructural. But this attitude discounts the importance of levels of organization (or form, as Aristotle and medieval philosophers would say) and the causal efficacy of things in virtue of their level of organization. This feature of reductionism perhaps helps explain why it has come under special attack in philosophy of biology.[110] Biological function is frequently a feature of the way in which the microstructural components of something are organized, rather than of the intrinsic properties of the microcomponents themselves. Proteins, for example, tend to be biologically active only when folded in certain ways, so that their function depends on their three-dimensional structure. But this is a feature of the organization of the molecule as a whole and can't be reduced to properties of the elementary particles that make up the atoms of the molecule. In fact, for large proteins, even an omniscient knowledge of the properties of elementary particles of the atoms that comprise the protein may not be enough to predict the shape of the folded protein, because the activity of enzymes is required to catalyze the folding of some proteins.[111]

In his magisterial treatment of reductionism in *The Disorder of Things*, John Dupré takes the examples in his arguments against reductionism not so much from molecular biology as from ecology and population genetics.[112] On reductionist views, Dupré says, "events at the macrolevel, except insofar as they are understood as aggregates of events at the microlevel—that is, as reducible to the microlevel at least in principle— are causally inert. This . . . is the classical picture of Laplacean determinism, except that it does not depend on determinism, only the causal completeness . . . of the microlevel."[113] But, as Dupré's examples from biology make clear, "there are genuinely causal entities at many different levels of organization. And this is enough to show that causal completeness at one particular level [the microlevel] is wholly incredible."[114] Dupré thinks that commitment to reductionism was strongly motivated by a belief in determinism, either of the classical variety, which supposes that there is a complete causal story, a sufficient antecedent condition, for everything that happens, or its quantum mechanical analogue, which supposes that there are antecedent conditions that determine particular probabilities for events. Consequently, Dupré thinks his arguments against reductionism are also part of an argument for either variety of determinism as well. His arguments against reductionism provide, he claims, an "inversion of the reductionist *modus ponens* (Causal completeness requires reductionism) into . . . [an] antireductionist *modus tollens* (the failure of reductionism implies the failure of causal completeness)."[115]

So O rests on philosophical views that aren't obviously true but are rather the subject of considerable controversy.

It seems, then, that neither science nor philosophy can demonstrate O's truth. Therefore, while it is uncontroversial that neural events are causally *influenced* by events outside the agent, it isn't at all clear that they are causally *determined* by events outside the agent. There may well be biological events, including biological events in the brain, where the ultimate causal determination of the event is internal to the agent. To take a simple example having nothing to do with mental events, prion protein is normally found on the outside of neurons, where it is innocuous; but it can mutate into a highly destructive form in some individuals, as a result of the internal environment surrounding the neuron.[116] If Dupré's rejection of reductionism and determinism is right, the mutation of prion protein may be an example of a genuinely contingent event, produced by causal efficacy at a level of organization higher than the level of elementary physical particles and resulting ultimately just from chance encounters among molecules within the brain. In such a case, if Dupré is right, events external to an agent may have some causal influence on the shaping of the internal environment of the brain, but there need not be any such external events causally sufficient for the neural chain of events culminating in the mutation of the prion protein.

The Larger Issue

Here we may seem to have reached a familiar impasse, which is just highlighted by bringing theories of the nature of the mind into discussions of free will. The objector supposed that all neural events must be causally determined by something outside the agent and that, therefore, if neural events and mental events are correlated as RCE assumes, RCE isn't compatible with L1'. I have tried to cast doubt on the objector's position; but, in the one example I have used to illustrate my point, the example of prion protein, chance instead of external causation produces the brain event in question. If the only way to defeat the objector is to claim that neural events are brought about by chance when they aren't causally determined by something outside the agent, then the victory over the objector is Pyrrhic. If the only options are external causal determinism or accident, the libertarian has lost the argument; his position is sunk either way.

Aquinas's position gives a helpful insight into why the libertarian can't avail himself of either option. An action is free on Aquinas's view in case the ultimate source of the action is the agent's own intellect and will. (Aquinas doesn't think that for an action to be free the agent has to have reasoned, consciously and rationally, about the action; the action could have been the result of unconscious and irrational cognitive processing and still count as ultimately stemming from operations of the agent's intellect and will.) But if either causes outside the agent or sheer accident is responsible for neural events correlated with the agent's acts of intellect and will, the ultimate source of the action isn't the mind of the agent.

Some contemporary philosophers share Aquinas's basic intuition about the nature of freedom. For example, Fischer's account of moral responsibility is like Aquinas's account of free actions in this respect: Fischer thinks that moral responsibility is a function of an agent's reasons-responsive mechanism.[117] And one way of understanding the point of contention between compatibilists and libertarians of any sort is this: is it possible for the brain to be a reasons-responsive mechanism if neural events are produced only by accident or by causes outside the agent? A compatibilist will say "yes"; libertarians such as Aquinas will say "no". That is why, if mental events are tied to neural events and neural events must stem either from accident or from causal determination by something outside the agent, the libertarian position has lost.

Part of what makes it hard to adjudicate between the compatibilist and the libertarian here is that we are so far from understanding how the brain can be a reasons-responsive mechanism at all, on anybody's theory of mind or free will. Except for extreme Cartesian dualists, most philosophers suppose the brain *does* constitute a reasons-responsive mechanism, but it is hard to see *how* a biological organ such as the brain can respond to reasons or process information. Neurobiologists are in no position to give anything other than promissory notes on this subject, and the best philosophical attempts are ultimately unpersuasive even if ingenious.[118] But unless we understand how a biological organ such as the brain can be an information-processor or a reasons-responsive mechanism, we won't be able to give a scientific account of our cognitive functioning that settles the question at issue between the compatibilist and the libertarian.

Looked at philosophically, rather than scientifically, compatibilism appears to be a sort of corollary to reductionism and determinism. If all macrophenomena are reducible to microstructural phenomena and if there is a complete causal story to be told at the microlevel, then whatever control or freedom we have as macroscopic agents has to be not only compatible with but in fact just a function of the complete causal story at the microlevel. But if reductionism and determinism are rejected, then, as Dupré argues, there can be causal efficacy at various levels of organization, including the level of human agents. A person's intellect and will can exercise real causal efficacy, from the top down, in the way Aquinas supposes they do. Dupré says, "Humans have all kinds of causal capacities that nothing else in our world has. . . . There is no good reason for projecting these uniquely human capacities in a reductionist style onto inanimate bits of matter. Nor is there anything ultimately mysterious about particular causal capacities being exhibited uniquely by certain very complex entities." He can take this position without what he regards as "metaphysical excesses," such as accepting extreme Cartesian dualism, because having rejected reductionism he is free to hold that "there is no reason why changes at one level may not be explained in terms of causal processes at a higher, that is, more complex level. In the case of human action, the physical changes involved in and resulting from a particular action may perfectly well be explained in terms of the capacity of the agent to perform an action of that kind."[119] If Dupré is right, compatibilism looks like an unnecessary concession, an attempt to preserve what we commonly believe about our control over our actions in the face of a mistaken commitment to reductionism and determinism.

Dupré's attitude toward reductionism and determinism is, of course, controversial; many philosophers of mind, in particular, are explicit adherents of reductionism. I myself find Dupré's case against reductionism persuasive, but the issue is much too large to adjudicate in passing here. Consequently, this is where the discussion stands. If RCE violates L1' because of the correlation between mental and neural states, as the objector supposes, then, for the same reasons, libertarianism is false, for all versions of libertarianism that are combined with a theory of the mind other than extreme Cartesian dualism. (And this result holds even if, contrary to my argument, libertarianism is committed to L1 rather than to L1', since if the correlation of mental and neural states implies that all mental events are caused by something outside the agent, it also implies that all mental events are caused.) On the other hand, if RCE does not violate L1', then it constitutes a viable Frankfurt-style counterexample to PAP, and L2 isn't a necessary condition for libertarianism any more than L1 is, contrary to what Widerker supposes.

Which of these possibilities is the right one depends on whether the objector is right in supposing that all neural events are the product of causal determination by something outside the agent. Since determining whether the objector is right requires either results from neuroscience far in advance of anything now available to us or the final adjudication of large and controversial philosophical issues, it isn't possible to show that the objection is mistaken; by the same token, it isn't possible for the objector to demonstrate the truth of O. Since this is so, it is open to the libertarian to hold that RCE is compatible with L1'. Furthermore, and more importantly for Widerker's position, unless the libertarian is an extreme Cartesian dualist, his choice is either to hold that the objector is wrong and RCE is compatible with L1' or to give up his libertarianism.

Conclusion: Adjudicating between Fischer and Widerker

We can now adjudicate the dispute between Fischer and Widerker.

I've argued that the first of the claims Widerker takes to constitute libertarianism is too strong, requiring libertarians to reject all theories of the mind except extreme Cartesian dualism. To avoid being committed to extreme Cartesian dualism, the libertarian needs to hold as a necessary condition L1', that decisions are free only if they aren't causally determined by anything outside the agent, and not L1, that decisions are free only if they aren't causally determined at all.

RCE doesn't violate L1', unless O is right. It's difficult to adjudicate the issues raised by O, but the libertarian's position requires a certain stand with regard to it. The libertarian is committed to a theory of freedom that requires him to deny that all mental acts are caused by something external to the agent. Consequently, unless he is an extreme Cartesian dualist and supposes that there is no correlation between mental acts and neural events, the libertarian must think that the objection to RCE is mistaken: it isn't the case that all neural events are caused by something external to the agent. So if the libertarian isn't committed to extreme Cartesian dualism, he must reject O and grant that RCE is a Frankfurt-style counterexample that is compatible with supposing that free decisions are not externally caused. Given the arguments that libertarianism is committed to (L1') but not (L1), he should consequently also grant that (RCE) is compatible with libertarianism.

Therefore, (RCE) can be construed as a Frankfurt-style counterexample in which an agent has libertarian freedom with respect to a mental act D, but could not have done otherwise than D. Widerker's argument against FFC doesn't apply to RCE. Consequently, Widerker's arguments against Frankfurt-style counterexamples to PAP fails, and RCE therefore shows that PAP isn't necessary for free will even in a libertarian sense.

Nothing in this argument has the implication that libertarian free will is never accompanied by alternative possibilities. It may be true that in most cases in which an agent acts with free will or is morally responsible, the agent can do otherwise. What Frankfurt-style counterexamples show is only that the ability to do otherwise isn't essential to a free action or an action for which the agent is morally responsible. It might nonetheless be the case that the ability to do otherwise is what the medievals called an associated accident, an accident that accompanies free will or moral responsibility much or even almost all of the time.[120]

Finally, this discussion of Frankfurt-style counterexamples shows what is essential to free will if the ability to do otherwise is not essential. In Widerker's view, libertarianism holds that

> L. A decision is free only if [1] "the decision [is] not . . . causally determined, and . . . [2] the agent could have avoided making it."

As I argued above, L1 is too broad and should be replaced with L1': the decision is not the outcome of a causal chain that originates in a cause outside the agent. The success of Frankfurt-style counterexamples shows that L2 is also too strong. What is necessary for libertarian free will is, as Aquinas says, that the ultimate source of the action be the agent's own will and cognitive faculties, whether or not the agent has alternative possibilities open to him in the circumstances. Widerker's definition of libertarianism can then be emended or reformulated in this way:

> LR. A mental or bodily act is free only if (1) the act is not the outcome of a causal chain that originates in a cause outside the agent, and (2) the ultimate cause of the act is the agent's own will and cognitive faculties.[121]

Libertarians thus need not accept PAP, and its acceptance isn't necessary for a rejection of compatibilism, since a compatibilist could not accept LR. Frankfurt-style counterexamples are successful against PAP; but, contrary to what Widerker supposes, the libertarian has nothing to fear from them. Unless extreme Cartesian dualism is the right theory of the mind, libertarianism would be in serious trouble if it could be shown that neural events are always caused by events external to the agent. But Frankfurt-style counterexamples can certainly not demonstrate that, and neither science nor philosophy gives any sign of being able to do so, either.[122]

5

Real Freedom

James Ross

Faciamus Hominem ad Imaginem et Similitudinem Nostram.
—Genesis 1:32

Preface

Some notions of freedom are philosophical and theological dead ends. Some make an antagonistic trade-off between human choice and the range of divine causation.[123] Others make the world necessitated (emanation) and fated, as in Islam. But some make creation an inexplicable preference for the cosmos over "more perfect" worlds lacking moral evil or physical pain.

To avoid the dead ends, I redeploy the idea that integral human freedom (and understanding) has *two modes*.[124] One is "natural" and the other "supernatural," though dividing the matter that way supposes the "natural" is the *residue* after the integrated whole is lost, because the supernatural contains the natural "eminently" the way olympic winning routines envelop the qualifying skills.[125] In my account, humans were never "merely" objects in nature at all—that is, objects, alongside stones and tigers and dinosaurs, that are entirely consequences of matter and biotic life, or explicable the way trees and volcanoes are. Humans never had a "completion"—a fulfillment—that can be defined by conditions of earthly life or attained by "flourishing," as other living things do.[126] Rather, humans have abilities that are positive natural mysteries because (1) they lack a causal account expressible in terms of the principles of nature (even in an *ideal* universal science of nature), and (2) humans have a fulfillment positively *beyond* the active abilities of any material being.[127]

89

Among "positive natural" mysteries, I include (1) such *natural* phenomena as our intellectual powers and rational responsibility; (2) psychic
energy and positive emergence, as well as the being of the cosmos as a
whole, which cannot be the consequence of the laws or necessities of
nature because it *contains* them, and the being of anything at all, which
cannot be accounted for by causation because causation presupposes
being; as well as (3) the outright *super*natural, which is defined strictly as
phenomena accounted for by God in the distinction of divine persons,
not merely by ascription but by the opposition of relations that constitutes the Trinity of Persons.[128]

Human nature, aimed at life with God, is supernature right from the
beginning; from creation and always thereafter. Human freedom is like
divine freedom.[129] Human freedom, integral freedom (the ability to attain
life with God), is restored by redemption and individual faith. Those are
my themes, themes that are central to St. Paul, St. Augustine, and
St. Thomas Aquinas but have not recently been exploited to resolve
philosophical problems. Yet even Zeno the Stoic (c. 300 B.C.) said, "all
bad men are slaves and only the good are free," as did Diogenes Leander
and Plato as well. How right they were, although under conditions they
could not know.

I mark the theological character of this discussion with a literary form
much like the Tenebrae Service for Good Friday: It has repeated antiphons (some lines from Psalm 8), nine lessons, and many lamentations
marked with Hebrew letters (on which there are medieval chants with
Spanish, even Moorish, variations); the point of the form being part of
the argument.

The aim of my reasoning is as follows: we can understand the freedom
of God only through its effects, most particularly, our own freedom.
But integral human freedom, the freedom that is the effect of God, is the
freedom that Adam lost and that the redeemer exercises. So we can
understand ourselves, and therefore God, only though the redemption.
We lost our integral freedom and our understanding of it with the Fall,
keeping only remnants of it: responsibility and a certain spontaneity.[130]
We lost the active ability to live with God but retained responsibility,
which is enough to earn damnation (separation from God). We also lost
the knowledge that life with God is our fulfillment. We can find our full
freedom only in response to "an inner divine invitation," as Aquinas put
it. In finding the redeemer, we can begin to understand the freedom of
the Creator that is not a response to the merits of things, but a freedom
that *makes* the good of things by the activity of the divine will, which is
love.[131] Thus, God does not love things because they are good things;

they receive their good, as well as their being, from God's love, the way a painting receives its beauty from the talent of the painter and a song, being and beauty from the breath of a singer. Thus, our only cognitive access to the freedom of the Creating God is by appreciating the freedom exercised by the New Adam; and *that* appreciation comes only by *mimesis*, by doing as he did.

Imagine, then, the music and liturgy: seven candles are extinguished one by one, with antiphons, psalms, lessons, and lamentations, like the passing ages of human wisdom after the Fall, until the last light is extinguished, to leave total darkness and total silence, "the silent infinity of empty space," that can be broken only by a new light, a resurrection.

I

Antiphon

What is man, Lord, That Thou art mindful of him, and the son of man that You visit him? You made him a little less than the angels and You crowned him with glory.

First Lesson: Flourishing and Fulfillment

Of the two modes of freedom, one closely approximates Aristotle's notion of the *voluntary*. It is the notion of responsible action, that is, action of a rational animal aimed and activated by its *bias* toward its own *understood* good.[132] Genuine volition (of which animals have a counterpart) makes the human a *moral* agent, subject to moral praise and blame.[133]

That is one focal notion of freedom—the voluntariness that is the basis of moral agency—which has triggered many competing analyses, mostly concerned with what we have to be *able* to do, or to avoid, in order to be responsible for our acts, and with the degree and kind of causal *determinism* that can coexist in three ways with moral responsibility: (1) physically, for example, by micromatter, by chemical and electrical forces; (2) psychologically, for example, by animal feeling and by unconscious and social causes; and (3) ontologically, for example, by divine causation of being.[134] Such analyses focus on the notion of freedom to ground the appropriateness of praise and blame, just as Aquinas argued that without freedom there would be no basis for moral praise or blame. We praise and blame domestic animals—"Good dog!" "Bad!"—to mold their activities from their desires, their imperfect volition; but we do not genuinely attribute merit or unworthiness to animals, except in the peculiar feeling toward a dog that pulls its master/mistress from a fire or saves him/her from drowning.

In contrast to this focus on *responsibility*, where actions originate in desire aimed at self-flourishing, there is another focal notion of freedom: *spontaneity*. We act spontaneously when we act (1) as if *for* the action itself; (2) as if without cause or motive, except for the self-expression or the enjoyment of what we do; (3) as if effortlessly, even gaining energy from the activity; and (4) as if we can explain our so acting from our ability to succeed, that is, explain our playing Chopin because we *can* play Chopin and like to, explain our walking from our ability to walk, explain our mode of living from our ability to *attain* human fulfillment.[135] Spontaneous action is explained by its own success, either instrumentally or by the enjoyment in the activity itself.

Spontaneity—to act for the action itself, out of one's ability to succeed at it—is an excellence. It can be *learned* in particulars for which we have a real talent, as in talking, thinking, walking, loving, or helping, or in more complex activities like playing Chopin, dancing, rock climbing, doing psychology and philosophy, making moral, political, and legal judgments, and even pitching baseballs. The reason we see, hear, feel, smell, and taste *actively*, is that doing so is an excellence satisfying in itself.[136] The very exercise of these faculties/capabilities is a mode of satisfaction. This is negatively illustrated by the *cancellation* of modes of apprehension when something has to be ignored or avoided at all costs, for example, the swelling of anger by the unconscious. So every area of human survival, ornament, expression, or relaxation is an appropriate range of spontaneity. But full-scale freedom, spontaneous energizing habitual action out of the ability to *succeed* at action aimed at life with God: *that* is a divine gift that completes human design with the elements forgone, or lost, by Adam's sin. It is restoration by God.

This second focus of concepts is theologically central: we are designed for life with God, in the Trinity of Persons, and are designed to attain that life by our own doing. To have freedom restored is to be *able* to do something *now* that amounts to living with God without *cognitio visionis Dei*, so that on death, the change is not in what we do, but in what we *see*.

On this view, humans are, by design, aimed at the Trinity, so that loving God, like seeing or hearing, is a joy to do, and so much part of our being, that the exercise of loving explains our continuing the activity. This is distinct from the power that has a purpose, a function; we continue loving not *for* some purpose, but *for* itself. Spontaneous loving or understanding or right acting is like our spontaneous seeing. Although there are some things we need to see and would seek to see, the fact is that, under normal conditions, we want to see because we *see*, and not vice versa. The negative side of spontaneity, as Augustine indicates in his *Confessions*, is that humans are eventually disillusioned with all creatures, and with everything that is not enjoyed as something that cannot be taken away against our will (and is a means to life with God). "All is vanity," as the scripture says; everything turns to dust, even us.

The *telos* for humans lies *beyond* nature (the cosmos) and beyond any power in nature to attain it. This is because it requires energy from our *envisioning* the object, an envisioning that requires a divine disclosure (revelation) *and* an enablement that, Aquinas says is a "supernatural dispositon" by grace.[137] (This is analogous to the potential intelligibility of matter, whose actualization lies beyond the matter, and requires intelligence, an immaterial power to actuate it, as with Aristotle's theory of *intellectus agens*.)

Furthermore, reason discloses against the conclusions of the ancients, that humans, while having many forms of natural *flourishing* to which rational action is ordered (such as art, philosophy, economy, agriculture, statesmanship, family love, service to humanity, etc.), have no natural *fulfillment, no completion in nature*, as do the plants and animals.[138] Philosophy, as understanding, is not, as the ancients thought, human completion. That is, for a plant or animal to flourish for its time *is* to be fulfilled.[139] Not so with a human: just to flourish is to be incomplete. In fact, it is to fail.

Now, the ancient philosophers had no inkling that human fulfillment requires an *encounter* (life) with God, the Person, and, thus, requires even more than acquaintance with the Good, itself, which was Plato's inspired guess. Therefore, they would and did reasonably think fulfillment lies in some specially effective flourishing, peculiar to humans and peculiar to which human it is.

In this way, careful reasoning produced one of the lasting confusions of Western thought: (1) flourishing, however fitting otherwise to a rational animal, that did not promise complete fulfillment was thought secondary, inferior; (2) it was thought that with luck, endowment, and goodness, one can attain human fulfillment by the highest human activity, that of the understanding (philosophy). Fulfillment was to be lived out in a life of virtue; and so the wisest of the ancients concluded that "responsible activity in accord with excellence" (virtue) applied to the highest power, that is, understanding (philosophy), is the actual ability to attain human fulfillment.[140] Thus "responsibility" and "fulfillment" were molded together as parts of one notion. This was a mistake, for it is by freedom alone that we attain life with God, and by responsibility alone that we attain separation from God and from ourselves.[141]

Aristotle, in particular among the ancient greats, thought that philosophical contemplation in a life of moral virtue was a genuine natural fulfillment for a human, without the mystical elements we find in Plato, but blinked away the paradoxical outcome: that is, by far most people fail, not just accidentally, or even by their own fault, but as the natural condition of their birth. It is as if, when not born blind, they are born in the dark and die there. For most people, just to be born where they are is to guarantee *un*happiness, the experienced failure of flourishing.[142] As Aristotle himself remarks in the *Rhetoric*: "Life is a bad business . . . most things turn out badly or worse than we expected." So the story sags, making fulfillment a matter of good fortune rather than good conduct: a lottery for the aristocracy. For one needs to be healthy, wealthy, and wise and morally lucky, besides, to be happy, as Greek drama makes clear. But it is still not guaranteed.[143] So, either humans cannot be happy (fulfilled) at all, or it consists of something else and is to be attained in another way.

What looks to reason like *one* ability, responsible action, and its natural (but unusual) success, happiness, are actually distinct. They are unified only in integral human nature, with happiness (either impossible or) requiring a *transcendent* object and a matching *ability* surpassing the forces of nature to attain it.[144]

Human fulfillment is not only beyond nature to attain, it is unintelligible and unimaginable (for lack of content) without a revelation. Without revelation, the human condition after the Fall is a broken symmetry, a fragmentation from which the whole prior state cannot even be conjectured without "enlightenment."[145] So, although reason discloses the brokenness of the human condition, it cannot reconstruct integral human nature. Genesis does not only reveal something *we* could have demonstrated (the being of God), but also *presents* the Creator, and begins the salvation history in which integral human nature is divinely revealed and restored.

First Lamentation

[Aleph] The philosophers' disabling notions of freedom, causation and being, come from (1) neuroses of the understanding and (2) an underappreciation of revelation.[146]

[Beth] A neurosis of the understanding is an enduring obsessive-compulsive retracing of nondispositive considerations.[147] It is a disorder, typically epidemic, like the compulsion to seem scientific, or to seem logically disciplined and skilled that shaped the collective consciousness of analytic philosophy for five decades.[148] Sometimes the disorder is individual, like Chisholm's resolving problems by drawing consequences from made-up definitions, or Quine's reiterated behaviorism, or Goodman's nominalism, a form of compulsive check-kiting. More commonly it is collective, with conviction usurping the place of reasoning: for example, that nothing is really necessary, that all science is underdetermined, that sentences are truth-bearers, that animal intentionality is computationality or connectivist, and so on.

Intellectual neuroticism took over the mind-body problem after 1640 and reached ludicrous extremes, in which physicalist philosophers promised a naturalized account of *thinking* now, when in actuality scientists cannot even explain the appetites of a worm. Where did philosophers expect to get the scientific cash for their intellectual junk bonds?[149] Only a scientific narcissism could promise epistemology naturalized while ignoring for a whole century the demand to explain animal awareness and animal cognition.

In fact, one of the disorders of understanding is the *misconstrual* of the import of the underdetermination of hypotheses by data, and the indeterminacy of reference. The justified consequences are not irrealism and hermeneutical impasses, skepticism about facts of the matter, or skepticism as to what we mean. Rather, they are signs that we *do* distinguish forms from matter, just as Aristotle said, and that there *are* dynamic propensities everywhere.[150] Each generation of philosophers traumatized and terrorized the next into the same routines, like circus bears, thus spreading the neuroses.[151]

[Caph] Disorders of thought stain the recent literature on free will with ritual arguments about alternatives, preferences, foreknowledge, determinism, compatibilism, and second-order preferences.[152] Contortions, practiced to no outcome, blot out the ideas from scripture, leaving theology homeless, an intellectual bag lady outside the arts and sciences, while the fastidious scientists look the other way passing by.

[Yodh] Energizing the neurotic, repetitive, dead-ended thought routines are *worn-out images* of how things have to be (say, that choice is motivated or reasoned preference, or that the ability exercised in wrongdoing is the same as that by which we act rightly), eluding conscious examination but they still transfer energy (by displacement of feeling) for the contorted thinking.[153]

The result? "Et factus sum sicut homo non audiens" (Psalm 37). The philosophers are like persons gone deaf from the violence of sound: in *bondage to their metaphors.*

So, consider the next lesson.

II

Antiphon

What is man, Lord, That Thou art mindful of him, and the son of man that You visit him? You made him a little less than the angels and You crowned him with glory.

Second Lesson: The Imagination Is the Master of Falsity

The imagination is the master of falsity.[154] First, *without* imagination, there is no falsity because for us there is no understanding without animal cognition, which requires imagination, as Aristotle and Aquinas both testify.[155] Understanding begins with a dematerialization of animal awareness, which requires imagination. As Aristotle said, "where there is appetite, there is imagination."

Second, nothing we *imagine* is ever true, in the strict sense that any thing or situation we imagine ever *becomes* (or could be) real.[156] There could never *be* anything as indefinite as any object or situation we imagine. And we can never imagine anything as definite as a real thing has to be.[157] So what the imagination makes is what is not real.

Third, and right to my point here, the imagination is the master of falsity as *coach* for the understanding. Imagination prompts and urges pictures for things, intellectually erotic sketches, by which we are "captured" (as Wittgenstein was himself captured by the "picture" theory of truth). Imagination typically makes the *local* appearance into the model for general belief,[158] and thus limits the thinkable. For instance, that the "fixed stars" do not move was believed even by great scientists for centuries (because such distances, as would be required for lack of movement to be merely apparent, were unimaginable [and inexpressible in available notation]). The imagination makes "the dreams and terrors of the night," prayed against in the Compline Hymn: "Procul recedant somnia et noctium phantasmata."

Infatuation with imagination is a nearly fatal disease for philosophy.[159] One is "captured by the pictures" as Wittgenstein called it; one is "thinking according to appearances only" or reasoning from "false imagination," as Aquinas calls it[160]; or, as Hume calls it in the *Treatise*, making "fictions" "by the mind's propensity to spread itself on things." *Even the Psalmist got carried away.* In Psalm 21 he says "salva me ex ore leonis, et a cornibus unicorum humilitatem meam."[161] "From the horns of unicorns, save my humility." Indeed! There is nothing, beyond the phantasmata, for the word "unicorn" to name. The Psalmist's words, for a *philosopher*, are a bottomless pit. To imagine that there can be *empty names*, names for sorts of things that have no cases, chimeras, manticores, martians, and antilichts, is to fall forever.[162]

"Wanting to be scientific" invites imagination to satisfy the demands of logical notation by saying that there are divine ideas "for" what never is to exist, so, we get conundrums about how God is to choose among worlds, considered as possible objects or their ideal surrogates (e.g., divine ideas).[163]

Third Lesson: There Are No Divine Ideas for Things Never to Be

Let it suffice that God no more has to contain by itemized representation what he knows and contains eminently by perfection, than the *Mona Lisa* has to have sections, slices, skimmings, or reflections, corresponding to "every possible adequate copy of it." The *one* self-knowing is an adequate "intention" for knowing all things, as Aquinas said.[164]

Furthermore, *being* (that is, "to be"), cannot be exhausted logically by "division" into possible things and kinds, for there is no "least [smallest] difference that makes a difference of thing."[165] Moreover, there is no "what" [e.g., "human"] that even an infinity of cases would logically exhaust.

Being is like a continuum: any division leaves just as much as there was to begin with. Therefore, to use a "line" model, no domain of differentiated possibilities (of kinds, species, or individuals) *diminishes* the domain of *undifferentiated* possibility.[166] Therefore, there cannot be a *domain*, a differentiated realm, of "everything that is possible," or of "every possible kind," to be the range of reference for (quanitified modal) logic, or for a theology of creation or of human freedom.

There is no point, then, in imagining that God picks among worlds and individuals, or among icons for them, like a child picking among pictures for toys to make. Possibility is consequent upon being, not prior to it or explanatory of it.

Pictures of divine ideas, as divine reflections in distorting mirrors (limited participation), are just metaphysical nightmares. The creator makes the *entire* being of the thing without an *intermediate* template, blueprint, or reflection. God does not model icons into matter. There are no such icons in the first place. The whole ontology is false.[167]

Certain lamentations are in order, from the lesson that there are no empty names, and no divine images for what is never to be.

Second Lamentation

[Aleph] *The contrary to fact is mostly empty.* So it is not by preference "over" what is never to be, that God has chosen what to make.

Consider a variation (like an ornamented Spanish Chant on the Hebrew letter [Aleph]) that explains this. What-might-have-been has content only so far as it is referentially rooted in the actual, and in so far as the "causal connections" (whatever *they* really are) in the actual "extend" to "what did not happen." Causality is really a problem because "if I had eaten powdered lead, a tablespoon per day for a month, I would have lead poisoning" seems quite determinate, whereas "if arsenic were not a poison, then giving a person arsenic would not be murder (unless it was like ground glass instead)," seems quite different, a truth by semantic inheritance alone.

"I might have been sick today" seems fully rooted in the actual. "I might have been president of Uganda" *seems* rooted, but only by *discourse*: for while "I" and "Uganda" and "being president of" are referentially anchored, the whole is *loose*, from reality and from real causation, as the laws of nature and history now stand. "*I* might have been president of Uganda" might be (1) a mere truth by inheritance, which is a verbal consequence of other truths, or (2) a *legal* consequence of Ugandan constitutional privilege that states "anyone whom the people choose may be president"; but that is *not* like "Mondale might have been president," when Mondale was the runner-up. Some counterfactuals are true only because being semantically well-formed, nothing known makes the condition (e.g., I might have been president of Uganda) false, in the way, say, that "I might have been Emperor of Rome" is.

Counterfactuals typically have truth-values, if at all—and most do not at all[168]—only by *inheritance*. They do not have *earned* truth-values from compliant realities (e.g., my having been or being sometime president of Uganda, or your having been an astronaut). Besides, truth about formal objects (like numbers) is a special case: *truth by inflation.*[169]

[Beth] *There are no truths about empty kinds.* There are no "ways things might have been" for things of sorts that never are. So, there are no "alternatives" for God to know, or make, or choose among.[170] Thus, salient problems about our and God's freedom dissolve.

[Caph] *There are no empty kinds. So, there are no merely possible individuals.* That follows from things said already.

[Daleth] *There is no divine knowledge of what might have been instead of anything that is.* That follows from the *absence* of any such objects. How what is might have been rearranged is another matter. But what there might have been instead is entirely empty even though God is exemplar of whatever might have been.

[Gimel] *God could not have chosen this world, instead of some other definite world* because God's knowing extends as far as his causation (*ST*, Ia, 14); God does not make what will never be, so there is nothing to know beyond what is. God knows his *ability* to do otherwise by knowing his actual doing, rather than by speculation on what he might have done, just as a dancer knows what she might have done in the ease and excellence of her *doing*.

[Heth] *There is no middle knowledge in God.*[171] That is because, for the most part, what even an actual thing *might* have done is too indeterminate to constitute a real alternative.[172] Alternatives are schematic, skeletal shadows of what is. And, what-might-have-been, involving empty individuals and kinds that have no cases, is simply without content, unknowable (and, so, impossible, of course).

[Vau] *The actual—and the potential in it—exhausts the possible with content ad extra for God.*

[Zain] *Thus, whatever God does, as creator, is antecedently impossible,* not impossible for inconsistency (which is only a consequence of thought and language), but impossible for lack of content, and, of course, cannot be referred to (or called impossible) except from the vantage (and supposition) of what is made.[173]

Variation on [Zain]. What God might have done is entirely without content because of untaken divine elections required for it to have content. Scotus says, as does Aquinas, that it is God's own being that is the source of all divine knowledge:

> Many things are said about the ideas, but even if they were never said, nay, even if the ideas were not mentioned, no less will be known about Thy perfection. This is established, that Thy essence is the perfect reason of knowing (ratio cognoscendi) every knowable whatsoever under every reason [aspect] of the knowable. Let him who wishes call it an idea. I do not intend to delay here over that Greek and Platonic word.[174]

Neither Scotus nor Aquinas thought there was any *range* of divine ideas that was the expatriated domain of Plato's ideas and the icons that determine the possibility of what might have been. *All* the knowable *ad extra* depends upon divine creation. All that is knowable is the work of love (*ST* Ia, 23). Thus, individuals, kinds, natural laws, and the arrangements of things to make the cosmos are from the divine wisdom. In fact, they are from the divine wisdom *alone*, as Aquinas says: "Given that he wished to make the universe such as it is, it was necessary that he should produce such and such creatures whence such a universe would arise. . . . Accordingly, we must conclude that the multitude and diversity of creatures proceeded from one principle . . . from the order of Wisdom."[175] Aquinas also says, along with Rabbi Moses, whom he cites, "that there is no other reason for the distance among the stars than the divine will. [Today, the values of the independent universal constants would be an apt example.] In fact, for the whole disposition of the universe, the only reason that can be assigned must be found in *the mere will* of the creator. . . . [So, too,] the appointment of a fixed quantity of duration for the universe *depends on the mere will of God*, even as does the appointment of a fixed quantity of dimension."[176] And Aquinas repeats at the end of his answer, "The fixing of the measure to time depends on *the mere will* of God, who willed the world should not always have been, but should have a beginning, even as he willed the heavens to be neither greater nor smaller than they are." Then Aquinas, in a flourish of his own imaginative fertility, goes on to say: "The last instant of all time will indeed be the end of the past but not the beginning of the future (*DP* 3, 5, ad 11), as the celestial movement will cease, [and] the subsequent rest will not be in time (*DP* 3, 5, ad 10), [and yet] the universe will remain forever (*DP* 5, 7.2c). When however, the heavens cease to be in motion, there will be another cause of their incorruptibility, namely that they cannot be destroyed except by an extrinsic cause, but when the heavenly movement ceases, that extrinsic cause will cease also" (*DP* 5, 7c).

Thus I conclude these second lamentations (that whatever God does is antecedently impossible) with Thomas's wild variation on [Zain], the end of things, to illustrate how *constructive imagination*, not trapped in old, debilitated pictures, opens new options in philosophy and theology. And here, next, is one constructive imagining that may help with the issues of freedom.

III

Antiphon

What is man, Lord, That Thou art mindful of him, and the son of man that You visit him? You made him a little less than the angels and You crowned him with glory.

Fourth Lesson: Double Truth and the Adornment of Things

Many of the problems about freedom are caused by our failure to acknowledge that there are vantaged truths with conflicting standpoints, and that there are incommensurable truths that cannot be intermingled. Let me show you.

Aquinas is surprising. He is known as a firm opponent of the "double truth" doctrine attributed to Siger of Brabant.[177] Yet he has a double truth doctrine of his own! Furthermore, it is not as unlike the doctrines to be found in Maimonides, Avicenna, and Averroes, as his clucking advocates have said, though he does not advocate teaching one thing about scripture to the unlettered and another to the learned, except insofar as further lessons are to be left out. Rather, his distinction serves to do what we now call "distinguishing conceptual schemes." I will explain what he says briefly and then broaden its scope.

Aquinas, answering a question about the interpretation of Genesis over "whether the firmament divides waters from waters," points out that a "superficial" reading might lead to a view like that "held by certain philosophers from antiquity, that the firmament of heaven might be said to divide the waters without from the waters within—that is to say, from all bodies under the heaven, since they took water to be the principle of them all."[178] But, he says,

> this theory can be shown to be false on solid reasons and, thus cannot be held to be the sense of Holy Scripture. It should rather be considered that Moses was speaking to ignorant people, and that out of condescension to their weakness he put before them only such things as are apparent to sense and avoids setting before ignorant persons something beyond their knowledge [that the air is corporeal]. In order, however, to express the truth to those capable of understanding it, he [Moses] implies in the words "Darkness was upon the face of the deep," the existence of air as attendant, so to say, upon the water.

Clearly, Aquinas acknowledges *two* messages, one based on what the people at large can understand from the appearances of things, and the other, the whole or further truth for those who are "capable of understanding it." Furthermore, he explicitly uses the principle that what is "shown to be false on solid reasons . . . cannot be held to be the sense of scripture."

No, this is not a passing lapse of his, but his worked-out position. In Question 70, "On the Work of Adornment," in Article 1, ad 3, Aquinas describes the view of Ptolemy that the "heavenly luminaries have their own movement," and Aristotle's opposed view "that the stars are fixed in their orbits and in reality have no other movement but that of the spheres," and goes on to say:

> and yet our senses perceive the movement of the luminaries and not that of the spheres" (*De Caelo*, ii text 42). But Moses describes what is obvious to sense, *out of condescension to popular ignorance*, as we have already said (*QQ* 67, 4; 68, 3) . . . even though the distinction is not apparent to the senses whose testimony Moses follows; for although to the senses there appears but one firmament, if we admit a higher and lower firmament, the lower will be that which was made on the second day, and on the fourth, the stars were fixed in the higher firmament.

This remarkable passage has parallels in *De Potentia*, for example, "Moses coming down to the level of an unlettered people, described things as they appear" (*DP* 4, 2, ad 30), and has parallels elsewhere when Aquinas says Moses describes the stars as "the adornment" of the heavens, when they are in fact "its substance," "out of condescension to the way things appear to ignorant and unlettered people," and when Aquinas says, "As to fire and air, seeing that the common people do not regard them as parts of the world, Moses does not mention them expressly" (*DP* 4, 2, ad 34).

In all of those contexts, Aquinas distinguished *truth according to appearance* to the senses from the "whole" or scientific truth, although he does *not* give a name, like "scientific" or "whole" for the things known to the learned. In each of these cases, except the last, the corporeality of air, what Aquinas took to be the "scientific," or "whole" truth, has turned out *not* to be true at all. This is instructive, for the "other truth," supposedly available to the learned, may *not* be as close to the way things really are as the vantaged truth, based in how things *look*, which is available to the unlettered.

That is a lesson. The "scientific" descriptions of things, designed to provide inner-mechanism explanations (e.g., Aristotle's theory that the stars are like jewels in spheres that move, like plates, the stars being unmoving in themselves), turn out, disconcertingly often, to have so many made-up elements that it is better to say that they are just false, and that their explanatory force is not the same as, and is independent of, their truth.[179]

Now why is this so important? Because there is a whole class of things that have to be said about God to explain the scriptures—especially to relate God's acts in history and in the liturgy, and to express the story of salvation—that can be counted truths only according to "unadjusted common sense," that is, only according to the "prescientific appearance" of things, by which persons of right faith and practical wisdom have to live out their salvation. Some of the "truths according to appearance" have false assumptions, and yet cannot be replaced because of their special positions in the proclamation of the faith (e.g., "God knows beforehand whatever will happen," with the false assumptions that God has temporally ordered knowledge and *pre*-plans the world). Other truths of appearance are simply not the whole truth, but are objective and without error as far as they go (e.g., "God endures forever," understood as "does not stop").

Consider all the accepted discourse—even *de fide formulations*—about foreknowledge and predestination, praying and the answering of prayers, the kingdom to come, the final judgment, divine action in the course of history, the role of Mary and the saints with God, and the bodily location of Jesus in "heaven," that is part of a correct understanding of the faith and yet (1) is as if God held a *temporal vantage* on nature, and thus (2) does not comport with the "scientifically" described *actus purus*, the reality of God's eternity and immutability.[180] Undeniably, there are complementary but disparate, even *imparate*, discourses (having distinct authorizations and distinct authentications) with which we have to describe divine realities: poetry, history, myth, law, synoptic gospels, prophecies, letters, creeds and hymns, prayer, liturgy, and counciliar proclamations. Moreover, "scientific" formulations have no credentials to replace the scripturally originated wording of the proclaimed faith, nor any ability to take over the pragmatic role of temporally and spatially vantaged truths about God, for example, about the effectiveness of prayer or the certainty of forgiveness to those who are moved by grace to seek it. "Scientific" truths have no superiority in practical realization over truths vantaged, both semantically and referentially, in the ways things objectively appear. (Sometimes even *subjective* appearance is a foundation for truths that cannot be scientifically replaced: thus Francis Thompson's sense of divine pursuit (in *Hound of Heaven*) may have been a truth about *him* for which we have no "scientific" replacement. The same holds for mystic raptures and encounters.)

Not only is there no license to conjoin one sort of truth with another (just because they are true, and without regard for the different vantages assumed); reason *prohibits* the incautious and artless conjunction of the proclaimed faith with "scientific" abstractions.[181] There is no analogy of "conjunction." Not just any pair of truths can be conjoined, and preserve truth. (So a simple principle of the propositional calculus—P or not-

P—has no general application due to the "belief-elements of meaning" that form semantic neighborhoods.[182])

Denial of religiously sanctioned commonsense, temporally and personally vantaged affirmations about God is to be avoided, no matter how well justified on "scientific" grounds. This is because it may invite the faithful to affirm a *contrary* commonsense claim that entails both a commonsense falsity *and* a scientific falsity about God. Thus we don't say, "No, you are wrong; God does *not* know what is going to happen," "because nothing is going to happen for God," because the believer is implicitly invited to say, "Well, then, there is something that God does not know, namely, what is going to happen, because, surely, something *is* going to happen." Discourse with diverse suppositions is a vivid enticement to error and equivocation.[183]

I think Aquinas adopted the principles that (1) you have to explain things within a framework that the hearer can understand (quidquid recipitiur, reciptur modo recipientis), (2) that not all of the relevant truth can be communicated to everyone, and (3) that not even enough can be communicated to correct all false suppositions in their faith, even perhaps when they are learned. His view is pretty much what Maimonides and the Moslem theologians thought, too. Commentators on Aquinas say that Rabbi Moses and the Arabs were willing to let secular science (Aristotle's metaphysics) dictate that portions of scripture are not literally true, whereas Aquinas stood for the position that the believing community, guided by the Spirit, is the authority on the meaning of Scripture, *except* that he also says, what is "shown on solid reasons to be false, cannot be the sense of Scripture," just as Rabbi Moses and the Islamic philosophers did.[184]

Fifth Lesson: Double Truth and More, about Nearly Everything

1. The prescientific appearance of things does not usually *change* when you find out the scientific truth (sometimes it does). The pillars of the Parthenon do not look slanted when we find out that they are.[185] This is for a very good reason: our experience is *vantaged* in the appearances; that is, the *standpoint*, the perspective, from which we explain things.[186] Moreover, in religious matters, that is where many of the things *appear* that need to be explained: sin, grace, repentance, salvation, the course of history, life, man, and the kingdom of God.

2. The scientific truth often has different assumptions and entailments that are not even suitable to replace the commonsense appearance of things. Despite some scientific realists who say that midlevel objects are

"just" illusions (e.g., W. Sellars, A. Eddington, P. Churchland), no one believes that you can see clouds of molecules *instead* of tables, or hear atmospheric compressions or frequencies instead of sounds (except P. Churchland) or perceive light frequencies instead of colors.[187]

3. Temporally vantaged beliefs about God are religiously necessary, just as sailing by the constellations was necessary for millennia of deep-sea navigation. There is a rightful, irreplaceable place for truths vantaged in appearances.

4. Cautious mixtures, with full knowledge, are characteristic of Christian theology (especially that of Aquinas). For example, it might be all right to say that the galaxy Andromeda is the last star in the handle of the Little Dipper (if it is), but it is not all right also to say that galaxies are stars, without qualifying the contexts. The same goes for God.

When you frame discussions of omniscience (God's knowing everything), first, by calling contents of knowing "propositions," second, by postulating that for every reality there is a content (proposition) to be known, and, third, by, postulating that some things to be known are *inherently* temporal (e.g., what time it is *now*, what John *will* do tomorrow), you create a conflict between the unchangeability of God and the requirements for knowing everything. The *contrived* nature of those problems can be "read off" the very statement of the problem. Yet, such conundrums have been taken seriously for years by many.[188] The artificiality of the problem, particularly its trading on the made-up features of obtuse abstractions like "propositions," strains one's patience. (Can these philosophers be serious?)

Without the needed qualifications, most discussions of divine freedom are surreal. For instance, the belief that God causes everything, without preempting nature or disabling the will (cf. *DP* 3, 7) is not supposed to be scrambled with the prescientific truth that free actions have no cause but the will. See the next lesson.

For now, note that there really is a *vantaged truth*: *double truth*, and more, not only about God, but about everything.[189] Many truths are ranged on different bases that cannot simply displace one another, that fit different purposes, social functions, and assumptions, but are *not* to be commingled arbitrarily or artlessly into intellectual goulash, or picked over like a teenager looking for the least fattening spaghetti strands.

Besides, as Aquinas's own scientific mistakes make clear, we need faith-assertions, founded in the authority of scripture and tradition, that do not depend on fashions in science.[190] The referential and conceptual bases of such assertions (e.g., "Jesus is bodily in heaven") will not coincide or readily translate into nineteenth- or twentieth-century cosmology, and, of course, *need* not. The same holds for "The Eucharist is really the body and blood of Christ." What has that to do with the molecular composition of bread and blood? The statements "This is my body" and "This is my blood" do not belong to a semantic network that immediately licenses any statement, one way or the other, about molecular composition. To take one's standard for "is the same stuff as" from molecular science, and *thus challenge* the real Eucharistic presence, is simply to conjoin what is disparate in vantage, to make theology into an Escher painting.

Aquinas went far enough in the direction of Rabbi Moses and Averroes, saying, with them, that what science rejects "on solid reasons" cannot be the sense of scripture. That is much further than we can go today with our diminished belief in the certainty of science. Aquinas's attitude is excusable because he, like the others, expected science to be *demonstrative* and, thus, fit to be a *negative* theological authority. But his expectations of science were unfounded, as his own false beliefs make clear.

Nevertheless, exaggerated claims that science is a *negative* authority for theology, indeed for understanding the scripture, have been reiterated and renewed every century since the Middle Ages. Recently those exaggerations have been counterbalanced by *philosophers* of science, who go too far in the other direction, claiming that science is *not* an authority on an independent reality at all. We can see this in antirealism and irrealism, not to mention odoriferous views about deconstructing the polarity of "true" and "false," drifting over from the Continent.[191] The extremes are both wrong: sciences, say, geology, can, if approved by the community of the faithful, negate a too literal earth-dating from scripture; but science cannot *show* that the Eucharist is not the body and blood of Jesus by showing that it is made entirely of wheat, yeast, and other molecules, whereas real bodies are made of meat molecules. The frameworks of discourse are incommensurable.

We should *not*, then, be contemptuous of biblical fundamentalists who insist upon the true principle that the community of the faithful (or the Spirit enlightening believers), not its scientists, determines the content of scripture. Rather, we should encourage a wider, more alert community of the faithful to exercise an understanding of scripture. A basic fundamentalist principle is right, that supposed science that conflicts with scriptural truth is wrong, just as Aquinas, Maimonides, and the Moslems were right that what is demonstrably false cannot be the sense of scripture. Still, the logical space between the two principles, and a *limited* respect for science, along with a moderate literalism about scripture, requires us to acknowledge a multiplicity of descriptive vantages, some with conflicting, and others with disparate, assumptions and "belief-elements of meaning." With all due care not to get mixed up between truths of appearance and made-up science (or between truths belonging to incommensurable referential and conceptual bases), we still want to know: *Is creation God's activity in space-time?*

In one sense, yes. In another, no, because the creature has being of its own. Aquinas says in *ST* Ia. 20, a1 and a2, God's love is the cause and measure of being; God's will is the *cause* of the goodness of things and God loves things by causing their being (goodness), and not on account of their being and goodness as we do. In *DP* 3, 1, ad 12, he says: "that which is made is a thing that subsists." But, like Michelangelo's legendary freehand drawing of a "perfect" circle, the being of the thing and its perfection is all from his hand, every feature of the thing (ignoring the material, the paint and surface for now). If the work is subsistent, as creatures are, in a material medium (the way a musical composition, even written out, subsists in the medium of sound), even though it has all its features from the creator (who makes the medium as well), it is still its *own* being and not the being of the composer. However, all its being depends on the composer throughout its whole time of being. So the problem here is to make it clear that divine creative *causation* is of *being*. Then, it is all right to say that the being of creatures *is* the creative activity of God, if only in the sense of something God *does*, the way a painting is what its painter *does*, or a playing of an etude is what a pianist does, or a song is the singer's modulated breathing (considered from the vantage of the form, the "what," inherent in the modulated breathing).

We have to jump from limited simile to limited simile, like crossing a stream on broken ice. Created being is like electromagnetic induction: it is the product of the charged source, continuously dependent on the source, has all its features from the source (or modified by other things from the one source supposed here), and ceases to be "instantaneously," "with the cessation of the source" (instantaneous cessation being a truth of appearance or imagination that Aquinas relies on in his account of annihilation [*DP* 5, 3]).[192] Created being is like a hologram: wholly from the light, yet not the same as the light.[193]

The movement of the stars can illustrate. "God operates in the operations of nature and the will," says Aquinas (*DP* 3, 7), "but not so as to defeat causation by created things" (as he says Rabbi Moses reports that the Moorish sages thought). Rather, says Aquinas, God "acts in every agent immediately and without prejudice to the action of the will and of nature." Yet, "creation is not mingled with the work of nature" (*DP* 33, 8, ad 20). How is that to be understood?

God does not, then, strictly, make the stars move; that is an unrefined commonsense belief. The reality that explains how things look that way, is that God *makes the thus-moving stars to be*. And that is the story for all of nature and for all free action. For, as Aquinas says, the proper effect of God, as cause, is being.

The edge of the distinction between cause of being and cause of change was blunted when seventeenth-century theory (e.g., Descartes) required God to explain the universal deterministic locomotion of matter. So God was seen as "giving" an initial motion that is deterministically transformed and conserved in mathematical laws. That was a deep reformulation of the "Unmoved Mover" notion from Aristotle, and placed God in an imaginary relation to the world that is opposed to a good "scientific" one.

God is not to be said to "preprogram, prevision or provide," in the same framework of assumption in which we say "God is the entire cause, without succession, of the whole spatiotemporal cosmos, the cause of the thus-acting-beings that are, the cause of the causing of things and of time." For one thing, the conserving cause of the cosmos must act without regard to limitations (light velocity) on physical causation, and without limitation to the relativity of time. Otherwise, it cannot conserve the being of a spatiotemporally extended cosmos. Besides, as Augustine said, God is the cause of Time, as well as Space and everything changing.

The vantages are divergent and even opposed, like for example, Newtonian theory with inertial mass versus Einsteinian General Relativity, with relativistic mass, or like the discourse in which we mean by "divine will" the effective *causing* will, versus other discourses in which we mean the legislative *prescriptive* will. To this you may say, like a learned objector, "well, which one is true? Because, of opposed assertions, not all are true." I reply, "that parade already passed." Getting it right is not just affirming some proposals and rejecting the rest; it is far more a matter of putting the items that belong together on the right shelves in the right order.

There are *objective* appearances, like the relativity of motion (under special relativity theory). That is, there are appearances containing no elements of illusion or error but, like the "being smaller" of objects at a distance, which is a direct effect of true optics, are the natural consequences of the micromechanisms of things. So it is also with large parts of the faith, stated from the viewpoint in time and history of those who are redeemed and who confidently expect the completion of the divine kingdom in the future.

It is true that God watches over his creatures instant by instant, preserving them in being, caring for his creation as a gardener, a lover, a parent, and a friend, answering appeals, helping from moment to moment, and inviting us to him with fervent personal enticements, like presents for a lover. Those are all truths, but truths vantaged in the appearance of things to a human situated temporally and locally on the earth. They are vantaged in the being that is the effect, rather than in the eternal cause. Nevertheless, those are objective appearances, the way things ought to appear, just as "the crab nebula is blue." The objective appearances of things are just as much part of the real being of things as are the undisclosed real natures that explain the appearances and are sought by the sciences.

So, do not get the idea that "truth according to appearances" is always "inferior truth," necessitating a false assumption. Sometimes it is exactly how things should appear, yet still not to be mixed up with accounts that distinguish appearance from the ontology, or the micromatter that causes them. Metaphysical accounts are at a different degree of abstraction from reports of religious events we experience. That is one reason why, as Aquinas says, "creation is not interference with or prejudicial to nature or will" (*DP* 33, 8, ad 20).

So this lesson is: Double truth is many truths, aspectual truths, some needing correction, some not, and some, with limited and even false assumptions, not suitably to be replaced because of their privileged position in the account of salvation history, on pain of incoherence, contradiction, and offense to the faith.

A third lamentation reminds us of the "hard facts" delimiting an account of creation.

Third Lamentation

[Aleph] God is unknowable in "whatness."

[Beth] God is incomprehensible.

[Caph] There is no content ad extra *given* to God by divine self-understanding (as the Platonists thought), and so no *domain* of "the possible" determined by God's being.

[Gimel] Thus, God's power is completely unlimited, encompassing whatever he chooses, since to make "ens et non-ens simul" is not, as Aquinas says, within any power whatever.

[Daleth] Creating is *the act* of God's full causal power (which is the same reality as his being), even though God is *able* to have made any number of other things whose natures would be determinate only *by creation*.

[**Yodh**] There is no unexercised ability or unfulfilled capacity in God (*actus purus*).

[**Heth**] Strictly, whatever God makes is antecedently "impossible" in the sense of "nonpossible," for lack of content.

[**Teth**] There are no divine ideas, except one, The Verbum.

[**Vau**] There are no eternal truths, except one.

[**Zain**] There is nothing necessary in creatures and therefore, "necessities of nature," the very natures of things, are merely suppositional, from God's will (from Practical Wisdom), as are all their actions, and "from the very fact that being is ascribed to a quiddity, not only is the quiddity said to be, but to be created" (*DP* 3, 5 ad 2).

That seems to leave the problems harder than ever. If God causes the thus-acting-creature to be, how can the creature be free?

IV

Antiphon

What is man, Lord, That Thou art mindful of him, and the son of man that You visit him? You made him a little less than the angels and You crowned him with glory.

Sixth Lesson: Futile Fatalism

The learned objectors say, "God causes me to do what I do, if God is the complete cause of the being of his creatures." But that cannot be right. For if God is the agent, and I only the instrument, then *I* do nothing. God can only be the complete cause of the being of a free agent if the agent *is* free. "If God makes me do it, I do not really do it," as every whining child who blames a sibling knows.

But could it really be that nothing that has a cause of all its being other than itself is ever genuinely free or ever genuinely a cause, as the Islamic occasionalists think? That is an outcome even the objector does not want. So what is wrong?

First, it cannot be true that both (1) I-the-thus-freely acting-creature am entirely caused to be by God, and (2) that God *causes me* to do what I do. The two are inconsistent, and it is the *second* that is false. Second, it cannot be true that God causes the sun to move as it does and that gravity (etc.) causes the sun to move as it does, because, as the Moslems reasoned, if God's causation is really the cause, then gravity causes nothing at all. Again, right.

The supposition that God causes the events in nature is incompatible with the scheme of natural causes. So we have to conclude that God's making the thus-causing natural events to be and the thus-freely-acting-humans to be, cancels neither natural causation nor free will, but rather is sufficient and necessary to *enable* each. That is exactly what Aquinas argued. It is like jazz improvisation with an active composing cause but *internal* explanatory structures for what follows what.

Now, I know the usual rejoinder is that my original supposition is inconsistent: that God can cause a thus-*acting*-creature to be, a thus-*freely*-acting-creature to be. Yet all Christians accept that God does, throughout nature, cause thus-*causing*-beings to be. Even *I* can do that: in a musical composition; in a magic drama; in a play; by a song, and so on, whose effect on you is *its* effect (e.g., to make you sad), but requires the *being* that is caused by me. I don't make you sad with my sad song in the same way the sad song makes you sad. Lerner and Lowe may delight you, but it is by the causation of "On the Street Where You Live."

Now, if the creator must make the thus-causing-beings to be, then evidently, the creator must make the thus-freely-acting-beings to be, *without* causing them so to act (by any natural causation), because that defeats freedom. Thus, the *only* way God can make and conserve free creatures is by making the thus-freely-acting-beings to be. And thus, while God could defeat any free action by withdrawing being from the agent before or during the action, God makes the creature *free*, by both nature and grace as herein described, and makes the free creature to be by constant (from the temporal creature's vantage) causation of being throughout its actions, "making the thus-acting creature to be." (See Aquinas, *ST* I, 105, a.5.)

It is a matter of revelation, as well as reason, that God makes the thus-acting elements of the cosmos to be, making the temporal being of all free creatures within it, throughout the whole of their being. It is like making a quarter note; there is no specified length, only a relative length; but to make one, you have to make the whole of it. So, to make humans and birds and protons, *relative* durations and causations are required by *what* is made. That is just what the creator does. The temporality of what is done is a feature of what is made, not of the making.

V

Antiphon

What is man, Lord, That Thou art mindful of him, and the son of man that You visit him? You made him a little less than the angels and You crowned him with glory.

Seventh Lesson: True Freedom Is Not of This World

There is a mystery about man. The mystery is abetted by misunderstandings. By misunderstanding our freedom, we misunderstand God's, in whose image we are made, and so further misunderstand our own. Creation is the paradigm of freedom, but is so far from what we expect that we have to understand other elements of the revelation and salvation to grasp what kind of human acting could achieve fulfillment, and thereby, understand creation, from which we finally understand ourselves.

I repeat in this fourth lamentation what freedom is not.

Fourth lamentation

[Aleph] Freedom is not the ability to act from preponderant desire in the absence of external causes. Even some *animals* have that.

[Beth] Freedom is not the ability to act from a rational principle in the absence of defeating conditions (ignorance, fear, violence, and passion). That is just responsibility.

[Daleth] Freedom is not just the ability to act from rational appetite, even on the rational preponderance of desire, as Aristotle thought, and Aquinas said (*ST* I-IIae, q.6, a.1), because (1) that will not achieve human fulfillment and (2) there may be other rational animals, such as higher apes, or whales, that have weaker reason, yet still have limited responsibility.

[Gimel] Freedom in a particular act is not "being able to have done otherwise than as I do under the very same conditions as I act willingly," because the better my reasons and habits are, the less free I would be. For a holy will, wrong action is not a live option. Further, I can act willingly, not knowing that I have no other choice (e.g., being locked in), and still act freely. Again, I can seek happiness (or God) freely (willingly), even though I would do it anyway by nature (willingly). I will have no choice in the presence of God, but all enjoy God freely (willingly). Besides, there is no active ability that *consists* in its counterfactual states. Freedom cannot *consist* in my being able to have done something I did not do. The *form* of analysis is defective.

[Heth] Freedom is not the ability to do otherwise, more broadly conceived, for example, as "a second order ability": "had I *chosen* otherwise, I would have done otherwise," because that condition might be satisfied when I was not free in my actions at all, for example, drugged, unwittingly locked up, or too sick to comprehend.[194] Moreover, that condition can be satisfied when there is no other live option. Further, the supposed analysis uses the very notion of free choosing to be explained. Again, the *form* of analysis is defective, as well as the content.

[Teth] Besides, freedom and liberty can be necessitated: as God's doing the right; and the blessed loving God. Even the saintly can each reach such a holy will that wrong actions are "dead options," just as murder would be to you; yet you are free in your conformity to the Fifth Commandment.

[Vau] Freedom is not just voluntariety, not just responsibility, though that is enough, wrongly exercised, for damnation. I understand Augustine, Aquinas, Calvin, Luther, and all the great Christian traditions, including the holy orthodox church, to affirm that.

[Zain] Creation determines the content of real possibility, and so, of all necessity ad extra with content.

Eighth Lesson: True Freedom Is the Spontaneous Choice of the Right from Abandonment to Love

St. Augustine, in *De Utilitate credendi* tells his Manichean friend (who wants the whole structure of his life to be founded on rational principles for which there are convincing arguments, and so wants to be argued into the faith), "you are suffering from an illness that only God can cure." He is urging that you have to believe in order to understand. So look at what there is to believe.

As St. Paul says, freedom comes only by faith, freedom from sin, and "adoption as sons of God." St. John, also, says, "dedit eis potestatem filios Dei fieri" (John 1:1–14). St. Paul is clear that without faith there is no freedom, though there is damnation. Some ability is lacking. No one is clearer that freedom comes by faith alone, that faith gives an ability to act, and that *caritas* is an activity possible to a person who has freedom, not to one "enslaved to sin." Aquinas says a supernatural dispositon, *deiformity*, is given to the understanding; the more perfectly, the more one has charity (*ST* I, 12, 5–6).

Is it possible then that "freedom," the gift of grace, is just a *condition*, a particularly favorable condition of responsibility-voluntariety? No, because the object aimed at in particular, life with God, is beyond the capacity of unilluminated reason to conceive, or the will to want. In fact, the essence of God cannot be presented to our understanding by abstraction from sensible appearance, and so requires a "created light" (*ST* I, 12, a 4–5).

St. Augustine (*De Lib. Arb.*) says that freedom (*liberum arbitrium*) is
the ability to act *rightly*. He makes it evident, I would have thought for
all time, that freedom does *not* consist in, or have any real expression in
our acting wrongly. In *Confessions*, Augustine says that before he had
faith, "being a prisoner, I might mimic a maimed liberty by doing
with impunity things unpermitted me, a darkened likeness of your
omnipotence."

So I respectfully disagree with those who say, "We are free to reject
God's invitation." You have to be *responsible* to reject God. Nor is our
basic *choice* to accept or reject God. Rejecting God is a condition that
requires freedom-on-offer, but it is the abandonment of it, not the
exercise of it.

Free choice is like running and winning, as opposed to falling down,
or not starting. It is like driving well, not an ability to have accidents.

St. Anselm (*Diag. De. Lib. Arbitrio*) is clear that "free will is the
ability to keep uprightness of will for its own sake." For Satan (see *De
Casu Diaboli*), damnation comes by fallout, by the *failure* to exercise
freedom that acknowledges God's moral sovereignty, when the opportunity is at hand. The story Anselm tells is somewhat different from mine:
Anselm tells that Satan, noticing that the difference that really counts is
that God is sovereign (acknowledging no superior, and is, thus, a moral
lawmaker without a lawmaker) chooses (wills by voluntariety) to be the
lawmaker to himself, deposing God and claiming to be sovereign for
himself. In a perverse way he achieves his objective, becoming sovereign
over chaos, but losing all ability for rightness of will (freedom). I think
the same effect is attained by positive responsibility to acknowledge
God's sovereignty as lawmaker and the failure to do so.

In a word, the "choice" to accept God or reject God is a conflict of
two abandonments: either we abandon ourselves to love, a kind of self-
giving-over, an absorption in God, thereby acting freely and being
habitually free, or we abandon right-living, thereby *not* acting freely,
though acting responsibly (in the sense that deserves blame), like wrong-
way Brown, and abandon our freedom along with ordered love.

We have to stand on revelation and against the philosophers here. I
propose to stand with Augustine and Aquinas, who do not think,
regardless of the role of evolution (whether as forms potential in nature
[*rationes seminales*] or even as many conceive it now, as a succession of
design changes worked out by natural selection), that humans *ever* had a
natural end, a fulfillment in nature.

Reason supports this view part of the way. It supports the conclusion
that human fulfillment is *individual*, by some kind of excellence of

activity. The pagan philosophers largely agreed that humans are *for* something, though they did not agree about what, or about how to attain it, though, in very broad terms, they did agree that it had something to do with wisdom and action in accord with reason.

Moreover, reason supports revelation negatively by the *failure* of any philosopher to put forward an end achievable by excellence that would fulfill the deepest human longings and not be terminated by death. Valiant tries have simply disclosed that there is no target fit for humans entirely contained in earthly life. Human capacity and nobility clearly surpass the cosmic power to satisfy.

So the fundamental question about whether we are genuinely free is this: is there a condition of fulfillment fitting to humans, and one that we have the means to achieve, one that is not a lottery, but actually offered to us all?

Ancient pessimism and paradoxes show up in Christian thinkers, too, for instance, Peter Geach's notion from *The Virtues*, that people are like acorns, most of which fall to the ground and rot, never making a tree, a full life, because, in effect, they have not "been chosen." Such views are often attributed, erroneously I think, to Aquinas. Nevertheless, giggly "universalism," in which God gives His countenance to everyone, seems equally implausible. There just does not seem to be a rationally formulable principle for the distribution of efficacious grace. Perhaps that should be no surprise.

True freedom is the spontaneous choice of the good from love of the good, from abandonment to love. For us, that choice has to be of God over self. The answer is given by Augustine: "Thou has made us for Thyself alone, O God, and our hearts are restless till they rest in Thee." But, as Augustine said about wisdom, we have to find a manner of life fitting to our end, a mode of suitable action. We find that only by being *shown* the new creation, the redemption.

For given that the objective is supernatural, that the enablement is supernatural, and that the essential mode of action is not what reason commands (though it is not *against* reason illuminated by faith), we have to be shown by revelation what these elements of our nature consist in. Once we believe, we can understand, harnessing the energy of understanding to the objective of eternal life. Yet it will still be a mystery whether our ability to survive death is some form generated in the natural world, or whether it is part of our design for our supernatural end.

We know also that mastery in any area, once attained, makes what seems impossible feel easy. "My yoke is sweet and my burden light." But it takes revelation to show us what being absorbed in love, as a form of right action, rather than of pleasure, consists in. Mastery of right love, once learned, is its own satisfaction. That is why it can withstand suffering and misunderstanding, even death. It has inextinguishable hope.[195]

So the *sort* of activity that achieves eternal life, absorption in God, becomes easy with practice, and exhibits itself as the compassionate cherishing and nourishing of those we find to care for (with a breadth delineated by our individual characters and cultures) because we see the divine love by which we exist. But the underlying energy of all such action has to be abandonment of self, absorption (virtually bemusement, entrancement) in the love for God and the desire to be with God. ("Where there is greater charity, there is greater desire" [Aquinas, *ST* I, 12, 6].) We know about it rationally, but need to know it by faith.

We could never have known about absorption in God as our fulfillment without revelation. We could never have known that *our* loving God parallels God's making us because he loves us, an activity God displays again, but in human form, by making us over in a new creation, an activity that had to be done to bring us back to God. It is an act by which we *fill* the ambit of our designed desire, just as creation *fills* God's capacity to love.

So what is this spontaneity that is naturally mysterious? What is human freedom? We can only find out by looking to the God revealed and the God understood as revealed by human actions in scripture, especially in the redemption.

True freedom is the spontaneous choice of the right from abandonment to love. For a human, that is the choice of God, complete commitment. God's creative freedom is the abandonment to love for what is made by which God invents all the natures of things, all the mysteries of things, all the good and allows all the limitations, and is absorbed in love of what he makes, with no activity left over. None at all. The model of human freedom is demonstrated in revelation.

The rationality of true freedom is upside-down from the rationality of what appears to be genuine freedom ("And all you asked from me was to change my own will and accept yours," says Augustine [*Confessions,* IV, 1]), but is mere voluntariness. The rationality of the voluntary is action based on reason (but in accord with trained feeling), apparently directed to fulfillment, but at best able to attain flourishing. The rationality of the truly free is directed at fulfillment beyond this life and seeks flourishing only incidentally and not as the means to fulfillment. Just as the meaning of life is the loving of God expressed in the fulfillment of the Law for the Jew; so, the meaning of life is to love God as Jesus did.

That is why suffering and death and deprivation and ignominy—all deathly threats to the rationality of the voluntary directed to flourishing—are no threat to those who love God above all else. The fulfillment of the human is to be united in life with God, a condition that only love can attain.

It should be no surprise that the apparently rational is not the really reasonable in the most important matters. That is generally the way where taste, feeling, and understanding have to be sensitized. Even virtue seems silly to the piggish. It is no surprise then that *caritas*, or the love of God above all else, expressed as unlimited concern for others, seems meaningless and irrational to those who expect it all ends here in a passing flourishing, like a flowering, that ends forever in death. Creative love gives up life to God, who made it, and is victorious over death. But once the light dawns, once grace transforms, once we believe, we can come to understand: freedom is spontaneous right action from abandonment to love.

Yet fully to understand we need a paradigm. And that comes mediated through this liturgy I traced, for as the last candle is extinguished when all the Psalms are sung, just before total darkness falls, we are told of the last and transforming effort of human freedom made in our behalf that set us free.

The story says, "and at the third hour, darkness fell."

Et in magna voce ait Jesus: Pater, in manus tuas, commendo spiritum meum.

Jonathan Edwards, William Rowe, and the Necessity of Creation

William J. Wainwright

The first section of this chapter explicates and defends Jonathan Edwards's claim that God creates the world to emanate His internal glory *ad extra*. I then discuss two implications of this contention—that God must create some world or other, and that He must create this one. I shall argue that the first consequence of Edwards's view is defensible but that the second is not. For it is inconsistent with the libertarian freedom that most Christian theists ascribe to God. I shall show, however, that God's libertarian freedom can be defended without jettisoning any essential claims that Edwards makes in *End in Creation*. I will conclude by examining William Rowe's powerful objection to my solution.

I

In the *The Nature of True Virtue*, Edwards argues as follows. Because "the first objective ground" of "virtuous love" or benevolence "is being, simply considered" and its "secondary ground" is "moral excellency," and because "God has infinitely the greatest share of existence" and is "infinitely the most beautiful and excellent," "he that has true virtue, consisting in benevolence to Being in general, and that complacence in virtue, or moral beauty, and in benevolence to virtuous being, must necessarily have a supreme love to God, both of benevolence and complacence" (TV 520–21).[196] It follows that *God's* rectitude and holiness "chiefly consists in a respect or regard to himself, infinitely above his regard to all other beings" and that, consequently, His works must be "so wrought as to show this supreme respect to himself" (EC 422). His ultimate aim in creation, in other words, must be Himself. Edwards concludes that God creates the world for His own glory.

But Edwards also believes that God creates so that He might communicate good or happiness to others. One of the earliest entries in his philosophical notebooks asserts that "happiness is the end of creation. . . . For certainly it was the goodness of the creator [viz., His benevolence or inclination to communicate happiness] that moved him to create" (Misc. 3, T 193). Furthermore, the creature's good is an end in itself. For, in the first place, the nature of goodness is to communicate good for its own sake and not for some further end.[197] And, in the second, God's inclination to glorify Himself by displaying His goodness *presupposes* its existence, that is, it presupposes the existence of a direct inclination to communicate goodness or happiness. Hence, the latter cannot be resolved into the former.[198]

Edwards's ambivalence about God's end in creation reflects an ambivalence in the Christian tradition itself. The first answer (that God's aim in creation is Himself) is dictated by His perfection. If God's excellence infinitely surpasses that of other things, then God's love of goodness (eros) must ultimately be directed toward Himself. He must, therefore, be His own ultimate end. The second answer (that God's end in creation is to communicate good to others) is dictated by His benevolence (agape). A benevolence that treats its objects as mere means isn't true benevolence.[199]

Is Edwards's position (and the tradition he represents) coherent? In a treatise written toward the end of his life, Edwards shows that it is.

End in Creation defines God's glory as "the emanation and true external expression of God's internal glory and fullness." It includes (1) "the exercise of God's perfections to produce a proper effect," (2) "the manifestation of his internal glory to created understandings," (3) "the communication of the infinite fullness of God to the creature, (4) the creature's high esteem of God, love to God, and complacence and joy in God; and the proper exercises and expressions of these" affections (EC 527).

Items 1 and 3 aren't ontologically distinct. For the principal effect produced by the exercise of God's perfections is "his fullness communicated." Furthermore, since God's internal fullness is the "fullness of his understanding," consisting in His knowledge of Himself, and the "fullness of his will," consisting in "holiness and happiness," His "external glory . . . consists in the communication of these," that is, in causing or bringing it about that "particular minds" know God, love God, and delight in Him. Hence, 3 includes 2 and 4; and 2 and 4 are thus parts of 3 which is ontologically identical with 1. They are, therefore, "one thing, in a variety of views and relations" (EC 527–28).[200]

In aiming at His own glory, God thus takes *both* Himself *and* the creature's good as ultimate aims. God's communication of happiness to created wills isn't a *means* to God's glory; it is *part* of it. The creature's happiness is an ultimate end because it is *included* in God's ultimate end, namely, His communication of Himself *ad extra*.

God's love of His glory (so understood) is an expression and consequence of His self-love.[201] For, in the first place, if one loves something one loves or esteems knowledge and love of it, and joy or delight in it. One also loves or esteems what participates in it and shadows it forth. Because God loves His own perfection, He consequently loves and esteems the knowledge and love of God, and joy in Him, which is its created image, that is, He loves His own glory. But, in the second place, if "the fullness of good that is the fountain is . . . excellent and worthy to exist, then the emanation, or that which is as it were an increase, repetition or multiplication of it, is excellent and worthy to exist" (EC 433). Therefore, if God prizes the first (i.e., loves Himself), He prizes the second. Or again, if God prizes His own attributes, He prizes their exercise, and if He prizes their exercise, He prizes the effects that are intrinsically connected with it. Hence, if God delights in His power to communicate good, He necessarily delights in communicating good, and in the created knowledge and love of God, and joy in Him, which are its principal effects, that is, He delights in His own glory. If these arguments are sound, then a God who loves Himself necessarily loves His own glory.

Edwards has another reason for thinking that God's regard for His glory (i.e., for Himself communicated *ad extra*) is included in His regard for Himself. The elect and/or their qualifications (their knowledge, holiness, and happiness) are in some sense *one* with Him. In the course of eternity, the saints move progressively closer to union with God, and to an identification of their interests with His. This has an important consequence. "As the creature's good was viewed . . . when God made the world . . . with respect to the whole of the eternal duration of it, and the progressive union and communion with him, so the creature must be viewed as in infinite strict union with himself. In this view it appears that God's respect to the creature, in the whole, unites with this respect to himself" (EC 459).

An obvious objection to this argument is that there is no point in time at which God and the elect are one or their interests identical. The creature or its good is *never*, that is, at *no* time, identical with God or His good. The identity in question is fictitious. In an apparent anticipation of this objection, Edwards points out that God can be said to really (and not fictitiously) inflict an infinite punishment on the damned and bestow an infinite good on the elect even though there is no time at which the punishment will have been completed or the gift fully bestowed (EC 536). Unfortunately this doesn't resolve the difficulty. The punishment and gift are infinite in the sense that they are everlasting. The whole punishment will actually be inflicted and the whole gift will actually be bestowed since each temporal part of the punishment or gift will actually occur. Union or identity with God, on the other hand, will never be actual. What corresponds to an infinite punishment or reward isn't identity with God (which is a fiction) but the endless process of approximation to Him. The argument thus fails. But a related argument from the Miscellanies is potentially better.

Edwards's theology is Christocentric. God's glory is most fully manifest in the history of redemption that culminates in Christ's victory over the powers of darkness. But Christ's triumph is the church's triumph for "the church [i.e., the elect] . . . is the completeness of Christ." It can thus be said that "the end of the creation of God was to provide a spouse for his Son Jesus Christ, that might enjoy him and on whom he might pour forth his love." "Heaven and earth were created that the Son of God might be complete in a spouse" (Misc. 1004, 710, and 103).[202] God's (i.e., the Father's) regard for the elect and their qualifications is ultimately *part* of His regard for His divine Son, that is, for the "perfect idea God has of Himself." But God's perfect idea of Himself "is properly God" (Misc. 179, T 259).[203] God's love of the elect and their qualifications is therefore included in His love of Himself.

II

An apparent consequence of these views is that God *must* create a world to display His glory. In *Observations Concerning the Trinity*, Edwards asserts that "God's determining to glorify and communicate Himself must be conceived of as flowing from God's *nature*; or we must look upon God from the infinite fullness and goodness of His nature as *naturally disposed* to cause the beams of His glory to shine forth" (OT 79, my emphasis). *End in Creation* contends both that God's perfections include "*a propensity of nature* to diffuse of his own fullness" and that it isn't "possible for him to be hindered in the exercise of his goodness and his other perfections in their proper effects" (EC 447, my emphasis). It follows from these assertions that God *must* diffuse His own fullness, that is, He *must* create.[204]

Other considerations reinforce this conclusion. Edwards clearly believes that God must act for the best. He speaks, for example, of "the *necessary* determination of God's will, in all things, by what he sees to be *fittest* and *best.*" It is impossible, on his view, for God "to do any other, than always choose what is wisest and best" (FW 377). Now a clear implication of Edwards's discussion of God's glory is that it is "fittest and best" that God diffuse Himself *ad extra*. God's will, therefore, is necessarily determined by this end, that is, He could not not will it. But God's will is essentially omnipotent; what He wills necessarily comes to pass. It follows that God necessarily diffuses Himself *ad extra*, that is, creates a world in which particular minds know Him, love Him, and rejoice in Him.[205]

Is Edwards committed to a kind of pantheism as some critics have suspected? Thomas Schafer has suggested that Edwards tried to preserve his system from "pantheistic necessity" by including the theological doctrine that the world had a beginning in time.[206] This may be correct. Malebranche had argued for a position of this sort in *Concerning Nature and Grace*, arguing that the fact that God "has made the world in time shows, that the creatures are not necessary emanations of the Divinity, but essentially depending on the free-will of the Creator."[207] Edwards had access to this work and was probably familiar with it. Although to my knowledge, Edwards nowhere says that he shares Malebranche's view, it is not unreasonable to suppose that he did.

Yet *if* he did, he was mistaken. Malebranche's argument is presumably this: (1) If God's will to diffuse Himself *ad extra* is a necessary or essential property of His being, there is no time at which He fails to possess it. Now (2) God's will is necessarily effective. So (3) if there is no time at which He fails to possess the will to diffuse Himself, He is always diffusing Himself and creation is everlasting. Hence, (4) if creation *isn't* everlasting, God's will to diffuse Himself *ad extra* isn't necessary.

But this argument won't do. For 3 confuses the time at which God possesses the property of willing to diffuse Himself with the time of its effect, namely, Himself diffused. These needn't be identical. Like many other classical theists, Edwards believes that God has eternally willed such things as my writing this paper on Edwards in the autumn of 1994. It follows that it is everlastingly true that I write it this fall. It fortunately does *not* follow that I everlastingly write this paper. Similarly, if God necessarily, and therefore eternally, wills to diffuse Himself, it is everlast-ingly true that God is diffused (at some time or other). It does not follow that God is everlastingly diffused. Whether He is or isn't depends on whether He (eternally) chooses to create an everlasting world or a world with a beginning. (Of course Edwards believes that God has chosen the latter.)

Since Edwards's belief that the world had a beginning is consistent with God's necessarily willing it, it does not preserve his system from "pantheistic necessity." Yet Edwards is not a pantheist. God's glory is indeed, "*Himself* exerted and *Himself* communicated" (Misc. 1218, T 152), part of the "fullness and completeness of *himself*" (EC 439, my emphasis). But while His glory (i.e., God's communication of Himself *ad extra*) entails creation, it can't be identified with it. For one thing, the divine glory (consisting in the knowledge and love of God, and joy in Him) is communicated to some (the elect) and not others (the reprobate). For another, creation is merely the *presupposition* of the history of redemption in which God's internal fullness is diffused *ad extra*. God may or may not be identical with His glory, He isn't identical with cre-ation.

But a more important point is this. God's self-communication is a communication of love, knowledge, holiness, and joy; it isn't a commu-nication of *being*. God's attributes "may be reduced to" His understand-ing or will, "or to the degree, circumstances and relations of these." "Infinite," for example, expresses the degree of the divine good, namely, the fullness of God's understanding (perfect knowledge) and the fullness of His will (perfect love and joy). "Eternity" expresses the divine good's duration, and "immutability" its imperviousness to change. "Power" expresses "the degree of these things, with a certain relation of them to effects."[208] But God's attributes are distinct from His being or substance. Edwards normally speaks as if there were three (real) things in God: (1) God, that is, the essence or being of divinity; "God (absolutely considered)," "the deity subsisting in the prime, unoriginated and most absolute manner, or the deity in its direct existence" (the Father); (2) God's understanding, or wisdom, or idea (the Son); and (3) His will or inclination, or love and delight (the Holy Spirit) (EC 528 and ET 118). God communicates His internal fullness, namely, His knowledge of Himself, love of Himself, and delight in Himself. That is, God communi-cates the fullness *of His real properties*. He does not communicate His being or substance.

But is this distinction viable? God is not only the immediate cause of the creature's love and knowledge of deity, and joy in Him; He is also the immediate cause of its existence. And neither the creature's existence, nor its holiness and knowledge, nor its joy are identical with their divine counterparts. Why say, then, that the fullness of God's understanding and will are communicated to creatures but the fullness of His being is not? For this reason, I think. The knowledge, love, and joy that God bestows upon the saints are faithful images of His own knowledge, love, and joy because they are of the same nature as His (though "infinitely less in degree" [RA 202]). Their being is not. For God is the only real substance and only true cause.[209] The creature's substantiality, that is, its "thinghood" and causal efficacy, don't differ merely in degree. They differ in kind.

It is also important to be clear in just what senses creation is and is not necessary. God's emanation *ad extra* is an end He consciously and willingly pursues. That is, God's self-communication is a voluntary act, an expression of His reason and will. It isn't a nonvoluntary consequence of His nature. (God doesn't emanate His internal glory in the way the sun spontaneously and unthinkingly emanates light or Plotinus's One emanates Nous and Soul.) It is true that God could not have voluntarily pursued any other end (or no end at all) for His nature is such that He could not have willed otherwise. This is no more inconsistent with God's freedom, however, than the fact that we can't help but will happiness is inconsistent with our freedom.

But even if Edwards's position isn't pantheistic, it does seem incompatible with God's independence, and with "his being . . . absolutely perfect in himself, and in the possession of infinite and independent good . . . perfectly and infinitely happy in himself . . . above all need and all capacity of being . . . made better or happier in any respect" (EC 445).

Edwards's response to the first worry seems reasonable. His view does not "argue any dependence in God on the creature for happiness" since, on that view, creatures and their qualities are "wholly and entirely from Him" (EC 447).[210]

Edwards's response to the second objection is more problematic. He appears to construe it as follows:

1. If (a) A and B are genuinely independent (i.e., if neither is included in, or part, of the other) and (b) one places one's happiness in both A and B, then (c) one's enjoyment of A constitutes only part of one's happiness and (d) one needs B in order to be completely happy.
2. God and His creatures are independent of each other. Hence, if (as Edwards believes)

3. God places His happiness in (i.e., delights in or enjoys) creatures as well as in Himself,
4. His delight in Himself constitutes only part of His happiness, and
5. He is not above all need.

Edwards's response to this objection is to deny 2.[211] Since God's delight in Himself entails a delight in the exercise of His perfections and its effects, His delight in Himself entails a delight in His creatures. His delight in His creatures is thus *included* in His delight in Himself.

But isn't this a non-sequiter? That God's delight in Himself "includes," that is, *entails*, a delight in His creatures doesn't alter the fact that God delights in *two* things, Himself and creatures. His delight in Himself constitutes only *part* of His happiness, and for Him to be as happy as He is two things are necessary—Himself *and* creatures. Even if a regard for creatures is necessarily included in His regard for Himself, God would be less happy than He is if He had no creatures to enjoy. There is a real sense then, in which God needs creatures in order to be completely happy. It follows that if creatures aren't part of God,[212] God needs *something other than Himself* to be completely happy.[213]

Edwards's defense requires a sense of "inclusion" which is more robust than entailment but doesn't commit him to pantheism. Perhaps the following will do. Creatures (or, more accurately, their holy qualifications, i.e., their holy knowledge, love, and joy) are *literally* Himself diffused *if* "self" is construed in an extended but not unreasonable sense, that is, if self is thought of as including not only the agent and the agent's activity but also any effects or products of this activity that are inseparable from it, and that reflect, or provide images of, the agent's perfections. The elect and their holy qualifications are parts of God in the real but attenuated sense in which an effect or product (a spontaneous song, dance, or daydream, for example) that is (1) absolutely dependent upon, and inseparable from, the activity that produces it, and that (2) expresses the character or inner being of the producer, is part of the producer.[214] In placing part of His happiness in the saints, God therefore places it in something that is other than Himself in the strict sense but part of Himself in a more extended one.

I conclude, then, that Edwards's somewhat unorthodox views on the necessity of creation are defensible.[215] Another consequence of his position is not.

III

Edwards's system doesn't just entail that God must create some world or other. It entails that He must create this one. For God necessarily does what is "fittest and best."[216] He must therefore create the best possible world.[217] It follows that He must create this world. For consider the following argument:

1. Necessarily, God creates the best possible world.
2. God has created Charly (where "Charly" is the proper name of the possible world that happens to be actual, namely, this one).

Therefore,

3. Charly is the best possible world. (From 1 and 2.)

Hence,

4. Necessarily, Charly is the best possible world. (From 3 and the proposition that "being the best possible world" is an essential property of the world that has it.[218])

It follows that

5. Necessarily, God created Charly. (From 1 and 4.)

There are two standard objections to the claim that God necessarily creates our world. It implies that there isn't any real contingency,[219] and that God isn't free.

Neither objection would have bothered Edwards. For Edwards thought that our world displays neither contracausal freedom nor real indeterminacy. He also believed that moral agency and freedom are compatible with metaphysical necessity. God can only do what is fittest and best. He is nonetheless free in the sense that He is aware of alternatives (the array of possible worlds), has the ability (i.e., the power and "skill") to actualize any of them, is neither forced, constrained, nor influenced by any other being, and does precisely what He wishes. Edwards believes that this is the only kind of freedom that is either relevant to moral agency or worth having.

Edwards's wholesale rejection of contracausal freedom would be unacceptable to libertarians. In addition, his denial of libertarian freedom *to God* is a "significant revision of a major stream of thought in traditional theism."[220] But the latter, at least, is defensible. Compatibilist notions of freedom are more plausible with respect to God than creatures.[221] As a classical theist, Edwards believes that the sources of God's actions are found in Himself. God is genuinely independent—neither determined nor causally affected by other powers. His activity, though necessary, is fully autonomous. If, on the other hand, determinists are correct, and human choices are causally necessary consequences of conditions that ultimately extend beyond the agent's control, then those agents *aren't* fully autonomous. The two sorts of necessity are thus significantly different. Hence, that the second is incompatible with morally significant freedom and responsibility doesn't imply that the first is.[222] Nevertheless, the Christian tradition has, by and large, ascribed libertarian freedom to God. Nor is this unmotivated. For if God possesses libertarian freedom, He seems somehow greater and His sovereignty more complete. How might advocates of divine (libertarian) freedom respond to Edwards's argument?

The most obvious move is to deny the existence of a best possible world. Perhaps there are several unsurpassable worlds none of which is better than the others. Or perhaps, for every world there is a better. Either way, no world is best or fittest. (Like Leibniz, Edwards seems not to have seriously entertained these possibilities—and for similar reasons. Suppose, for example, that there were several unsurpassable worlds. God would have no reason for creating one world rather than another. And if for every possible world there were a better, then, for any world, God would have a better reason for creating another. Assuming that a reason for creating a world can't be sufficient if there is a better reason for creating another, then, for any world, God doesn't have a sufficient reason for creating it. But God's actions can't lack sufficient reasons. If they did, the Principle of Sufficient Reason would be violated, and God's actions would be irrational.)

There are two ways, then, of preserving God's libertarian freedom. We can postulate several unsurpassable creatable worlds or insist that for every creatable world there is a better one.[223] I prefer the second solution. The first unduly restricts God's freedom (God can only create unsurpassable worlds), and is intrinsically less plausible. If (as Aquinas argues[224]) creatable worlds are images or imitations of God's perfect being, various ways in which (in Edwards's terms) God can express His perfections *ad extra*, and if God's perfection is infinite, then it seems reasonable to assume that for any creatable world there is a better one. Unfortunately, William Rowe, has offered a powerful argument that this solution isn't available.[225]

God can't be morally faulted for failing to create a world that is better than the one He has created. For no matter what world He creates, He would be exposed to the same charge. And an accusation that is always in place is never in place. An agent can't be blamed for a fault to which it would be exposed no matter how it acted.[226] But even, though God can't be *morally faulted*, if for every creatable world there is a better one, He can't create and be *morally perfect*. For if every creatable world is surpassable, then no matter what world God creates it is logically possible for Him to have created a better world and, if He had, He would have been morally better than He is. Yet no agent A is morally perfect if a logically possible agent B is morally better than A. Hence, given that every creatable world is surpassable, God can't create and be morally perfect, that is, He can't create and be God.

Rowe is appealing to two principles:

(I) If a being creates a world when there is a morally better world that it could have created, then it is possible that there exists a being morally better than it.

(II) If a being is essentially perfectly good, then it is not possible that there exist a being morally better than it.

If these principles are sound, then "no omnipotent, omniscient being who creates a world is essentially perfectly good. Moreover, if we add to this . . . that a perfectly good, omnipotent, omniscient being *must* create, it will follow that there is no omnipotent, omniscient, perfectly good being."[227] Indeed, if Rowe's reasoning is valid, his conclusion can be stated more strongly, namely, that on the supposition that for every creatable world there is a better one, then, if principles I and II are true, there *can't* be an essentially omnipotent, omniscient, and perfectly good being, that is, that either principle I or II is false, or God (so defined) is impossible. For if "For every creatable world there is a better" is true, it is necessarily true.[228] Principles I and II are also necessarily true if they are true at all. Hence, if every creatable world is surpassable, principles I and II entail that it *isn't possible* that an essentially omnipotent, omniscient, and perfectly good being exists.[229] I shall argue, however, that principles I and II are both questionable.

The intuition behind principle II appears to be that it isn't possible that there exists a being that is better than an essentially perfect being. But whether this is true or not depends on how "perfect being" is construed—as an unsurpassable being or (following Charles Hartshorne) as a being surpassable only by itself.[230] The most that Rowe's argument shows is that, given that it is better for God to create than not to create and that for each creatable world there is a better, God can't be perfect in the first sense. It doesn't show that He can't be perfect in the second. Rowe's conclusion should trouble theists only if the concept of an unsurpassable being best expresses what the tradition was trying to capture by employing such phrases as "a being greater than which none can be thought" or "a being with all pure perfections." While it may seem to, two things suggest that the concept of a being that is unsurpassable in those respects in which unsurpassability is a logical possibility (power, for example, or knowledge), and is surpassable only by itself in those respects in which unsurpassability is not a logical possibility (happiness, for example, or, if Rowe's argument is sound, goodness), may be as good an approximation to traditional notions of perfection as the concept of an unsurpassable being.[231]

First, theists like Anselm and Descartes were trying to articulate the notion of the most perfect *possible* being. If Rowe is right, however, and all worlds are surpassable, unsurpassable beings aren't possible. Second, the comparisons these theists primarily had in view were comparisons between God and *other beings*. But a being that is perfect in the second sense is at least as great as any *other* possible being.[232] Principle II thus doesn't seem compelling. Principle I is even more suspect, for it obscures the splendor of God's grace.

Does the fact that the *product* of an agent's action is morally better in the sense that it is a morally better state of affairs (i.e., more closely approximates some moral ideal such as the greatest happiness of the greatness number, happiness in proportion to virtue, or a "kingdom of ends") entail that the agent is (all things considered) a *better or more perfect moral agent*? I think not. Suppose that John and Sarah are morally good, and that x and y are (very) good moral actions although the state of affairs brought about by x is morally better than the state of affairs brought about by y (because, it includes more units of good, for example). John does x because he wishes to maximize the good. Sarah also wishes to produce good but chooses to do y rather than x because y benefits Steve and Sarah loves Steve. John may be better from certain narrowly circumscribed points of view. (For example, he is better from the point of view of a consequentialism that restricts its attention to a consideration of the moral value of the states of affairs that an agent produces.) But is John better *uberhaupt*? It isn't obvious that he is. Some valuable forms of love are *necessarily* gratuitous. Platonic eros and Aristotelian friendship are *responses* to value. But romantic love and agape *confer* or *bestow* it. Nor are Tristan or Iseult, or St. Francis, value maximizers.

Compare now three morally good, omnipotent, and omniscient agents A, B, and C, and three morally good worlds w1, w2, and w3, such that w3 is morally better than w2, w2 is morally better than w1, and no world (let us suppose) is morally better than w3. A creates w1 because it gratuitously loves (some of) the creatures in w1. B creates w2 because it gratuitously loves (some of) the creatures in w2.[233] C chooses w3 because it wishes to create the morally best world. Is C a better agent than A or B? Or is B a better agent than A? It isn't obvious that the answer to either question is "yes." For gratuitous love is a great good and a highly desirable character trait. Nor is an agent morally better because she gratuitously loves a better person or a person whose life is better (happier or, in some other way, more fortunate). The value of this sort of love isn't, and indeed *can't* be, a function of the value of its object or of its consequences. Principle I thus won't seem compelling to theists who prize love of this sort, that is, to theists with a high doctrine of grace. Acts of grace which bestow more good may be more splendid than those that bestow (much) less. But that the value of acts of grace, and of the agents who perform them, should be measured by standards of objective value that agents must meet to qualify as perfectly good seems inconsistent with grace's spontaneity and gratuitousness.

Rowe has a response to this argument. He concedes that "A creates a world better than the world created by some other omnipotent agent B" doesn't *entail* "A is morally better than B." He also concedes that "gratuitous love . . . is a great good" whose "value is not a function of the value of its object."[234] But he denies that these concessions imply that principle I is false.

Suppose that although w1 and w2 are both very good worlds, w2 is better than w1. Aren't the following two omnipotent, omniscient, and superlatively good beings, G1 and G2, both possible? G1 is unwilling to settle for a world less good than w1 while G2 is unwilling to settle for a world less good than w2.[235] G1 gratuitously loves (some of) the creatures in w1 and creates w1 for that reason. G2, on the other hand, creates w2 because it gratuitously loves (some of) the creatures in *it*. Neither surpasses the other with respect to gratuitous love. (The value of gratuitous love isn't determined by the value of its object or by the value of its consequences.) But, as we have seen, G1 is willing to settle for less than G2 is willing to settle for. Isn't G2 therefore better? It would seem so. And yet, of course, there *also* appears to be a possible omnipotent, omniscient, and superlatively good being, G3, who is unwilling to settle for a world less good than w3 (where w3 is better than w2) and who just happens to gratuitously love (some of) the beings in w3 and creates w3 for that reason. And so on. Thus, if for every creatable world there is a better one, there will be an infinite series of possible omnipotent, omniscient, and superlatively good creators, G1, G2, G3 . . . , each better than the last. And this will be true *even if*, for each of these beings, gratuitous love is its reason for creating the world it does, and *even if* none of these beings surpasses the others with respect to gratuitous love. Principle I thus emerges unscathed: "If a being creates a world when there is a morally better world it could have created, then it is possible that there exists a being morally better than it."

I have two responses to this objection. First, it presupposes the following principle:

III. Other things being equal, if an omnipotent and omniscient being, A, is willing to settle for a creatable world which is less good than the world which another omnipotent and omniscient being, B, is willing to settle for, A is less good than B (and hence isn't perfect).

But given that for every creatable world there is a better one, *no* omnipotent and omniscient being can set a standard for itself that can't be surpassed by an even higher standard. No matter what standard it sets, there is a possible being like it in all morally relevant respects except that it is unwilling to settle for as little. Now Rowe admits that we can defeat the claim that God has failed to discharge a moral obligation by pointing out that a criticism that is always in place is never in place. So why can't we defuse the charge that God is imperfect because He fails to set (and meet) a sufficiently high standard for Himself by appealing to considerations of the same kind?

My second (and possibly more important) point is this. Rowe's response doesn't fully accommodate the central role God's gratuitous love plays in Christian theism. Note that while G2 creates w2 because it gratuitously loves (some of) the beings in it (and not because it wants to produce the better or best), if worlds containing the beings G2 gratuitously loves hadn't been good enough (i.e., as good as w2 actually is), G2 wouldn't have created those beings. Of course, something similar can be said of G1. For *any* omnipotent, omniscient, and superlatively good being will set *some* standard for itself, that is, there will be some good world w*, such that it would be unwilling to create a world less good than w*.[236] Hence, even if it should love Rebecca and Chantal, for example, it wouldn't create them if any world containing them would be less good than w*. Its desire not to create a world less good than w* would trump its gratuitous love of these persons.

But note two things. First, because G2's standard is higher than G1's, the odds that its desire not to settle for a substandard world will trump its gratuitous love are greater. Or to put this another way: the higher the standard an omnipotent, omniscient, and superlatively good being sets for itself, the less scope it has for the exercise of gratuitous love.[237] Second, the less worthy the vessel, the more splendid the grace. Yet views like Rowe's imply that an omnipotent, omniscient, and superlatively good being, G1, who creates (and bestows good lives upon) less worthy vessels because it gratuitously loves them, may be morally inferior to an omnipotent, omniscient, and superlatively good being, G2, who, because it is unwilling to create worlds with as little objective value as G1 is willing to create, would *not* create those vessels *even if* it gratuitously loved them. And this seems to imply that the production of objective value is a greater good than grace.[238]

Rowe contends that G2 is morally better than G1 because G2 is unwilling to settle for as little as G1 is. The considerations of the previous paragraph suggest that Rowe is mistaken. His response obscures a salient feature of divine perfection as Christians construe it, namely, that God's gratuitous love (and not His desire to meet standards like "Don't settle for a world less good than w*," or to minimize evil, or to maximize good) is the dominant or defining feature of His actions *ad extra*.[239] Those who appreciate this, and who also recognize that every creatable world is surpassable, are unlikely to find Principle I compelling.

IV

What can we conclude? I have argued that Jonathan Edwards's version of the traditional claim that God creates in order to display His glory is attractive and defensible. But I have also argued that his views commit him to two controversial claims—that God must create some world or other and that He must create this one. Both are somewhat heterodox. The first seems to me defensible. The second is inconsistent with the libertarian freedom that most theists ascribe to God. Fortunately, we can avoid committing ourselves to the second by asserting what is independently plausible, namely, that all creatable worlds are surpassable. This attractive solution is only viable, however, if Rowe's powerful objection to it can be met. I have argued that it can.

Part III

Rationality

7

"It Is Wrong, Everywhere, Always, and for Anyone, to Believe Anything upon Insufficient Evidence"

Peter van Inwagen

My title is a famous sentence from W. K. Clifford's celebrated lecture, "The Ethics of Belief."[240] What I want to do is not so much to challenge (or to vindicate) the principle this sentence expresses as to examine what the consequences of attempting consistently to apply it in our lives would be. Various philosophers have attempted something that might be described in these words, and have argued that a strict adherence to the terms of the principle would lead to a chain of requests for further evidence that would terminate only in such presumably unanswerable questions as "What evidence have you for supposing that your sensory apparatus is reliable?", or "Yes, but what considerations can you adduce in support of the hypothesis that the future *will* resemble the past?"; and they have drawn the conclusion that anyone who accepts such propositions as that one's sensory apparatus is reliable or that the future will resemble the past must do so in defiance of the principle. You will be relieved to learn that an investigation along these lines is not on the program tonight. I am not going to raise the question whether a strict adherence to the principle would land us in the one of those very abstract sorts of epistemological predicaments exemplified by uncertainty about the reliability of sense perception or induction. I shall be looking at consequences of accepting the principle that are much more concrete, much closer to our concerns as epistemically responsible citizens—

137

citizens not only of the body politic but of the community of philosophers.

I shall, as I say, be concerned with Clifford's sentence and the lecture that it epitomizes. But I am going to make my way to this topic by a rather winding path. Please bear with me for a bit.

I begin my indirect approach to Clifford's sentence by stating a fact about philosophy. Philosophers do not agree about anything to speak of. That is, it is not very usual for agreement among philosophers on any important philosophical issue to be describable as being, in a quite unambiguous sense, common. Oh, this philosopher may agree with that philosopher on many philosophical points; for that matter, if this philosopher is a former student of that philosopher, they may even agree on *all* philosophical points. But you don't find universal or near-universal agreement about very many important theses or arguments in philosophy. Indeed, it would be hard to find an important philosophical thesis that, say, 95 percent of, say, American analytical philosophers born between 1930 and 1950 agreed about in, say, 1987.

And why not? How can it be that equally intelligent and well-trained philosophers can disagree about the freedom of the will or nominalism or the covering-law model of scientific explanation when each is aware of all of the arguments and distinctions and other relevant considerations that the others are aware of? How—and now I will drop a broad hint about where I am going—how can we philosophers possibly regard ourselves as justified in believing much of anything of philosophical significance in this embarrassing circumstance? How can *I* believe (as I do) that free will is incompatible with determinism or that unrealized possibilities are not physical objects or that human beings are not four-dimensional things extended in time as well as in space, when David Lewis—a philosopher of truly formidable intelligence and insight and ability—rejects these things I believe and is already aware of and understands perfectly every argument that I could produce in their defense?

Well, I *do* believe these things, and I believe that I am justified in believing them. And I am confident that I am right. But how can I take these positions? I don't know. That is itself a philosophical question, and I have no firm opinion about its correct answer. I suppose my best guess is that I enjoy some sort of philosophical insight (I mean in relation to these three particular theses) that, for all his merits, is somehow denied to Lewis. And this would have to be an insight that is incommunicable—at least *I* don't know how to communicate it—for I have done all I can to communicate it to Lewis, and he has understood perfectly everything I have said, and he has not come to share my conclusions. But maybe my best guess is wrong. I'm confident about only one thing in this area: the question must have some good answer. For not only do my beliefs about these questions seem to me to be undeniably *true*, but (quite independent of any consideration of which theses it is that seem to me to be true), I don't want to be forced into a position in which I can't see my way clear to accepting any philosophical thesis of any consequence. Let us call this unattractive position "philosophical skepticism." (Note that I am not using this phrase in its usual sense of "comprehensive and general skepticism based on philosophical argument." Note also that philosophical skepticism is not a thesis—if it were, it's hard to see how it could be accepted without pragmatic contradiction—but a state: philosophical skeptics are people who can't see their way clear to being nominalists or realists, dualists or monists, ordinary-language philosophers or phenomenologists; people, in short, who are aware of many philosophical options but take none of them, people who have listened to many philosophical debates but have never once declared a winner.) I think that any philosopher who does not wish to be a philosophical skeptic—I know of no philosopher who *is* a philosophical skeptic—must agree with me that this question has some good answer: whatever the reason, it must be possible for one to be justified in accepting a philosophical thesis when there are philosophers who, by *all* objective and external criteria, are at least equally well qualified to pronounce on that thesis and who reject it.

Will someone say that philosophical theses are theses of a very special sort, and that philosophy is therefore a special case? That adequacy of evidential support is much more easily achieved in respect of philosophical propositions than in respect of geological or medical or historical propositions? Perhaps because nothing really hangs on philosophical questions, and a false or unjustified philosophical opinion is therefore harmless? Or because philosophy is in some sense not about matters of empirical fact? As to the first of these two suggestions, I think it is false that nothing hangs on philosophical questions. What people have believed about the philosophical theses advanced by—for example—Plato, Locke, and Marx has had profound effects on history. I don't know what the world would be like if everyone who ever encountered philosophy immediately became, and thereafter remained, a philosophical skeptic, but I'm willing to bet it would be a vastly different world. (In any case, I certainly *hope* this suggestion is false. I'd hate to have to defend my own field of study against a charge of adhering to loose epistemic standards by arguing that it's all right to adopt loose epistemic standards in philosophy because philosophy is detached from life to such a degree that philosophical mistakes can't do any harm.) In a more general, theoretical way, Clifford has argued, and with some plausibility, that it is *in principle* impossible to claim on behalf of any subject-matter whatever—on the ground that mistaken beliefs about the things of which that subject-matter treats are harmless—exemption from the strict epistemic standards to which, say, geological, medical, and historical beliefs are properly held. He argues,

> [That is not] truly a belief at all which has not some influence upon the actions of him who holds it. He who truly believes that which prompts him to an action has looked upon the action to lust after it, he has committed it already in his heart. If a belief is not realized immediately in open deeds, it is stored up for the guidance of the future. It goes to make a part of that aggregate of beliefs which is the link between sensation and action at every moment of all our lives, and which is so organized and compacted together that no part of it can be isolated from the rest, but every new addition modifies the structure of the whole. No real belief, however trifling and fragmentary it may seem, is ever truly insignificant; it prepares us to receive more of its like, confirms those which resembled it before, and weakens others; and so gradually it lays a stealthy train in our inmost thoughts, which may some day explode into overt action, and leave its stamp upon our character forever. . . . And no one man's belief is in any case a private matter which concerns himself alone . . . no belief held by one man, however seemingly trivial the belief, and however obscure the believer, is actually insignificant or without its effect on the fate of mankind.

Whether or not you find this general, theoretical argument convincing, it does in any case seem quite impossible to maintain, given the actual history of the relation between philosophy and our social life, that it makes no real difference what people believe about philosophical questions.

The second suggestion—that philosophy is "different" (and that philosophers may therefore properly, in their professional work, observe looser epistemic standards than geologists or physicians observe in theirs) because it's not about matters of empirical fact—is trickier. Its premise is not that it doesn't make any difference what people believe about philosophical questions; it's rather that the world would look exactly the same whether any given philosophical thesis were true or false. I think that that's a dubious assertion. If the declarative sentences that philosophers characteristically write and speak in their professional capacity are meaningful at all, then many of them express propositions that are *necessary* truths or *necessary* falsehoods, and it's at least a very doubtful assertion that the world would look the same if some necessary truth were a falsehood or if some necessary falsehood were a truth. (Would anyone argue that mathematicians may properly hold themselves to looser epistemic standards than geologists because the world would look the same whether or not there was a greatest prime?) And even if it were true that philosophy was, in no sense of this versatile word, "about" matters of empirical fact, one might well raise the question why this should lend any support to the suggestion that philosophers were entitled to looser epistemic standards than geologists or physiologists, given that philosophical beliefs actually do have important effects on the behavior of those who hold them. Rather than address the issues that these speculations raise, however, I will simply change the subject.

Let us consider politics.

Almost everyone will admit that it makes a difference what people believe about politics—I am using the word in its broadest possible sense—and it would be absurd to say that propositions like "Capital punishment is an ineffective deterrent" or "Nations that do not maintain a strong military capability actually increase the risk of war" are not about matters of empirical fact. And yet people disagree about these propositions (and scores of others of equal importance), and their disagreements about them bear a disquieting resemblance to the disagreements of philosophers about nominalism and free will and the covering-law model. That is, their disagreements are matters of interminable debate, and impressive authorities can be found on both sides of many of the interminable debates.

It is important to realize that this feature of philosophy and politics is not a universal feature of human discourse. It is clear, for example, that someone who believes in astrology believes in something that is simply indefensible. It would be hard to find a philosopher—I *hope* this is true—who believed that every philosopher who disagreed with his or her position on nominalism held a position that was indefensible in the same way that a belief in astrology was indefensible. It might be easier to find someone who held the corresponding position about disputed and important political questions. I suspect there really are people who think that those who disagree with them about the deterrent effect of capital punishment or the probable consequences of unilateral disarmament are not only mistaken but hold beliefs that are indefensible in the way that a belief in astrology is indefensible. I can only say that I regard this attitude as ludicrous. On each side of many interminably debated political questions—it is not necessary to my argument to say *all*—one can find well-informed (indeed, immensely learned) and highly intelligent men

and women who adhere to the very highest intellectual standards. And
this is simply not the case with debates about astrology. In fact, it is
hardly possible to suppose that there could be a very *interesting* debate
about the truth-values of the claims made by astrologers.

Everyone who is intellectually honest will admit this, will admit that
there are interminable political debates with highly intelligent and well-
informed people on both sides. And yet few will react to this state of
affairs by becoming political skeptics, by declining to have any political
beliefs that are disputed by highly intelligent and well-informed people.
But how can this rejection of political skepticism be defended? How can
responsible political thinkers believe that the Syndicalist Party is the last,
best hope for Ruritania when they know full well that there are well-
informed (even immensely learned) and highly intelligent people who
argue vehemently—all the while adhering to the highest intellectual
standards—that a Syndicalist government would be the ruin of Ruritania?
Do the friends of Syndicalism claim to see gaps in the arguments of their
opponents, "facts" that they have cited that are not really facts, real facts
that they have chosen not to mention, a hidden agenda behind their
opposition to Syndicalism? No doubt they do. Nevertheless, if they are
intelligent and intellectually honest, they will be aware that if these
claims were made in public debate, the opponents of Syndicalism would
probably be able to muster a very respectable rebuttal. The friends of
Syndicalism will perhaps be confident that they could effectively meet the
points raised in this rebuttal, but, if they are intelligent and intellectually
honest, they will be aware . . . and so, for all practical purposes,
ad infinitum.

I ask again, what could it be that justifies us in rejecting political
skepticism? How can *I* believe that my political beliefs are justified when
these beliefs are rejected by people whose qualifications for engaging in
political discourse are as impressive as David Lewis's qualifications for
engaging in philosophical discourse? These people are aware of (at least)
all the evidence and all the arguments that I am aware of, and they are (at
least) as good at evaluating evidence and arguments as I. How, then, can
I maintain that the evidence and arguments I can adduce in support of
my beliefs actually justify these beliefs? If this evidence and these
arguments are capable of that, then why aren't they capable of convincing
these other people that these beliefs are correct? Well, as with philosophy,
I am inclined to think that I must enjoy some sort of incommunicable
insight that the others, for all their merits, lack. I am inclined to think
that "the evidence and arguments I can adduce in support of my beliefs"
do not constitute the totality of my justification for these beliefs. But all

that I am willing to say for sure is that *something* justifies me in rejecting political skepticism, or at least that it is *possible* that something does: that it is not a necessary truth that one is not justified in holding a political belief that is controverted by intelligent and well-informed political thinkers.

I have now accomplished one of the things I wanted to do in this chapter. I have raised the question how it is possible to avoid philosophical and political skepticism. In the remainder of this chapter, I am going to turn to questions about religious belief. My point in raising the questions I have raised about philosophy and politics was primarily to set the stage for comparing religious beliefs with philosophical and political beliefs. But I think that the questions I have so far raised are interesting in their own right. Even if everything I say in the remainder of the chapter is wrong, even if my comparisons of philosophical and political beliefs with religious beliefs turn out to be entirely wide of the mark, the interest of the questions I have raised so far will remain. How can we philosophers, when we consider the matter carefully, avoid the uncomfortable suspicion that the following words of Clifford might apply to *us*: "Every one of them, if he chose to examine himself *in foro conscientiae*, would know that he had acquired and nourished a belief, when he had no right to believe on such evidence as was before him; and therein he would know that he had done a wrong thing."?

Now as to religion: is religion different from philosophy and politics in the respects we have been discussing? Should religious beliefs perhaps be held to a stricter evidential standard than philosophical and political beliefs? Or, if they are to be held to the same standard, do typical religious beliefs fare worse under this standard than typical philosophical or political beliefs? It is an extremely popular position that religion *is* different. Or, at least, it must be that many antireligious philosophers and other writers hostile to religious belief hold this position, for it seems to be presupposed by almost every aspect of their approach to the subject of religious belief. And yet this position seems never to have been explicitly formulated, much less argued for. Let us call it the Difference Thesis. An explicit formulation of the Difference Thesis is a tricky matter. I tentatively suggest that it be formulated disjunctively: Either religious beliefs should be held to a stricter epistemic standard than beliefs of certain other types—of which philosophical and political beliefs are the paradigms—or, if they are to be held to the same epistemic standard as other beliefs, they typically fare worse under this standard than typical beliefs of most other types, including philosophical and political beliefs. I use this disjunctive formulation because, while I think

I see some sort of difference thesis at work in much of the hostile writing on the epistemic status of religious belief, the work of this thesis is generally accomplished at a subliminal level and it is hard to get a clear view of it. I suspect that some of the writers I have alluded to are thinking in terms of one of the disjuncts and some in terms of the other.

A good example of the Difference Thesis at work is provided by Clifford's lecture. One of the most interesting facts about "The Ethics of Belief" is that nowhere in it is religious belief explicitly discussed. There are, to be sure, a few glancing references to religion in the lecture, but the fact that they are references to religion, while it doubtless has its polemical function, is never essential to the point that Clifford professes to be making. Clifford's shipowner, for example, comes to his dishonest belief partly because he puts his trust in Providence, but Clifford could have made the same philosophical point if he had made the shipowner come to his dishonest belief because he had put his trust in his brother-in-law. Clifford's other main illustrative case is built round an actual Victorian scandal (described in coyly abstract terms: "There was once a certain island in which . . .") involving religious persecution. But he could have made the same philosophical point if he had described a case of purely secular persecution, such as those that attended the investigations of Senator McCarthy; his illustration turned simply on the unwillingness of zealous agitators, convinced that the right was on their side, to examine certain matters of public record and to obtain easily available testimony. In both of Clifford's illustrative cases, there is a proposition that is dishonestly accepted, accepted without sufficient attention to the available evidence. In neither case is it a religious or theological proposition. And at no point does Clifford come right out and say that his arguments have any special connection with religious beliefs. It would, however, be disingenuous in the extreme to say that "The Ethics of Belief" is simply about the ethics of belief in general and is no more directed at religious belief than at any other kind of belief. "Everyone knows," as the phrase goes, that Clifford's target is religious belief. (Certainly the editors of anthologies know this. "The Ethics of Belief" appears in just about every anthology devoted to the philosophy of religion. It has never appeared in an anthology devoted to epistemology.[241] I know of only one case in which anyone writing on general epistemological questions has mentioned Clifford's lecture, and that is a very brief footnote in Chisholm's *Perceiving*, in the chapter entitled "The Ethics of Belief." In that note, Chisholm simply says that he holds a weaker thesis about the ethics of belief than Clifford's. Given that he had borrowed Clifford's title for his chapter-title, I suppose that that was the least he could have done.) The real thesis of Clifford's lecture, its subtext as our friends in the literature departments say, is that religious beliefs—belief in God; belief in an afterlife, belief in the central historical claims of Judaism or Christianity or Islam—are always or almost always held in ways that violate the famous ethico-epistemic principle whose quotation-name is my title: It is wrong always, everywhere, and for anyone, to believe anything upon insufficient evidence. If, moreover, he is of the opinion that beliefs in any other general category are always or almost always (or typically or rather often) held in ways that violate his principle, this is certainly not apparent.

This conviction that Clifford's specific target is religious belief is no knee-jerk reaction of overly sensitive religious believers or of antireligious polemicists eager to find yet another stick to beat churchgoers with. If the conviction is not supported by his argument, in the strictest sense of the word, it is well grounded in his rhetoric. For one thing, the lecture abounds in biblical quotations and echoes, which is not a usual feature of Clifford's prose. For another, there are the inessential religious elements in both of his illustrative examples. Much more importantly, however, there are two passing allusions to religious belief, which, although they go by rather quickly, are nevertheless writ in letters that he who runs may read. First, one of the dishonest comforts provided by certain beliefs that are not apportioned to evidence is said to be this: they "add a tinsel splendor to the plain straight road of our life and display a bright mirage beyond it." Secondly, when Clifford raises the question whether it is fair to blame people for holding beliefs that are not supported by evidence if they hold these beliefs as a result of their having been trained from childhood not to raise questions of evidence in certain areas, he refers to these unfortunates as "those simple souls . . . who have been brought up from the cradle with a horror of doubt, and taught that their eternal welfare depends on what they believe."

Let us call Clifford's principle—"It is wrong always, everywhere, and for anyone . . ."—Clifford's Principle, which seems an appropriate enough name for it. I should note that there seems to be another principle that Clifford seems sometimes to be appealing to and which he neither articulates nor distinguishes clearly from Clifford's Principle. Call it Clifford's Other Principle. It is something very much like this: "It is wrong always, everywhere, and for anyone to ignore evidence that is relevant to his beliefs, or to dismiss relevant evidence in a facile way." Clifford's Other Principle is obviously not Clifford's Principle. It is very doubtful whether someone who satisfied the requirements of Clifford's Principle would necessarily satisfy the requirements of Clifford's Other

Principle (it could be argued that it would be possible to have evidence
that justified one's accepting a certain proposition even though one had
deliberately chosen not to examine certain other evidence that was
relevant to the question whether to accept that proposition) and it is
pretty certain that someone who satisfied the requirements of Clifford's
Other Principle would not necessarily satisfy the requirements of Clifford's Principle. I suspect that Clifford tended to conflate the two
principles because of a combination of his antireligious agenda with an
underlying assumption that the evidence, such as it is, that people have
for their religious beliefs is inadequate because it is incomplete, and
incomplete because these believers have declined to examine certain
evidence relevant to their beliefs, owing to a subconscious realization
that examination of this evidence would deprive even them of the power
to continue to hold their cherished beliefs. However this may be, having
distinguished Clifford's Other Principle from Clifford's Principle, I am
not going to discuss it further, beyond pointing out that there does not
seem to be any reason to suppose, whatever Clifford may have thought,
that those who hold religious beliefs are any more likely to be in violation
of Clifford's Other Principle than those who hold philosophical or
political beliefs. We all know that there are a lot of people who have
violated Clifford's Other Principle at one point or another in the course
of arriving at their political beliefs and a few who have not. As to
philosophy, well, I'm sure that violations of Clifford's Other Principle
are quite rare among professional philosophers. No doubt there are a few
cases, however. One might cite, for example, a recent review of a book
by John Searle, in which the author of the review (Dan Dennett) accuses
Searle of gross violations of Clifford's Other Principle in his (Searle's)
descriptions of current theories in the philosophy of mind. If Dennett's
charge is not just, then it is plausible to suppose that *he* is in violation of
Clifford's Other Principle. So it can happen, even among us. But let us,
as the French say, return to our sheep, prominent among which is
Clifford's Principle—Clifford's Principle proper, that is, and not Clifford's Other Principle.

It is interesting to note that Clifford's Principle is almost never
mentioned by writers subsequent to Clifford except in hostile examina-
tions of religious belief, and that the antireligious writers who mention it
never apply it to anything but religious beliefs. (With the exception
of illustrative examples—like Clifford's example of the irresponsible
shipowner—that are introduced in the course of explaining its content
and arguing for it.) It is this that provides the primary evidence for my
contention that many antireligious philosophers and other writers against

religion tacitly accept the Difference Thesis: the fact that they apply Clifford's Principle only to religious beliefs is best explained by the assumption that they accept the Difference Thesis. The cases of Marxism and Freudianism are instructive examples of what I am talking about. It is easy to point to philosophers who believe that Marxism and Freudianism are nonsense: absurd parodies of scientific theories that get the real world wildly wrong. Presumably these philosophers do not believe that Marxism and Freudianism were adequately supported by the evidence that was available to Marx and Freud—or that they are adequately supported by the evidence that is available to any of the latter-day adherents of Marxism and Freudianism. But never once has any writer charged that Marx or Freud blotted his epistemic escutcheon by failing to apportion belief to evidence. I challenge anyone to find me a passage (other than an illustrative passage of the type I have mentioned) in which any devotee of Clifford's Principle has applied it to anything but religious belief. And yet practically all philosophers—the literature will immediately demonstrate this to the most casual inquirer—subscribe to theses an obvious logical consequence of which is that the world abounds in gross violations of Clifford's Principle that have nothing to do with religion.

An explanation of the widespread tacit acceptance of the Difference Thesis among those who appeal to Clifford's Principle in their attacks on religious belief is not far to seek. If Clifford's Principle were generally applied in philosophy (or in politics or history or even in many parts of the natural sciences), it would have to be applied practically everywhere. If its use became general, we'd all be constantly shoving it in one another's faces. And there would be no comfortable reply open to most of the recipients of a charge of violating Clifford's Principle. Use every man after his desert, and who shall scape whipping? If, for example, I am an archaeologist who believes that an artifact found in a neolithic tomb was a religious object used in a fertility rite, and if my rival, Professor Graves—a professor, according to the German aphorism, is someone who thinks otherwise—believes that it was used to wind flax, how can I suppose that my belief is supported by the evidence? If my evidence really supports my belief, why doesn't it convert Professor Graves, who is as aware of it as I am, to my position? This example, of course, is made up. But let me mention a real and not entirely dissimilar example that I recently came across in a review (by Malcolm W. Browne) of several books about the Neanderthals in the *New York Times Book Review* (4 July 1993, p. 1). The review includes the following quotation from the recent book *The Neandertals* by Erik Trinkhaus and Pat

Shipman. The authors are discussing a debate between two people called Stringer and Wolpoff, who are leading experts on the Neanderthals. "What is uncanny—and disheartening—is the way in which each side can muster the fossil record into seemingly convincing and yet utterly different syntheses of the course of human evolution. Reading their review papers side by side gives the reader a distinct feeling of having awakened in a Kafka novel." Assuming that this description of the use Stringer and Wolpoff make of their evidence is accurate, can it really be that their beliefs are adequately supported by this evidence? Will someone say that Stringer and Wolpoff are scientists, and that scientists do not really *believe* the theories they put forward, but rather bear to them some more tentative sort of doxastic relation? "Regard as the best hypothesis currently available," or some such tentative attitude as that? Well, that is certainly not the way the author of the review sees the debate. Stringer, one of the parties in the debate, has written his own book, also discussed in the review, of which the reviewer says, "*In Search of the Neanderthals* is built around Mr. Stringer's underlying (and highly controversial) belief that the Neanderthals were an evolutionary dead end, that they simply faded away after a long and unsuccessful competition with their contemporaries, the direct ancestors of modern man." (That the Neanderthals were an evolutionary dead end is, by the way, the proposition that was at issue in the debate between Stringer and Wolpoff that was said to give the reader the feeling of having awakened in a novel by Kafka.) Later in the review, summarizing the book of another expert on human origins, the reviewer says, "In another section of the book, Mr. Schwartz defends his belief that modern human beings are more closely related to orangutans than to either chimpanzees or gorillas." It is hard to see how to avoid the conclusion that it is very common for scientists *qua* scientists to have beliefs that are vehemently rejected by other equally intelligent scientists who possess the same scientific qualifications and the same evidence. Even in the more austere and abstract parts of science, even in high-energy physics, the current queen of the sciences, where there is some real plausibility in the thesis that investigators typically hold some more tentative attitude than belief toward the content of the controversial theories they champion, it is possible to find clear examples of this. To find them, one need only direct one's attention away from the *content* of the theories to the judgments that physicists make *about* the theories, their judgments about such matters as the usefulness of the theories, their "physical interest," and their prospects. A former colleague at Syracuse University, an internationally recognized quantum-gravity theorist, has told me, using a simple declarative sentence that contained no hedges

whatever, that superstring theory would come to nothing. Many prominent physicists (Sheldon Glashow, for example) agree. They really *believe* this. And many prominent physicists (such as Steven Weinberg and
Edward Witten) vehemently disagree. They really *believe* that superstring
theory has provided the framework within which the development of
fundamental physics will take place for a century.

But let us leave the sciences and return to our central examples,
philosophy and politics. If we applied Clifford's Principle generally, we'd
all have to become skeptics or agnostics as regards most philosophical
and political questions—or we'd have to find some reasonable answer to
the challenge, "In what sense can the evidence you have adduced support
or justify your belief when there are many authorities as competent as
you who regard this evidence as unconvincing?" But no answer to this
challenge is evident, and religion seems to be the only area of human life
in which very many people are willing to be agnostics about the answers
to very many questions. (When I say "very many people," I mean very
many people like *us*: people who write books. It is, of course, false that
a very high proportion of the world population consists of people who
are willing to be agnostics about religious questions.)

It might, however, be objected that what I have been representing as
obvious considerations are obvious only on a certain conception of the
nature of evidence. Perhaps the Difference Thesis is defensible because
the evidence that some people have for their philosophical and political
(and archaeological and historical . . .) beliefs consists partly of the
deliverances of that incommunicable "insight" that I speculated about
earlier. This objection would seem to be consistent with everything said
in "The Ethics of Belief," for Clifford nowhere tells his readers what
evidence is. If "evidence" is evidence in the courtroom or laboratory
sense (photographs, transcripts of sworn statements, the pronouncements
of expert witnesses, records of meter readings—even arguments, provided that an argument is understood as simply a publicly available piece
of text, and that anyone who has read and understood the appropriate
piece of text thereby "has" the evidence that the argument is said to
constitute), then "the evidence" pretty clearly does not support our
philosophical and political beliefs. Let such evidence be eked out with
logical inference and private sense experience and the memory of sense
experience (my private experience and my memories, as opposed to my
testimony about my experience and memories, cannot be entered as
evidence in a court of law or published in *Physical Review Letters*, but
they can be part of *my* evidence for *my* beliefs—or so the epistemologists
tell us) and it still seems to be true that "the evidence" does not support

our philosophical and political beliefs. It is not that evidence in this sense is necessarily impotent: it can support—I hope—many life-and-death courtroom judgments and such scientific theses as that the continents are in motion. But it does not seem to be sufficient to justify most of our philosophical and political beliefs, or our philosophical and political beliefs, surely, would be far more uniform than they are. (Socrates told Euthyphro that people do not dispute about matters that can be settled by measurement or calculation. This is certainly false, but there is nevertheless an important grain of truth in it. There is indisputably significantly greater uniformity of opinion about matters that can be settled by measurement and calculation than there is about the nature of justice and the other matters that interested Socrates.) If "evidence" must be of the courtroom-and-laboratory sort, how can the Difference Thesis be defended?

If, however, "evidence" can include "insight" or some other incommunicable element—my private experience and my memories are not necessarily incommunicable—it may be that some of the philosophical and political beliefs of certain people are justified by the evidence available to them. (This, as I have said, is the view I find most attractive, or least unattractive.) But if evidence is understood in this way, how can anyone be confident that some of the religious beliefs of some people are not justified by the evidence available to them? (I say some people; and that is probably all that anyone would be willing to grant in the cases of philosophy and politics. Is there anyone who believes that it makes sense to talk of philosophical beliefs being justified and who also thinks that the philosophical beliefs of both Carnap and Heidegger were justified? Is there anyone who holds the corresponding thesis about the political beliefs of both Henry Kissinger and the late Kim Il-Sung?) If evidence can include incommunicable elements, how can anyone be confident that all religious believers are in violation of Clifford's Principle? If "evidence" can include the incommunicable, how can the Difference Thesis be defended?

What I have said so far amounts to a polemic against what I perceive as a widespread double standard in writings about the relation of religious belief to evidence and argument. This double standard consists in setting religious belief a test it could not possibly pass, and in studiously ignoring the fact that very few of our beliefs on any subject could possibly pass this test.

Let me summarize this polemic by setting out some Socratic questions; a complex, in fact, of alternative lines of Socratic questioning laid out in a sort of flowchart.

Either you accept Clifford's Principle or not. If not, game ends. If so, either you think that religious belief stands convicted of some epistemic impropriety under Clifford's Principle or not. If not, game ends. If so, do you think that other important categories of belief stand convicted of similar epistemic impropriety under Clifford's Principle—preeminently philosophical and political belief? If you do, are you a skeptic as regards these categories of belief, a philosophical and political skeptic (and, in all probability, a skeptic in many other areas)? If not, why not? If you do think that the only important category of belief that stands convicted of epistemic impropriety under Clifford's Principle is religious belief—that is, if you accept the Difference Thesis—how will you defend this position? Do you accept my disjunctive formulation of the Difference Thesis: "Either religious beliefs should be held to a stricter epistemic standard than beliefs of certain other types—of which philosophical and political beliefs are the paradigms—or, if they are to be held to the same epistemic standard as other beliefs, they typically fare worse under this standard than typical beliefs of most other types, including philosophical and political beliefs"? If not, how would *you* formulate the Difference Thesis (and how would you defend the thesis you have formulated)? If you do accept my disjunctive formulation of the Difference Thesis, which of the disjuncts do you accept? And what is your defense of that disjunct? In formulating your defense, be sure to explain how you understand evidence. Does "evidence" consist entirely of objects that can be publicly examined (photographs and pointer readings), or that can, at least for purposes of setting out descriptions of the evidence available for a certain thesis, be adequately described in public language (sensations and memories, perhaps). Or may what is called "evidence" be, or be somehow contained in or accessible to the subject in the form of, incommunicable states of mind of the kind I have rather vaguely called "insight"? If the former, and if you have chosen to say that a single standard of evidence is appropriate to both religious beliefs (on the one hand) and philosophical and political beliefs (on the other), and if you have decided that religious beliefs fare worse under this one standard than philosophical and political beliefs—well, how can you suppose that philosophical and political beliefs *are* supported by that sort of evidence, public evidence, to any significant degree? If the evidence available to you provides adequate support for, say, your adherence to a certain brand of functionalism, and if it is evidence of this straightforward public sort, then it is no doubt readily available to most philosophers who have paid the same careful attention to questions in the philosophy of mind that you have. But then why aren't most of these philosophers functionalists of your particular stripe? (Why, some respectable philosophers of mind aren't even functionalists at all, shocking as that may seem to some of us.) Wouldn't the possession and careful consideration of adequate, really *adequate*, evidence for a proposition induce belief in that proposition? Or, if evidence that provided adequate support for a philosophical proposition was readily available throughout a sizable population of careful, qualified philosophers, wouldn't this fact at least induce a significant uniformity of opinion as regards that proposition among those philosophers?

If you take the other option as to the nature of evidence, if you grant that evidence may include incommunicable insight, can you be sure, have you any particular reason to suppose, that it is false that there are religious believers who have "insight" that lends the same sort of support to their religious beliefs that the incommunicable insight that justifies *your* disagreement with Kripke or Quine or Davidson or Dummett or Putnam lends to *your* beliefs?

This is the end of my Socratic flowchart. I will close with an attempt to forestall two possible misinterpretations. First, I have not challenged Clifford's Principle, or not unless to point out that most of us would find it awkward to live by a certain principle is to challenge it. Clifford's Principle could be correct as far as anything I have said goes. Secondly, I have not argued that religious beliefs—any religious beliefs of anyone's— *are* justified or enjoy any particular warrant or positive epistemic status or whatever your own favorite jargon is. (For that matter, I have not argued that philosophical and political beliefs—any philosophical or political beliefs of anyone's—are justified or enjoy any particular warrant or positive epistemic status. I have recorded my personal conviction that some philosophical and political beliefs are justified, but I have not *argued* for this conclusion. I do not mind—just for the sake of literary symmetry—recording my personal conviction that some religious beliefs are justified, but that they are is not a part my thesis.)

There is one important question that bears on the epistemic propriety of religious belief that I have not even touched on: whether some or all religious beliefs may go clean contrary to the available evidence—as many would say the belief in a loving and all-powerful deity goes clean contrary to the plain evidence of everyone's senses. To discuss this question was not my project. My project has been to raise certain points about the relevance of Clifford's Principle to the problem of the epistemic propriety of religious belief. These are different questions: it suffices to point out that the philosopher who argues that some religious belief—or some belief of any sort—should be rejected because it goes contrary to some body of evidence is not appealing to Clifford's Principle. If what I have said is correct, then philosophers who wish to mount some sort of evidential or epistemic attack on religious belief (or, more likely, not on religious belief in general, but on particular religious beliefs) should set Clifford's Principle aside and argue that religious belief (or this or that religious belief) is refuted by the evidence they present.[242]

8

Theism and the Mind-Body Problem

Robert Audi

There are many challenges to theism as a rational perspective on the world. The most widely known, and probably the most extensively discussed, may be the problem of evil. But in the present age there may be an even more influential challenge, one that very likely affects even more people overall and many people more deeply. This is the challenge from the scientific orientation of our time. Those who consider the challenge insurmountable tend to think of it as the challenge from the scientific habit of mind; those who regard it as a failure tend to think of it as the challenge from scientism.

Unlike the problem of evil, this challenge from the scientific orientation of our time is not commonly expressed in a single argument, such as one comparable to the argument from evil.[243] We could say that the challenge presupposes an argument to the effect that since a rational person takes a scientific view of the world, and theism is clearly incompatible with that view, a rational person should reject theism. But this argument, as stated, is not often defended by major thinkers (at least not directly), perhaps in part because it is fraught with vague terms.[244] That weakness does not, however, prevent the argument, or variants of it, from exercising an influence below the surface of discussion. This essay will attempt both to indicate some respects in which the argument might be clarified and strengthened and to assess the reasoning thereby obtained. This will be done, however, only in connection with the second premise: that theism is clearly incompatible with a scientific view of the world. I am happy to grant the first premise—that a rational person takes a scientific view of the world—at least for the sake of argument and as applied to people who have an appropriate opportunity to form such a view.

The relation between religion and science has long been a major concern of the philosophy of religion, particularly since Darwin. There are many elements in the relation, but the most important may be those connected with the concept of mind. In an unqualified form, the central question here is whether the truth of theism can be squared with a scientific conception of mind, or, to change at least the emphasis of the question, whether there is a scientifically acceptable conception of mind that squares with a plausible theistic concept of a person—human or divine. One difficulty in answering the question is that we cannot presuppose any widely accepted definitions of "theism," "science," "mind," or other pivotal terms. Even the most plausible definitions of these terms remain highly controversial. The best course in a chapter of limited scope is to establish, for each pivotal term, a working characterization that enables us to address the most important philosophical issues associated with the problem. This is my first task.

Sketch of the Main Concepts Central to the Problem

To make the issue manageable, and to maintain contact with the mainstream of discussion on our problem—that of the harmony or disharmony between theism and a scientific view of mind—we may consider only monotheism and indeed what might be called "standard" Western theism. I take this to be the kind of theism illustrated by (at least) Christianity, Judaism, and Islam and centering on God as the omniscient, omnipotent, omnibenevolent creator of the universe.

If these four terms are taken to imply, as they commonly are in the literature of the philosophy of religion, more than what intelligent lay people would ordinarily mean by "all-knowing," "all-powerful," "wholly good," and "creator"—if, for example, omnipotence entails being able to do anything "logically possible" and "creator" implies producing the universe "from nothing"—then it is arguable that the God of standard Western theism is a philosophical construction and, hence, the concept of God is not (or not entirely) a religious notion rooted in scripture or everyday religious practice. Even if this "deflationary" view is correct, however, the traditional notion of God as creator of the universe and as having these four attributes is both central in the literature on our problem and one that ordinary theists readily arrive at upon reflecting on what is implicit in their initially simpler conception of

God. One need not start with a philosophical conception of the divine attributes to find the path thereto almost irresistible once reflection begins. For a child, "all-knowing" may be a vague superlative; for a reflective adult, it is readily seen to imply knowledge of whatever there is to be known.

A brief discussion of theism and the mind-body problem need not, however, presuppose that God has certain other, more "technical" attributes often considered essential to the divine nature, for instance, impassibility, necessary existence, simplicity, and timelessness. For one thing, there is less consensus about whether these are indeed essential to God; for another, they are in any event not central, or not central in the same way as omniscience, omnipotence, and omnibenevolence, to the conception of God possessed by ordinary intelligent believers in the traditions of standard Western theism. It may also turn out that the points emerging below can be applied to these attributes as well as to omniscience, omnipotence, and omnibenevolence.

It may seem that science is less difficult to characterize than theism, but that is by no means clear. Again, it is best to center our attention on some of the natural and social sciences as paradigms—particularly biology, chemistry, physics, and psychology—and to frame the discussion with reference to them. We may also presuppose some widely accepted basic properties of scientific theorizing. (1) It aims at constructing an account of the phenomena of experience, psychological as well as physical, where this implies providing both a classification of these phenomena and a kind of understanding of them. (2) The kind of account it seeks to articulate is one that has explanatory and predictive power and is in some way testable through the use of observation or experiment. (For some philosophers, explanatory power *implies* predictive power, at least predictive power in principle, but we need not presuppose any position on that issue here.)[245]

There is less agreement on what constitutes a scientific understanding—the kind that is an upshot of successful scientific theorizing. Some philosophers of science would say that we understand phenomena, such as those of human behavior, only if we can predict them from underlying states or processes, such as movements of subatomic particles. There would, however, be disagreement among philosophers of science about whether the relevant underlying states or processes are causal. There is even disagreement among them over whether the basic, unobservable items that, at any given time, are explanatorily fundamental are real or, instead, to be understood instrumentally, say as posits that facilitate the activities of explanation and prediction crucial for negotiating the world.

There is also disagreement over the status of scientific generalizations: do they express necessary connections or simply *de facto* regularities? *Must* metals expand when heated or is this simply a regular pattern that we have confirmed sufficiently to warrant our accepting it?

It is impossible to resolve these disagreements here, but we may be guided by the idea that the degree of harmony between science and theism is most readily probed if we consider rich conceptions of each. Standard Western theism is a rich version of theism. It attributes to God not only far-reaching attributes but, by implication, the associated mental properties of (minimally) knowledge and goodwill. Knowledge is plausibly taken to be mental because it is apparently constituted by, or at least entails, belief or some other "intellectual" attitude; and goodwill is plausibly considered mental because it is apparently constituted by, or at least entails, intention or some similar conative (desiderative) attitude. If there is not an equally standard conception of science, we may certainly say that, at least for many who understand science, its theories do provide an account of phenomena that has explanatory and predictive power, represents events as playing causal roles, and, commonly, describes them as falling into patterns that admit of explanation in terms of underlying states or processes, such as those involving configurations, movements, and forces among elementary particles. Taking this fairly rich conception of science together with the suggested, comparably rich conception of theism enables us to address a number of the persistent problems centering on the relation between scientific and religious conceptions of mind.

Some Scientific Perspectives on the Nature of Mind

Even with a conception of science before us, there remains much to be said about what would constitute a scientific understanding of mind. The first point to be made here is that neither psychologists nor biological scientists interested in mind need countenance any *substance* that can be called "the mind." Rather, talk of the mind—for example of someone's having a good mind—may be considered a kind of discourse about people and their mental properties, such as thinking. To have a good mind, on this view, is not to possess something like a mental organ that functions well; it is (roughly) to have a nature in virtue of which, as a person, one functions well in intellectual activities.

To be sure, many educated people tend to think of the mind as the brain. This is not, however, a considered view: it comes of oversimplifying the multitude of connections between our brains and our mental properties, and (outside philosophy) it is not often put to the basic test it must pass as a serious identity claim: every property of the brain must be a property of the mind and vice versa. Do we want to assign the mind a weight in grams? Could it be dyed bright red, as the brain could? Can we, as in the case of the brain, remove parts of the mind, hold them in our hands, and discard them, without affecting its mental function? And when the mind is wholly occupied with the relation between religion and science, must the brain be so occupied also? Given everything we know about what the brain must do to keep us alive, the answers are surely negative. It must, for instance, control heartbeat and respiration in order to sustain thought; but exercising that control, in the automatic way in question, is not thinking, nor can any clearly mental process be plausibly identified with the brain's exercising the relevant kind of control over heartbeat and respiration or over other involuntary bodily processes.

There may be a few who will dig in their heels and defend the view that the mind is the brain. Rather than continue to discuss this, we would do better to note that what, in a scientifically minded person, motivates the brain-mind identity view is the desire to construe a person as a physical system. *That* desire, however, can be accommodated by simply taking every mental property to be some kind of brain property—a view commonly called the *identity theory*. The identity theory goes well with a materialistic conception of the universe, and that, in turn, seems to go well with a scientific worldview. Physics, for instance, is commonly taken to understand phenomena in terms of matter and motion, especially contacts between concrete material entities. This conception is, however, naive: even Newtonian physics countenanced action at a distance, and the relevant gravitational forces do not require a stream of material particles traversing the entire distance between the mutually attracting bodies.

As scientists report progressively smaller and less "corpuscular" elementary particles, we may wonder how material the basic entities postulated by current physics *are*. We might also ask what scientists, as such, must say about the status of numbers, which are indispensable for their work. The number 3 is not a numeral or even a set of numerals (destroying them all would not destroy it, or undermine the truths in which it figures). Granted, a scientific materialist may care only about concrete entities; but even if all of these can be conceived as material, numbers and properties (such as the property of being square) are at best not easily interpreted as such. The point is that while materialist *metaphysicians* want to conceive everything real as material, this aim is not essential to science, which, arguably, presupposes rather than seeking to explain, the nature and truth of pure mathematics, and appears quite uncommitted to restricting its posited entities to those properly conceived as material.

There are two broad conceptions of science that are not commonly distinguished and that we must not allow to be conflated. One, which perhaps deserves to be called the loose and popular conception, takes science to be concerned with accounting for everything that is real. This in turn is often identified with everything "in the world" or "in the universe." The second, more guarded view, takes science to be concerned with accounting for everything that is empirical, in the sense of being accessible, directly or through the use of instruments, to normal human sensory experience. The paradigms of what is empirical are physical, but psychological phenomena are often included as well. On the first, but not the second, conception, science must apparently account for abstract entities such as numbers. On the second conception, science must give an account of psychological phenomena, but is not committed to identifying them with physical phenomena, particularly if explaining their interrelations and their role in producing overt behavior does not require that identification.

A natural step to take here is to distinguish the material from the physical and to maintain simply that mental properties are physical. Now, however, the contrast between the mental and the canonical basic elements of science is weakened. Suppose, for example, that physical properties are understood as those having causal and explanatory power with respect to observable events. "Mentalists"—those who believe that mental properties like thinking and sensing are real—will respond that, clearly, mental properties have this kind of power.

But, one might ask, how can a mental phenomenon like a decision, cause a physical phenomenon like my telephoning a friend? With action at a distance, there are two physical phenomena in a causal relation; here, the relation is cross-categorial, at least in its linking of physical properties that are not material to those that, like the moving of a hand, are material. There may be no obviously cogent answer to this question, but it should help to recall that physics itself seems to be appealing to less and less familiar kinds of entities in explaining observable events. It should also be said that if there is something mysterious here, a mystery is not an impossibility. Indeed, there is, as Hume saw, something mysterious about causation of any kind once we look for more than a mere regularity linking causes to their effects.

Suppose, however, that it should be true that a scientifically minded thinker must opt for the identity theory. Is there good reason to think the theory true? It has been ably and plausibly attacked in the literature[246] and is presently not held by most scientifically minded philosophers who count themselves physicalists. There are many other conceptions of the mental available to such philosophers. Two should be noted here: *philosophical behaviorism*, roughly the view that mental properties are behavioral (and hence physical) properties; and *eliminative materialism*, roughly the view that there are no mental properties, and, hence, mental terms represent false postulations (it is usually coupled with the hypothesis that neuropsychology will ultimately enable us to do without those terms in explaining behavior). Philosophical behaviorism is widely agreed to have been refuted, in part because it seems to undermine the distinction between convincingly pretending to be in a mental state, such as pain, and actually being in that state. Eliminative materialism, though currently defended by a small number of theorists, does not provide a positive conception of the mental that can be readily used in pursuing the problem central here. Even if it should be successful in showing that certain apparently mental concepts are empty, its proponents have not provided a plausible general account of the concept of the mental and shown that this broad concept is empty.[247]

A view that may promise to avoid the pitfalls of both behaviorism on one side and the identity theory on the other is *functionalism*, roughly the thesis that mental properties are to be understood in terms of certain input-output relations; for example, to be in pain is to be in a state of the kind caused by a burn and causing outcries. Mental properties are, as it were, *role defined* rather than defined in terms of any quality they have or type of material constituting them. On this view, a person has only physical and functional properties, and the latter are defined in terms of relations among the former. This may be taken to leave open precisely how functional properties are to be classified in the physical-nonphysical dimension, but it undermines the view that any of them are either irreducibly mental or commit us to positing mental substances as their possessors.

Functionalism is defensible, but is widely (though not universally) agreed to leave us at least unsatisfied with respect to understanding qualities of experience, such as the painfulness of pain and the redness of an afterimage. Whereas the identity theory could claim that the experience of (say) being in pain is identical with a brain state, functionalism must maintain that there is nothing it "is like" to be in pain, no intrinsic character of the experience: talk of the experience is talk of mediation between inputs and outputs, and that mediation has no intrinsic charac-

ter. Thus, if my sensory impressions of red and green were inverted with
respect to those of normal people, functionalism would apparently have
to say that I am still having the same experience (am in the same
perceptual mental state) when I approach a red light because, being
taught in the same way as everyone else, I respond to red stimuli as they
do regardless of my internally "seeing green."[248]

These and other difficulties with the identity theory and functionalism
have led a number of scientifically minded philosophers to maintain a
nonreductive materialism: mental properties are grounded in (supervene
on, in a currently much-discussed terminology) physical ones, but are
not identical with them, hence not reducible to them. This view allows
us to anchor the mental in the physical and biological world without
either the difficulties of identifying mental with physical properties or
those of trying to account for qualities of experience.[249]

Granting that nonreductive materialism does not have to countenance
mental *substances*, such as Cartesian minds, it remains a *property dualism*. It will thus be unsatisfactory to those who take physical properties
to be the only kind there are, as well as those who do not see how mental
phenomena as such can have any explanatory power if they are not really
physical. If, for example, my decision to telephone someone merely
depends on my brain properties and is identical with none of them, how
does my decision produce my physical behavior, as opposed to being,
say, a mere shadow of the real productive work done by something in
my brain that really has the power to move my fingers over the buttons?

It may help to stress that whatever supervenience relation obtains in
the mental case is, like the physical instance, also presumably a causal or
nomic relation. Perhaps, then, the mental elements inherit causal power
from the base elements, as the magnetism of iron, say, apparently inherits
its causal power from the base properties in virtue of which iron is
magnetic. Let me develop this idea.

On the assumption that causation is a transitive relation, if certain
physical events cause certain mental ones, and the latter apparently cause
certain further events, both mental and physical, it would be natural to
think there is a causal chain. Granted, epiphenomenalism, taken to be
roughly the view that mental events are effects of physical events but
causes of nothing, cannot be ruled out *a priori*. But apart from arguments
for it that to my knowledge have not been offered, its plausibility is
matched or exceeded by the implausibility of supposing that physical
events produce events that themselves have no causal power. Indeed,
there are surely no uncontroversial examples of *any* concrete events that
clearly have no causal power; and such models of causation as we best

understand seem to involve what it is natural to call *transfers* of power or energy from cause to effect: think of pushing, pulling, heating, freezing, coloring, wetting, crushing, and inflating. Not only is something affected in these cases; it also acquires or at least retains causal power (not all of these relations are transitive, of course, but a nontransitive relation can imply a transitive one).

When we add to these points that it is partly by virtue of its content that the mental plays the role it does in explaining action, we can see how the mental might be a crucial link in any causal chain from the physical to action: through the map provided by their content, mental factors such as beliefs give direction to physical forces that, so far as we can tell, would otherwise be blind. Granted that mental factors might have no causal power apart from their nonmental bases, they might both exercise the power they derive from the latter and, in so doing, direct that power. Desire might move our limbs in part because of its roots in our brains; but this does not entail that it has no causal power itself: a lever that can move a stone only when anchored still moves the stone.

This kind of problem is receiving much discussion, and nonreductive materialism is still in development.[250] What has not been generally noticed that is highly relevant to our problem is that if there should be mental substances, their mental properties might still depend on physical ones in much the way posited by nonreductive materialists: nothing prevents my mind from being integrated with my body so as to respond to neural stimuli, say from my color perception, just as reliably as, for an identity theorist, the brain responds to them by going into "color states." If the nonphysical property of having a red sensation or being in pain can depend on a brain property, then in principle it can do this even if it is a property of a Cartesian mind. Descartes famously said (in Meditation VI), "I am not lodged in my body as a pilot in a vessel, but . . . am very closely united to it, and so to speak so intermingled with it that I seem to compose with it one whole." If one thinks there are mental-physical causal interactions, one might well suppose that the mental depends on the physical even if it also has causal powers over (other) physical phenomena. Reflection on this sort of possibility may lead to the hypothesis that in the end one must either live with a deep mystery in nonreductive materialism or choose between a version of the identity theory and a version of substance dualism.[251]

Is a substance dualism compatible with a scientific worldview? If such a worldview includes the metaphysical drive for monism, and especially for materialism (or at least physicalism) that is so prominent among philosophers of science (and indeed other thinkers in and outside of science), it is not. But if one conceives science as seeking a testable, explanatory account of the phenomena we experience and appealing to causal connections with underlying states or processes as basic, then there is no strict incompatibility. Indeed, one can do psychology, and scientifically connect the brain with our mental life, in all the ways psychologists do, without presupposing either that substance dualism is right or that it is wrong. For neither the kinds of laws one seeks, say those linking mental states to each other or to behavior, nor the empirical criteria for the application of mental terms, need be affected by this metaphysical assumption. Pain properties, for instance, may be linked to other phenomenal properties and to behavior whether they supervene on physical ones or are identical to certain of the latter.

In framing an overall conception of the human person, much depends on the status of the principle of intellectual economy (Occam's razor), which tells us not to multiply kinds of entity beyond necessity. This is a widely accepted principle, especially among the scientifically minded. But when is it *necessary* to posit a kind of entity? That is simply not obvious. The jury seems to be still out on the question of what philosophy of mind, taken together with all the scientific data, best harmonizes with this principle. This is not to say that a philosophy of mind that does not harmonize well with this principle must be either false or at least not a rational position. The point is that there is apparently no decisive reason to think the harmony cannot be achieved.

Theism, Mind, and Body

We may assume (for our purposes here) that standard Western theism centers on a personal God, a God conceived as having a sufficiently rich set of mental properties to count as a person of a special kind. Usually, God is conceived as a spiritual being; commonly, God is also considered a nonphysical substance. If, however, one wants to say that in the "typical" view, God is a kind of Cartesian mind, this would go too far. Those who speak, religiously and not philosophically, of the divine mind do not conceive it as identical with God but as essential to God. It is not common, however, for believers—apart from special cases like the incarnation of Jesus—to speak of God as embodied, and here we may leave the incarnation aside in order to avoid presupposing any specific theology.

Still, any theist convinced that a person must have a body can make a case for God's having a body—for instance, the physical world as a whole. At least three points are important if this view is to be taken seriously: God can move any part of the physical world at will, as we can move our limbs at will (roughly, without the mediation of any other action, such as a prior movement of special muscles that in turn control our limb muscles); God has noninferential knowledge (roughly, knowledge not based on premises) of the position of every part of the physical world, as we (often) have such knowledge of the position of certain of our limbs; and insofar as God has experiences (which might be taken to be a matter wholly up to God), the entire physical world might be experienced in the divine mind in something like a perceptual way, producing the appropriate sensations with as rich phenomenal qualities as God wishes them to have.[252] An omnipotent God can bring it about that divine knowledge of the physical world be through, or accompanied by, sensory states or more purely cognitive, and in either case it might be noninferential.

To be sure, it is not clear how the states of the divine mind would have to *depend* on anything physical, as our perceptual states often do; on one view, they would immediately depend on the physical, as where a divine perception is produced by my moving my head, but *ultimately* depend on God, as (at least the sustaining) creator of everything physical. The view in question—that the physical world is God's body—also implies that we human beings are part of God. This consequence brings its problems, but most of them, such as the harmony between divine sovereignty and human freedom, are already with us.[253]

Still another possibility is that the notion of a body need not be tied to that of physical matter. As some philosophers imagine resurrection, it takes place not by disembodiment of the mind or soul and the person's survival therein, but through God's providing a resurrection body in place of the physical one (note that in 1 Corinthians 15: 43–44, Paul speaks of a "spiritual body" as what is "raised").[254] Matter as we know it is not required, for instance, for having a perceptual point of view, for mobility of that point of view in space, or even for perceptibility construed as a causal potentiality to affect other persons (those who perceive one); and it would also seem that functional divisions of "the mind" into, say, intellect, imagination, and will does not require materiality. Theism as such, however, does not immediately entail the possibility of personal resurrection; it entails this only on the assumption that such resurrection is logically possible. If one's philosophy of mind forced one to conclude that it is not, unless some suitable physical embodiment occurred, then one could harbor a hope of resurrection only insofar as one took God to supply an appropriate body. That, however, is apparently logically possible, as are various kinds of embodiment on the part even of God.

So far, our discussion has presupposed a kind of realism: that there are things, such as physical objects, whose existence is mind-independent and material. For idealists, such as Berkeley, this view is a mistake; and some current antirealisms also reject such views. One intelligible form of antirealism would be, like Berkeley's, theistic: the primary reality would then be not only mental but also constituted by the divine mind.[255] The divine mind would sustain the physical (as opposed to material) world that other minds perceive. Idealism need not, however, be theistic, and it is arguable that each person's experience can be as vivid and stable on an idealist view as on the realism usually thought to be a commitment of common sense.

An idealist view, with or without the idea that the world is God's "body," can make sense of both the relation of God to human persons and the commonsense world known though perception and scientific investigation. The central problem here is to make good sense of the regularity and familiar features of experience, and this can in principle be done without taking perceptual experience to reflect the causal impact of mind-independent objects. If the picture is as coherent as it seems, the task is arguably quite within the scope of omnipotence.

Compatibility, Harmony, and Mutual Support

Several points seem clear from our discussion above: that standard Western theism, taken apart from specific theological commitments that cannot be addressed here, provides considerable latitude in the conception of God, that there is no universally acceptable notion of science that rules out the existence of God, and that most of the leading views in the philosophy of mind are either not materialist at all or at least not reductively so. Even reductive materialism is not strictly incompatible with theism: God could have created us as material systems, and God could also have a body some of whose properties would be the physical identicals of divine mental properties.[256] Even omniscience, omnipotence, and omnibenevolence may not be simply assumed to be by their nature properties of a nonphysical being. Granted, if there is an independent argument that they can belong only to minds and that minds are necessarily mental substances, then they could not belong to a nonphysical being; but apart from such a general (and highly contestable) argument, theism has the option in principle of taking God to have a body.

I am speaking, of course, about sheer logical compatibility between theism and various conceptions of mind and thereby going well beyond theological plausibility in any tradition of standard Western theism. As important as compatibility by itself is, one naturally wants to ask whether there can be something more: a harmony between theism and the scientific conception of mind.

Here we might begin with a question so far left in the background: Does a scientific conception of *anything*, mental or physical, require the assumption that all explanations of its existence and career must be natural? It is by no means clear that this is so, in part because it is not clear what counts as a natural explanation. It is certainly not clear that if a mental property, such as my making a decision, is not identical with a physical one, then that property's explaining something, such as my telephoning a friend, is not natural, or indeed not a case of a naturalistic explanation. The natural need not be identified with the physical; it should be a substantive question, not to be resolved by stipulation, what counts as natural—or at least this is a plausible assumption if we take natural properties and events to be the kind fundamental in the natural world: the world of hills, brooks, standing lakes and groves, and of people and animals.

Suppose, then, that a divine decision explains a physical event. It might be said that this *must* be a non-natural explanation because it is supernatural. That may seem true if God has no body, but even on that assumption there is a danger of going too fast. If it is even possible that we human beings are essentially mental substances, then the way events in our minds cause physical events could be a model for one way in which divine decisions do: cross-categorially. This could be harmonized with the view that we are created in God's image: for us, too, there are causal interactions between the mental and the physical, and our actions, too, represent just such a thrust from the mental to the physical.

There remains the disanalogy concerning the different kind of dependence of our mental states on the physical and of God's mental states on the physical (or anything else outside God). But it is not clear that a scientific approach to the world—as opposed to certain metaphysical interpretations of such an approach—cannot accommodate that disanalogy. Causation across different metaphysical categories may be mysterious, but (as noted earlier) causation—taken to be something more than Humean constant conjunction—may be somewhat mysterious in any case. If a scientific worldview is possible without it, that would at least not be a typical case of such a view. To many scientifically minded people, moreover, it would seem explanatorily impoverished.

At least four further responses to our problem should be mentioned if we are to indicate the range of main options. The appeal of these different responses will depend on one's intellectual and other priorities, but all of them show that the proverbial stark choice between science and theism is not inevitable for people inclined toward worldviews incorporating both.

First, a person attracted both to theism and to a scientific conception of mind and unable to harmonize them could agnosticize: simply hold theism as a perhaps ultimately unknowable hypothesis deserving regular reflection and meriting certain responses in one's daily life. Some people in this intellectual position are capable of living their day-to-day lives in a substantially religious manner. They might act on a kind of presumption of theism without believing (or, of course, disbelieving) that it is true or even that it is better confirmed than its negation.

Second, one could treat one's favorite position in the philosophy of mind similarly, being agnostic about that while taking one's theism to be true. This would certainly permit one's comfortably *doing* science, including psychology; it would simply require suspending judgment about certain philosophical theses regarding the mental.

Third, one could opt for theological *noncognitivism*, roughly the view that religious language is expressive rather than assertive: providing a picture of the world and prescriptions for human life, but not describing how reality in fact is. Here the task is to harmonize religious *attitudes* with scientific *beliefs*, rather than to harmonize two sets of beliefs having apparently disparate kinds of content. The former task is less demanding, intellectually at least, than the one we have been exploring.

Fourth, one could try to work out a naturalistic conception of God harmonious with one's scientific outlook.[257] Unless this conception proceeds through taking God to be embodied, as it often does not in the theologians in question, it tends to lose contact with the idea of God as a person. That tends to make it an unattractive option for many committed to a version of standard Western theism, but an ingenious naturalism can be adapted to preserve certain elements in that tradition and can, in any case, be argued to be a version of theism. God need not be identified with nature, but can be seen as a power felt in human experience and sustaining us in ways similar to those traditionally associated with divine conservation.[258]

There is a bolder approach for those who want to be both theists and scientifically minded: to employ the points made here (and others) in working toward not only a harmony between the two sets of commitments but also mutual support between them. From this perspective, scientific discovery is viewed as a *prima facie* indication of God's structuring of the world; divine sovereignty is seen as an assurance that the search for truth will tend to lead to valuable results; the intimate connection between one's physical and one's mental life, and especially our autonomy in directing our conduct, are conceived as possibly reflecting free agency in a sense that is applicable to divine sovereignty over the world. For people proceeding in this way, scientific results may lead to revisions in theology, as theology may lead to scientific hypotheses or changes in scientific direction. Different people with different theologies and philosophies of science will proceed in diverse ways; but so far as we can see, the compatibility between the two worldviews is clear, and possibilities for harmonious interactions between them are wide.[259]

9

Miracles as Violations of Laws of Nature

Martin Curd

There are two distinct kinds of philosophical questions about miracles: (1) What are miracles? and (2) When, if ever, would we be rationally justified in believing of an event that it is miraculous? Any answer to the second, epistemological, question presupposes an answer to the first, conceptual, question. Similarly, adopting a particular conception of the miraculous is likely to have epistemological implications. In this chapter I shall be mainly concerned with the standard modern conception of the miraculous as a violation of the laws of nature and its implications for justifiedly believing that a miracle has occurred.[260]

I

According to the standard modern concept of a miracle, shared by many theists and skeptics alike, there are at least two necessary conditions for an event to be miraculous:

M1. E violates at least one law of nature, and
M2. E is caused directly by God or some other supernatural agent.[261]

What is the logical relation between M1 and M2? As far as I can tell, neither condition entails the other. M1 does not entail M2 since, as William Rowe has argued, it would seem to be logically possible for an event to violate a law without that event having a supernatural cause (or, indeed, any cause of any kind).[262] Similarly, there is reason to doubt that

M2 entails M1. Again, Rowe is correct when he writes, "But if an event is due solely to the direct activity of God then, if it is an event covered by a natural law, it will also violate that law and thus be a miracle."[263] The second "if" here is crucial. It is only if one thinks that every event must be covered by at least one law that one would move automatically from "God acts directly in the world" to "a law is violated." But, presumably, it is possible that there are events that, in one or more respects, are not subject to laws of nature.[264] Thus, it is possible that God might intervene directly with regard to those respects without violating any law. Thus, paradoxical though it might sound, it is possible that God might intervene directly in the world without the divinely caused event being a miracle according to the modern conception of the miraculous.

The last point brings out a matter of considerable epistemological importance. One motivation for the insistence on law violation in the modern definition of a miracle has to do with evidence. One wants the occurrence of the anomalous event to be good evidence for positing God as the event's supernatural cause. If the event in question were not subject to any natural law—if it were merely not determined by laws of nature rather than *contrary* to them—then the event would not, by itself, point to God as its cause. It is because miraculous events (in the modern sense of miracle) are violations of law that they are strong evidence for divine intervention. If no law were violated by an event, then the case for God as its cause would be harder to make since it would have to involve making assumptions about God's nature and dispositions.

We can illustrate the general point with a pair of examples. Imagine that lightning strikes are not subject to any natural law (at least with respect to when and where they hit). An Old Testament prophet calls down the wrath of God on a pagan temple and soon thereafter the offending building is struck by lightning. The prophet might very well think that the destruction was caused by God because he believes that this is the kind of thing that God is disposed to do and that God pays special attention to the prophet's imprecations. But the case for this being an instance of divine intervention is hard to make because the event in question is one that could have happened anyway in the natural course of events and its timing (shortly after the prophet's curse) could have been a coincidence. (If a prophet of Baal had cursed a synagogue that was subsequently destroyed by lightning, then the Hebrew prophet would be very unlikely to regard *that* event as supernaturally caused.) Contrast this example with a second in which a man is raised from the dead, or plain water is converted into wine (*genuine* wine). Such events are *physically* impossible because, in some sense to be explicated, they *violate* laws of nature. Here, the case for supernatural causation is deemed to be much stronger because although M1 does not entail M2, it is, nonetheless, strong evidence for M2. We have, supposedly, good grounds for the event being a genuine case of law violation; those grounds do not presuppose or involve assumptions about God's nature and dispositions; and the event's being a case of law violation points strongly to God as its supernatural cause.

The second example illustrates the way in which the modern conception of miracles uses M1, law violation, as evidential grounds for M2, supernatural causation. For this strategy to work, it is crucial that M1 and M2 are *epistemically independent* in the sense that it is possible to justifiedly believe that M1 is true without first having to believe that M2 is true. This requirement of epistemic independence is vital for anyone who wishes to appeal to the occurrence of a purported miracle (such as a resurrection) as strong, non-question-begging evidence for God's existence.[265] Miracles could not serve as strong, independent evidence for theism if the recognition of an event as a violation of law required a prior determination that God exists and had caused the event, or involved assumptions about God's nature and dispositions. In other words, epistemic independence is the requirement that judgments of law violation should not depend on prior judgments concerning God's existence, nature, or actions: in short, the evidence for M1 must be theistically neutral.

The other feature of the modern conception of the miraculous that merits close attention is the assumption that condition M1 could be satisfied. Several authors have denied this. These authors claim that the modern concept of miracles entails that miracles cannot occur since it is logically impossible for an event to violate a law of nature.[266] After laying out the core argument for this conclusion, I consider three attempts by Rowe, Smart, and Swinburne to refute it. I shall argue that none of these attempts is an unqualified success. My thesis is that insofar as these attempts succeed, they do so at the expense of the epistemic independence condition.

II

Explaining how a miraculous event could possibly violate a law of nature is difficult because if L is a (universal) law of nature, then L has no exceptions.[267] In other words, if "All A's are B" is a genuine law of nature then it has no counterinstances; there are no cases whatever of A's

that are not also B's. Thus, it is logically impossible for the law of nature
"All A's are B" to be violated by the miraculous counterinstance of an A
that is a non-B. Thus, if all violations of natural laws are counterinstances
of them, it is logically impossible for any event to be a miracle.

Notice that this problem is not confined to the regularity theory of
laws (which Hume is commonly assumed to have held[268]) but afflicts
equally the necessitarian account; for the necessitarian, no less than the
regularity theorist, regards laws as being *at least* universal generalizations.
Adding the further requirement of nomic necessity, physical necessity,
or factual entailment to hold between the antecedent and the consequent
of lawlike generalizations does nothing to solve *this* problem.[269]

There are, of course, conceptions of laws of nature other than the
regularity theory according to which violations are possible. For example, Del Ratzsch has recently defended the traditional Christian view that
laws of nature are expressions of God's free will.[270] But adopting this
conception (and regarding miracles as expressions of God's extraordinary
will) would violate the epistemic independence condition since an event
would violate a law just in case it is caused directly by God. Indeed,
Ratzsch admits that his proposal is tantamount to occasionalism, since,
apart from those events that are the exercise of human free will, all
events, miraculous and nonmiraculous alike, would have God as their
agent cause.

Douglas Odegard has tried to make sense of the notion of law violation
by giving an epistemic interpretation of the necessity of laws.[271] On this
view, to say that a proposition is necessary implies that there is (in the
tenseless sense of "is") absolutely no good reason for doubting that
proposition. But, then, as Odegard points out, it follows from the
epistemic interpretation of laws that there would be no good reason to
believe that a law-violating event had occurred unless there were good
reason to think that a god had produced the event, thus compromising
the epistemic independence condition.

Finally, there are several authors who advocate interpreting laws of
nature, not as universal generalizations, but as ascriptions of powers
and dispositions to particular kinds of objects.[272] This dispositional
interpretation of laws traces its ancestry to John Stuart Mill.[273] It regards
laws of nature not as descriptions of the *actual* behavior of bodies, but as
descriptions of the *tendency* that bodies have to behave in certain ways.
This tendency will manifest itself as actual behavior of the relevant type
only if the body is free from counteracting causes. When God acts
directly to produce a miracle, God is a counteracting cause. So, when a

miracle violates a law, the law in question survives unimpugned even though the tendency asserted by the law is not realized.

The dispositional interpretation of laws is most plausible when it is applied to causal laws, or what Mill called "uniformities of succession"; for, in these cases, we are often dealing with forces, and it is natural to regard statements about forces as ascriptions of a tendency or power rather than as descriptions of actual behavior. But the dispositional interpretation is less plausible when it is applied to what Mill called "uniformities of coexistence."[274] The laws of coexistence include many of the fundamental laws of physics such as the laws of conservation of matter, energy, and momentum. Consider the law that men are mortal. What power or tendency is being attributed to each man by such a law? If anything, what is being attributed to each man is a *lack* of a power since, if all men are mortal, no man has the power to avoid death. Similarly, the law of the conservation of matter asserts that if no matter enters or leaves a system, then the quantity of matter in the system remains constant. Again, what power or tendency is being attributed to each body in a closed system by the law of the conservation of matter? Even if a way could be found to interpret all laws as attributions of dispositions, there would still remain the problem of epistemic independence; for, on the dispositional account of laws, what is necessary and sufficient for a violation of a law is the direct causal activity of God. An argument for the conclusion that the dispositional account of law violation must compromise epistemic independence is given in the next section of this chapter in which I criticize a closely related account of law violation that has been proposed by William Rowe. Rowe's account and the dispositional account share in common the thesis that law-violating events are not counterinstances of the laws that they violate.

Let me now summarize. We can analyze the difficulty in understanding miracles as violations of law by noticing that the following four statements form a logically inconsistent set.

1. E is a miracle.
2. If E is a miracle then there is at least one law of nature, L, such that E violates L.
3. If E violates L then E is a counterinstance of L.
4. If L is a law of nature then L has no counterinstances.

If statements 2, 3, and 4 are true, then there are no miracles. Moreover, if 2, 3, and 4 were necessary truths (because they are conceptual or definitional truths), then this would show not merely that 1 is false, but also that it is logically impossible for any event to be miraculous. This is the core argument against the possibility of miracles as violations of law. Since statement 2 comes directly from M1, anyone wishing to defend the modern notion of miracles must deny either 3 or 4. In the next two sections I consider several such attempts.

III

William Rowe denies 3 in chapter 9 of his *Philosophy of Religion*. He defends the view that a law of nature can be violated by an event even though that event is not a counterinstance of the law. Rowe considers a stone that remains stationary when released ten feet above the earth's surface. He reasons as follows. Either the event of the stone's suspension is *not* due to any natural force, cause, or process or it is. In the former case (in which no natural force is keeping the stone in place), Rowe says that "some law of nature—presumably, the law stated by the principle of gravitation—has been violated" (118). In the latter case (in which the stone is kept in place solely by a natural force), there are two possibilities: "either that [natural] force [keeping the stone in place] is accounted for by the principle of gravitation or the principle of gravitation is false and not really a law of nature." Of the second of these two alternatives he says, "If there is a natural force keeping the stone in the air, but that natural force is *less than* what, *according to the principle of gravitation*, is required to prevent the stone from being drawn to the earth, then the principle of gravitation is false as stated and, therefore, not a true law of nature" (118).

Thus, according to Rowe's analysis, there are three different cases, in all of which the stone remains in place when released. Let N be the magnitude of the net natural force acting on the body apart from the gravitational force, let G be the magnitude of the gravitational force actually acting on the body, and let P be the gravitational force that, *according to the principle of gravitation*, should be acting on the body given its mass and position above the earth's surface.

Case 1. $G = P$, and $N = 0$. The principle of gravity is correct but violated.

Case 2. $G = P$, and $N = G$. The principle of gravity is correct and unviolated.

Case 3. $G < P$, or $G > P$, and $N = G$. The principle of gravity is incorrect.

I have interpreted case 3 in what seems to me to be the most plausible way given Rowe's statement quoted above. The point is that in case 3, the principle of gravity makes a false prediction about the magnitude of the gravitational force acting on the body. Thus, the actual gravitational force is either less than *or greater than* the value implied by the principle. Thus, the principle is false, and hence not a law of nature.

The difficulty with Rowe's account lies in its characterization of case 1. We can agree that this case is not a counterinstance to the principle of gravity since the principle correctly predicts the actual gravitational force acting on the body. But why should we regard the principle of gravity as *violated* in this case? In fact, if any law is violated in case 1, it would seem to be Newton's second law of motion, since the body is not accelerating even though a net external (natural) force is acting on it.

In order to make sense of the notion that in case 1 event E violates the second law of motion but is not a counterinstance of it, there are two alternatives: either the law still applies when God intervenes, or it does not. It is clear from Rowe's text that he means to embrace the second alternative. On page 123 of *Philosophy of Religion*, for example, Rowe writes, "the laws of nature tell us what must happen only if what happens is due entirely to natural forces." I understand this and similar remarks to entail that we should regard statements of laws to have conjoined to their antecedents a *ceteris paribus* clause that excludes the supernatural.[275] Thus, on this proposal, Newton's second law would read: "All bodies subject to a net external force *when only natural forces are present*, are bodies that accelerate with an acceleration proportional to the magnitude of the force and in the same direction." But, thus understood, the second law says nothing about what will happen when a supernatural force is present. So, it is hard to see how this proposal can adequately capture the notion of law violation. For, how can a law be violated by a situation to which, by definition, it does not apply?[276]

Rowe's response to this objection is to go counterfactual. What makes E a violation of law, he argues, is not that E is contrary to what the law predicts but that E is contrary to what the law *would* predict if no supernatural forces *were* acting. We could then define law violation as follows:

V. Event E violates law L if and only if E is not a counterinstance of L and E would have been a counterinstance of L if only natural forces had been present.

When applied to case 1, V gives the desired verdict: the stone's suspension in midair is now a violation of Newton's second law.

We are led to much the same account of violation if we embrace the first alternative, that is, if we regard laws of nature as applying to all situations, whether supernatural forces are present or not. On this alternative, case 1 is a violation but not a counterinstance to Newton's second law because the net external force acting on the body is zero: the *natural* gravitational force, G, acting downward (correctly predicted by the principle of gravity) is exactly counterbalanced by an equal and opposite *supernatural* force acting upward. If gravity were suddenly switched off, the body would accelerate upward under the pull of this supernatural force, but at no time would it behave contrary to the second law.

On this proposal, Newton's second law has no proviso attached to its antecedent. The law asserts, without qualification, that "All bodies subject to a net external force are bodies that accelerate with an acceleration proportional to the magnitude of the force and in the same direction." In case 1, the consequent is false: the body is not accelerating. So, if there is no counterinstance, the antecedent must also be false. Thus, there is no net external force acting on the body. Case 1 is a violation of the second law only because if a supernatural agent were *not* at work, we *would* have a counterinstance to the second law. Thus, we end up with essentially the same account of law violation as on the second alternative.

Is Rowe's account of law violation summarized in V a plausible demonstration that statement 3 in the inconsistent tetrad is false and that we can have violations of law without counterinstances? I suspect not. Rowe's own hesitation is marked at one point by the use of scare quotes around the term "violates." Rowe writes, "The important point to note here is that if an event is not due to a natural force, process, or cause, it 'violates' a law of nature but does not show that the statement of the law is incorrect" (118). The basic problem is that, on Rowe's account, nothing that actually happens, whether naturally or supernaturally, conflicts with what the laws of nature assert. Rowe's explication of law violation uses the word "violates" but seems to sacrifice the spirit of that notion. When the relevant counterfactual in V is unpacked and examined, it simply asserts that a supernatural cause is at work, producing an event that must defy lawlike explanation. Thus, either the violation condition merely collapses into the divine causation condition or the violation condition should be replaced by something else, something that eschews the notion of violation entirely and reflects the traditional view that miracles are events that lie outside the order of nature and, hence, are insusceptible of lawlike explanation.[277]

Does Rowe's explication of law violation run afoul of the epistemic independence condition? When understood correctly, Rowe's violation condition, V, will be satisfied when and only when both of the following propositions are true:

V1. The occurrence of event E is not determined by the laws of nature (and hence E is incapable of lawlike explanation).

V2. Event E is the result of a supernatural force (or, in other words, God acts directly in producing E).

V2 is an essential part of V since it would not be true both that E is not a counterinstance of L and that E would have been a counterinstance of L if only natural forces had been acting unless E were the result of a supernatural force. V2 entails V1, but V1 does not entail V2. Clearly, we can imagine collecting evidence for V1 without having to make any assumptions about God's nature and dispositions—we simply keep failing in our attempts to explain the occurrence of E using the known laws of nature. Thus, we can confirm V1 without compromising the epistemic independence condition. Since V2 entails V1, does not this suffice to show that we can confirm V2, and hence that we can confirm V in its entirety, without begging the question against the nontheist? The answer to this question depends on whether one accepts converse entailment as a valid principle of confirmation. The principle of converse entailment asserts that whatever confirms a proposition, P, also confirms any proposition, Q, that entails P. The usual objection to converse entailment as a principle of confirmation is that it is far too liberal. Consider, for example, any one of a variety of "demon" hypotheses each of which entails we have sensations and experiences that appear to be of an external world of physical objects. Surely the fact that we have exactly the kind of sensations and experiences entailed by a demon hypothesis does not confirm that the hypothesis is true or give that hypothesis any measure of evidential support. Thus, there is good reason to suppose that converse entailment is not a valid principle of confirmation. In any case, quite apart from these doubts about confirmation, my main criticism of Rowe's proposal is that it is tantamount to giving up the standard modern concept of a miracle. In effect, Rowe has replaced the problematic violation condition, M1, with V1 (which does not mention violation at all), and then amalgamated V1 with V2 (which is equivalent to M2).

IV

Given the difficulties encountered in attempting to deny 3, that violations of laws are counterinstances of them, we now turn to consider 4. Are there any plausible grounds for denying that laws of nature have no counterinstances? Both Ninian Smart and Richard Swinburne have proposed that it is possible for a genuine law such as "All A's are B" to have a single (miraculous) counterinstance of an A that is not B, just as long as the single exception is *nonrepeatable*.[278] Thus, both authors would advocate that 4 be replaced with something like 4*:

4*. If L is a law then L has no repeatable counterinstances, but L can have a single nonrepeatable counterinstance.

Since both Smart and Swinburne are aware of the logical inconsistency between "All A's are B" and "There is an A that is not a B," it is difficult to see why they think a law can have even one counterinstance. A careful analysis of their positions reveals that what they are really advocating is a shift in the meaning of the term "law."

Smart begins by distinguishing large-scale laws (such as the principle of gravitation) from small-scale laws (such as the law describing the rate at which balls roll down an inclined plane). Small-scale laws are derivable from large-scale ones given relevant information about masses, distances, angles, and so on.[279] Smart then contends that what he calls "negative instances" of large-scale laws are not single events but repeatable events described by small-scale laws. He writes: "Miracles are not experimental, repeatable. They are particular, peculiar events occurring in idiosyncratic human situations. They are not small-scale laws. Consequently they do not destroy large-scale laws. Formally, they may seem to destroy the "Always" statements of the scientific laws; but they have not the genuine deadly power of the negative instance."[280]

Smart's term "negative instance" and his phrase about "destroying" large-scale laws, suggest that what he is really talking about here is the logic of falsification. In other words, Smart is discussing the circumstances in which scientists abandon or modify their lawlike hypotheses in the face of contrary evidence. At this point it is helpful to distinguish scientific laws from laws of nature.[281] Laws of nature are the (universal) regularities that hold in the world regardless of human thought and belief. Scientific laws are those generalizations that, at a given time, are believed to correspond to laws of nature. They are, so to speak, our best available candidates for laws of nature.

With the distinction between scientific laws and laws of nature in hand, Smart's position no longer seems quite so strange or shocking. We can regard him as saying that scientists will not abandon or modify a large-scale *scientific* law unless it has been compromised by several well-attested counterinstances. In fact, Smart thinks that only a small-scale (scientific) law can count as a genuine "negative instance" of a large-scale (scientific) law. If, by their very nature, miracles are nonrepeatable, then they are not instances of small-scale laws. Hence, miracles cannot falsify the large-scale scientific laws with which they are inconsistent.

For the moment, let us leave aside doubts we may have about whether there is any nontrivial sense in which an event, miraculous or otherwise, can be nonrepeatable.[282] The key issue is whether Smart has given us a plausible reason to believe that laws of nature can have counterinstances. I do not think that he has. At best he has shown that single counterinstances are consistent with *scientific* laws, that is, with lawlike generalizations that we believe to be laws of nature. In fact, Smart's analysis of falsification provides no support to those wishing to appeal to miracles as evidence for theism. If a scientist were asked to justify a decision not to abandon or modify a currently accepted scientific law in response to a single reported counterinstance, the scientist's reply would probably be as follows: "Given the wealth of evidence supporting the current scientific law L, I continue to believe that L is a genuine law of nature. Thus, I regard the reported counterinstance to L as spurious, since it would be inconsistent to continue to accept L as a universal law and also admit that it has a counterinstance." In other words, our decision to retain L as a law of nature implies that we do not believe that the reported counterinstance is genuine.

I now turn to consider the views of Swinburne who adopts essentially the same position as Smart in chapter 3 of his monograph *The Concept of Miracle*. Where Swinburne differs from Smart is in his explicit insistence that laws can have counterinstances even though "law" means "law of nature." It is important to stress that Swinburne, like Smart, is committed to the truth of statement 3; that is, he accepts that violations of laws are counterinstances of them since he defines "violation" as "an occurrence of a nonrepeatable counterinstance to a law of nature" (26).

Swinburne begins by supposing that we have good reason to believe that an event E has occurred contrary to the predictions of a scientific law L. (Swinburne calls L a "formula.") We now have two choices: either we say that L is not a law of nature; or we say that L is a law of nature but that it has a nonrepeatable counterinstance.[283] In defense of the latter alternative, Swinburne writes:

> The advantage of saying the latter is however this. The evidence shows that we cannot replace L by a more successful law allowing us to predict E as well as other phenomena supporting L. For any modified formula which

allowed us to predict E would allow us to predict similar events in similar circumstances and hence, *ex hypothesi*, we have good reason to believe, would give false predictions. Whereas if we leave the formula L unmodified, it will, we have good reason to believe, give correct predictions in all other conceivable circumstances.[284]

What Swinburne is proposing, in effect, is that we change our concept of laws of nature to allow for the possibility that they hold in all cases but one, the "nonrepeatable" violation. Notice that Swinburne is not suggesting that we change the form of laws of nature so that the exceptions are built into their statement, for he still wants violations to be counterinstances. (If law L read: "All A's are B, except in case E," E would no longer a counterinstance of L.) Rather, he is proposing that "All A's are B" is a genuine law even though there is a nonrepeatable instance of an A that is not B. But this is logically impossible: if "All A's are B" is a genuine law then *all* A's are B without exception. At best what Swinburne has described is a set of possible circumstances in which we might decide to call a universal generalization "a law of nature" despite our knowledge that it is false if we also believed that it could never be replaced with anything better. But the possibility of a change in our linguistic habits does not amount to a demonstration that laws of nature can have counterinstances given the *current* meaning of those terms.

Swinburne's position becomes even less convincing when one realizes that an event being "nonrepeatable" in his sense does not entail that that same type of event cannot recur. The problem for Swinburne is that events can be regarded in two different ways: either they are spatiotemporal particulars (in which case none of them is repeatable), or they are spatiotemporal instantiations of general descriptions. Unless these descriptions entail that the events that satisfy them are unique (e.g., the conception of Yasir Arafat, the completion of the Eiffel Tower), they can, in principle, be instantiated on many different occasions, and hence the instantiating events are repeatable. Indeed, many biblical miracles are instances of general types of events such as restoring sight to the blind, speaking in tongues, and raising the dead to life; and, purportedly, they took place on several different occasions. Thus, events that in Swinburne's technical sense are "nonrepeatable" are not unique; they can be repeated any number of times. This destroys, I think, whatever plausibility Swinburne's position might possess. For while we might be willing to concede the propriety of talking about a genuine law of nature that has a *single* counterinstance, Swinburne is actually committed to the logical possibility of a natural law having any number of counterinstances.[285]

Finally, there is the epistemic problem. Under what circumstances would we believe that E is a "nonrepeatable" counterinstance that violates law of nature L? Swinburne's answer is that we would believe this when we believe that L will continue to hold "in all other conceivable circumstances" and that the particular event E is fundamentally nonlawlike, that is, when we believe that there is no true law or "formula" of which E *could* be an instance. But that E is incapable of lawlike instantiation is scarcely something that follows from the mere description of E or that the "evidence" shows us. My conjecture is that Swinburne is assuming that we would believe a miraculous event is fundamentally nonlawlike when and only when we believed that it is an instance of agent causation, specifically, that the event is caused directly by God. And, of course, if this conjecture is correct, then Swinburne has implicitly violated the requirement of epistemic independence.

V

Hume once complained about "this custom of calling a *difficulty* what pretends to be a *demonstration*, and endeavouring by that means to elude its force and evidence."[286] In this chapter I have examined several attempts to elude the force and evidence of a demonstration that miracles are impossible. My conclusion is that none of these attempts is fully successful because even the most plausible of them violates the requirement of epistemic independence. Either violations of laws of nature are logically impossible or, on an amended understanding of "violation," the first condition for a miracle (law violation) collapses into the second (supernatural causation). If this conclusion is correct, then no reasonable person could believe that a miracle (according to the modern definition) has occurred without, from the outset, having good grounds for believing that the event in question was caused directly by God. Thus, if I am right, one of Hume's characteristic positions is vindicated: miracles cannot rationally persuade anyone to accept theism if that person is initially neutral on the issue (where neutrality entails that the person does not already accept certain assumptions about God's nature and dispositions). In short, the inference from "law violation" to "supernatural causation" fails to confer on miracles any special force as evidence for theism.

10

Aquinas's Disguised Cosmological Argument

Norman Kretzmann

Introduction

Aquinas's project in *Summa contra gentiles* (SCG) is different from all his other large-scale projects in theology in that he expressly declares that in the arguments of its first three books, he will not base any conclusions on any data derived from any source other than those available to human experience and human reason apart from any putative revelation. He begins his general introduction to SCG saying that in it he intends "to take up the role of a wise person" (2.9), and, as he conceives of wisdom here, "considering the highest causes is part of what it is to be a wise person" (1.3).[287] Therefore, the most fundamental truths making up the profoundest explanations involving primary (or ultimate) things, events, and states of affairs must be wisdom's concern. And this means that the one subject matter indispensable to anybody intending "to take up the role of a wise person" is the subject matter of metaphysics as Aristotle and Aquinas envisage it. For, Aquinas says, Aristotle "intends [metaphysics or] first philosophy to be the science of truth—not of just any truth, but of the truth that is the origin of all truth, the truth that pertains to the first source *(primum principium)* of being for all things" (1.5).[288] (It seems clear that Aquinas sees his natural theology in SCG I–III as the extension of metaphysics understood along these lines, and that his taking up the role of a wise person consists primarily in his developing that extension.)

So, if God exists, then, of course, God will be this broadly character-

185

ized universal source, the first source of being for all things. That's simply part of what it is to be God, considered pretheoretically, and any natural theology that aims at being taken seriously by theists would have to present God in that guise. It certainly seems possible, however, that there should be a universal first source of being, but no God—possible that metaphysics, even when conceived along these Aristotelian lines, should not culminate in *theology*, as Aristotle thought it did. Any entity that could count as the first source of being for all things would have to be breathtakingly extraordinary, but even breathtakingly extraordinary isn't yet divine.

Still, Aquinas ends his general introduction to SCG by declaring, unsurprisingly, that his project of a natural theology based on Aristotelian metaphysics could not get started without a satisfactory argument for God's existence (9.58). And he then duly begins the natural theology proper by devoting a long chapter (13) to the presentation of five arguments, mostly Aristotelian, by means of which, he says, it has been proved that God exists.

The first of those arguments—G1, I'll call it—does look promising as an argument for the existence of an ultimate explanatory principle, if it's appropriately supplemented along the lines proposed in MacDonald's recently published analysis of it and its younger relative, the more famous First Way (of ST Ia.2.3).[289] For my purposes in this discussion, however, I will simply set G1 aside. G2, the second of chapter 13's arguments, is, I think, the most complex of all Aquinas's existence arguments. It deserves a careful analysis (which I'll try to provide elsewhere), but it is fatally flawed and so can't be considered philosophically acceptable evidence for the existence of a primary, universally explanatory being— the sort of being the argument has in its sights. None of the remaining three arguments in the chapter is as impressive a candidate as G1 (or, in some respects, even G2) is for being an argument of the sort Aquinas thinks he has to have in order to get his project started.

Since Aquinas himself insists that the investigation he intends to carry out can't be begun without a good argument for the existence of God, it's only reasonable to expect that the moves he makes in the chapters immediately following chapter 13 will be based, explicitly or implicitly, on what he considers to be the just-proved proposition "God exists." So, even if we suppose for a moment that every one of his five existence arguments in chapter 13 succeeds, then, if Aquinas observes his own rules, in the immediately following chapters he should not be setting out to investigate the nature of an entity any more Godlike than is warranted by the conclusions of the existence arguments in chapter 13. And those conclusions, taken one by one, describe the entity whose existence is inferred as "an immovable first mover" (G1), a "separated, altogether immovable first mover" (G2), "a first efficient cause" (G3), "something that is a being in the fullest possible sense *(aliquid quod est maxime ens)*" (G4), and "someone by whose providence the world is governed" (G5).[290]

The G5-conclusion does unmistakably describe *God*, a supernatural, knowing, universally governing person. However, in the chapters immediately following chapter 13, Aquinas never draws on or alludes to argument G5, nor does he use the G5-description to pick out the being whose nature he is investigating. Since argument G5's conclusion is more unmistakably theistic and thus presumably more to his purpose than any of the other four, the most likely explanation for his not making use of it would ordinarily be that he considers G5 a weak argument.[291] And, although it appeals to evidence that might be developed more persuasively, G5 is a weak argument.[292] But Aquinas introduces all five as "arguments by which philosophers as well as Catholic teachers *have proved* that God exists" (9.81), and he provides no explicit indication that he thinks less of G5 than of the others. I have no satisfactory explanation for his ignoring it after having gone to the trouble of including it among the arguments of chapter 13.

To varying extents, Aquinas does use the descriptions in the conclusions of the other four arguments, and some of them are fuller than others, a little more nearly theological than merely cosmological. But none of them is full enough to provide an unmistakably sufficient condition for deity, and so I'll adopt the further working hypothesis that when Aquinas uses the word "God" in the chapters immediately after chapter 13 we could, without giving up information we're entitled to have, read "God" as "Alpha" (where "Alpha" designates a hypothetical ultimate universal explanatory principle).[293] The development of this natural theology could then proceed as an inquiry into the sort of thing an ultimate explanatory principle would have to be, into what sort of thing Alpha would have to be. If that inquiry turns up evidence for the existence of Alpha, so much the better; but in this development, the question of Alpha's nature would precede the question of its existence.

Aquinas ends the first nine chapters of SCG, his general introduction, by describing the rest of book I as devoted to "the consideration of matters having to do with God in himself" (9.57) as distinct from the consideration of other things in relation to God, the business of books II and III. And so, in keeping with the Aristotelian program we've already noted, he thinks of the rest of book I as divided into two main parts, the first consisting of four chapters devoted to the question of God's existence, culminating in chapter 13's arguments, the second part consisting of eighty-eight chapters devoted to the question of God's nature. But the first part is separated from the second by a short chapter 14, which provides presuppositions for the rest of his natural theology.

The first of these presuppositions I want to consider is Aquinas's explicit statement of the only basis he thinks he really needs, now that he is about to start the new investigation. And it is interesting that the basis he cites is not an explicitly existential claim. Instead, he merely ascribes to the subject of his investigation a single characteristic, the one associated particularly with argument G2: "Let us take as a starting point *(principium)* that which is already manifest from the above [arguments]—I mean, that *God is altogether immovable*" (14.119). Since by "altogether immovable" *(omnino immobilis)* he means incapable of being changed in any way, there's nothing unmistakably divine about this characteristic.[294] Some of G2's argumentation does offer good grounds for denying mutability to anything that, like Alpha, could count as an ultimate explanation of change. But I think it is in any case self-evident that Alpha can count as the ultimate explanation of change only if it is itself altogether unchangeable in at least the aspect of it that is supposed to account for all change. Following Aquinas in taking the absolute immutability of the ultimate explanatory principle as an already established starting point for the investigation of Alpha's nature does not involve either accepting an existence claim or associating with Alpha a characteristic that only God could have.[295]

In the order in which I'm considering them, the second of chapter 14's presuppositions is an epistemological observation that I consider uncontroversial, whether applied to God or to Alpha. Aquinas puts it this way: "In virtue of its immeasurability the divine substance is beyond every form our intellect acquires, and so we cannot apprehend it itself by discerning *(cognoscendo)* what it is" (14.117). He hasn't provided any argument for the first being's "immeasurability," nor does he claim to have done so. But what he's noting here really amounts to no more than our inability to locate Alpha within any of our taxonomic schemes or conceptual frameworks, which have all been developed, naturally, as means of knowing the ordinary phenomena of which Alpha is supposed to be the ultimate explanatory principle. This comes out more clearly when he argues, a little later, that God (or Alpha) can't be found in any of the nine Aristotelian categories of accident (chapter 23) or in the first Aristotelian category, substance (25.236), and that God (or Alpha) can't be given a full-fledged definition (25.233). What's uncontroversial here is the underlying idea that anything that could count as the ultimate explanation of physical reality could not be apprehended, measured, or classified in any of the ways human beings have discovered or could devise for apprehending, measuring, or classifying things in nature. Quarks, gluons, the strong force, and all the other ingredients in currently fundamental physical explanations conform to or manifest natural laws, the basic conceptual framework in which standard scientific explanations terminate. But anything that could count as an ultimate explanation would have to explain natural laws as well.

This epistemological presupposition of Aquinas's can also seem to defeat his purpose in going on to investigate the nature of ultimate reality. For what could be the goal of that investigation if not to "apprehend it itself by discerning what it is"?

Aquinas's answer to that question is the third and last presupposition provided in chapter 14. "We have a kind of knowledge of" the first being, he says, "by discerning what it is *not*, and we come closer to a knowledge of it to the extent to which we can through our intellect *eliminate* more [characteristics] from it; for the more fully we observe anything's differences from other things, the more completely do we discern it" (14.117). And, of course, he's right. Negative discoveries do carve out affirmative information. Just think of the assured progress you'd be making in a game of Twenty Questions by getting nothing but negative answers to your cleverly framed series of questions. "For example, if we say that God is not an accident"—that is, doesn't belong in any of the nine categories of accident—"he is on that basis distinguished from all accidents." Therefore, if God can be fit into the Aristotelian categories at all, he belongs in the first category: substance. "If we then add that he is not a body, we will distinguish him also from some substances" in the first category, and we will know that God is an incorporeal substance, if he is a substance at all (14.118). And so on.

So the third of chapter 14's presuppositions is methodological, and Aquinas himself calls this indirect route to cognition "the eliminative method" *(via remotionis)* (15.117,119). It is exactly suited to the project of acquiring cognition of the characteristics of the hypothetical Alpha, coming "closer to a knowledge of it to the extent to which we can through our intellect eliminate more [characteristics] from it." That is why Aquinas introduces as his new starting point only the already accomplished *elimination* of the characteristic of being in any way subject to change: "Therefore, in order to proceed by the eliminative method as regards the cognition of God, let us take as a starting point that which is already manifest from the above [arguments]—I mean, that God is altogether immovable" (14.119).

Drawing on the arguments of chapter 13 for no more about the first cause initially than that it must not be subject to any change, Aquinas carries his investigation of its nature forward by applying the eliminative method again and again in chapters 15 through 28, arguing for the elimination of at least nineteen characteristics that an altogether immutable first cause couldn't have. For instance, Aquinas's opening move in chapter 15 is to show that anything "altogether immutable," regardless of any causal function it might have, would also have to be beginningless and endless, since, as he says, "everything that does begin or cease to exist undergoes it through motion or change" (15.121). Immutability's incompatibility with ceasing to exist is more obvious than its incompatibility with beginning to exit. Still, even though a thing's beginning to exist can't count as a change in that thing, which didn't exist until then, it must count as a change in the way the world is. And so Alpha, which is by hypothesis the ultimate explanation of all change and of the way the world is, could never have begun to exist any more than it could ever cease to exist.[296]

But, as Aquinas goes on to observe in that same chapter 15, the world Alpha is supposed to be the explanation of is full of things that do, and therefore can, begin and cease to exist. On the basis of that observation, he develops another argument, one that focuses on Alpha's causality as the earlier argument focused on its immutability. As we'll see in just a minute, he presents this argument simply as another application of the eliminative method, not as an argument for the existence of anything. But I think that part of it can and should be considered as an argument for Alpha's existence, a disguised cosmological argument, and that's how I will now consider it. The part I am interested in I will call *Argument G6*.

We see things in the world that can exist and can also not exist *(sunt possibilia esse et non esse)*—I mean those that can be generated and can be destroyed. Now everything that can exist [and can also not exist] has a cause. For since on its own it is related indifferently to those two—existing and not existing—if existing is its status *(ei approprietur)*, that must be on the basis of some cause. But one cannot go on ad infinitum in [a series of] causes, as was proved above on the basis of Aristotle's reasoning. Therefore, one must posit something the existing of which is necessary *(aliquid quod sit necesse esse)*.[297] Now everything necessary either has the cause of its necessity in something else, or it doesn't but is, instead, necessary through itself. But one cannot go on ad infinitum in [a series of] necessary beings that have the cause of their necessity in something else. Therefore, one must posit some first necessary being that is necessary through itself. (15.124)

General Observations

The sentence with which I end my translation of this passage, the conclusion of argument G6, is not the final conclusion of Aquinas's argument, which, like the other arguments of chapter 15, is intended to show that God is eternal. Accordingly, his complete argument includes these two additional sentences: "And that is God, since he is the first cause, as has been shown. Therefore, God is eternal, since everything necessary through itself is eternal." I'm leaving out the first of those two sentences because I'm now concerned with Alpha rather than with God, and because I'm only supposing that there is a first cause, not claiming that that has been already shown.[298] The second omitted sentence, Aquinas's final conclusion for this argument, is what makes the argument appropriate for chapter 15. His complete argument is a product of the eliminative method because "eternal" as used in that final conclusion must mean existing beginninglessly, endlessly, and probably also timelessly.[299] G6, the argument I'm now interested in, is only the part of Aquinas's argument that purports to show that "one must posit some first necessary being that is necessary through itself." I'm not interested now in deriving another characteristic from that kind of necessity.[300]

G6's "first necessary being that is necessary through itself" is inferred as the explanation for the existence of all the things "we see . . . in the world that can exist and can also not exist," the things that make up the observable world. So the entity to which argument G6 concludes is Alpha, the hypothetical first cause of the existence and nature of the observable world.

The fact that G6 deals in possibilities and positings might give the impression that the argument is merely hypothetical , concluding only to a necessity that Alpha would have to have if Alpha really does exist. But G6 clearly is an inference to the explanation of the most familiar kind of actual existence, the kind exemplified by ordinary things that "we see . . . in the world." And so the conclusion of G6 is to be read as a claim that a certain extraordinary sort of thing must actually exist, and that it must exist differently from the way the things we see in the world exist, just in virtue of its serving as the ultimate explanation of their existence.

Considered in that way, as an argument for Alpha's existence, G6 is clearly within the extended family of the "cosmological" arguments, those that attempt to argue from the undoubted existence or occurrence of ordinary things, events, or states of affairs to the existence of an extraordinary being whose existence and nature constitute the ultimate explanation of the existence or occurrence of everything, including itself.[301] That observation about G6 invites comparisons between it and others of Aquinas's cosmological arguments for God's existence. It will become clear that G6 is specifically different from any of the three cosmological arguments in chapter 13 (G1, G2, and G3). As for the cosmological arguments among ST's Five Ways, what I am calling G6 has been described in the literature, much too simply, as "the version of the *Third Way* given in the *Summa Contra Gentiles.*"[302] Since the Third Way, too, is an argument based on the contingency of ordinary existence, it might count as G6's closest relative among the Five Ways. But there are more than enough significant differences between the two arguments to rule out taking G6 to be merely a version of the Third Way, differences that warrant considering G6 on its own.

Double Dependence

G6 begins with propositions immediately inferable from commonplace observations about familiar things. We regularly observe the more impermanent things around us being generated and being destroyed, and we have good reasons to think that all the less impermanent things we see, such as mountains and planets and stars, have been generated and will be destroyed. The world is full of existing things that *can* also not exist, things that did not always exist but have been (and so "can be") generated and *can* be destroyed—in short, contingently existing things (lines 1–3).

As G6 implies, Aquinas thinks that a contingent being's present existence is dependent in two respects. First, it has been generated and so depends on something else for having come into existence. Second, it depends on something else for existing, because it has no intrinsic tendency to continue to exist: "on its own it is related indifferently to *(de se aequaliter se habeat ad)* . . . existing and not existing" (lines 4–5).[303]

The dependence of a contingently existing thing in this second respect may at first seem overstated because it entails the denial of an altogether natural, practically universal background belief, which might be thought of as the presumption of existential inertia—the presumption that many or most contingent beings *do* have a tendency to continue to exist, other things being equal. And there's nothing objectionable in that presumption, as long as it is recognized that a contingent being is by definition something the existing of which is utterly dependent on other things' being equal, on the fulfillment of many necessary conditions.[304] Aquinas's denial of existential inertia applies only to such an utterly dependently existing thing considered "on its own," not within a context normal for its existing. So the cause or causes inferred in lines 3–6 must be whatever it takes to explain some contingent being's presently existing despite its doubly dependent existential status. What it takes is answers to these two questions, into which the question about a thing's existence can be analyzed: (Q1) What explains its having come into existence? and (Q2) What explains its presently existing? The causes inferred in lines 3–6, then, may at first seem to be both generating and sustaining (or continuating) causes. But, as we'll see, generating causes are not at issue in argument G6.

The natural sciences provide answers to questions Q1 and Q2 about very many sorts of dependently existing things, and their answers are in terms of other dependently existing things. But, of course, both questions can and, at least from the standpoint of metaphysics, should be asked again about each dependent explanatory being referred to in such explanatory answers, no matter what level of generality they're formulated at, no matter how pervasive or simple may be the dependent things, events, or states of affairs they refer to. And the crux of Aquinas's line of reasoning in G6 is his denial that it is theoretically possible to trace back explanatory beings in this way ad infinitum (line 6). What does he mean by that?

A Series of Generating Causes

He might mean that it is theoretically impossible for the series of explanatory dependent beings to be beginningless, theoretically impossible for Q1 to be correctly answered again and again in terms of generating causes that "go on ad infinitum" into "the dark backward and abysm of time."[305] He might; but he doesn't. Aquinas argues elsewhere in SCG and in other works *against* the impossibility of the infinite temporal and causal regress entailed by the notion of our world's having existed always.[306] In doing so, he sometimes expressly supports the theoretical possibility of a regress that is infinite, as he says, only accidentally *(per accidens)*. For instance, "in connection with efficient causes a regress that is infinite *accidentally* is *not* considered impossible—if, that is, all the infinitely many causes have the order of only one cause, but their being many is accidental. A carpenter, for example, acts by means of accidentally many hammers because one after another of them breaks; and so it is an accidental characteristic of this hammer that it acts after the action of another hammer. Similarly, it is an accidental characteristic of this man, insofar as he begets, that he has been begotten by another; for he begets insofar as he is a man and not insofar as he is the son of another man, since all men considered as begetters have a single status among efficient causes, the status of a particular begetter. And so it is not impossible that a man be begotten by a man ad infinitum" (*ST* Ia.46.2, ad 7). For many things to "have the order of only one cause" *(non teneant ordinem nisi unius causae)* or "to have a single status among efficient causes" *(habent gradum unum in causis efficientibus)* is for their plurality to be irrelevant to the causal activity of any one of them, whether or not they are elements in a single causal series. The many hammers successively owned and used by the carpenter, one at a time, are not elements in a single causal series but are altogether causally independent of one another: each of them does its hammering without in any way depending on its predecessors. On the other hand, each human begetter in a single line of biological descent is causally dependent on his immediate predecessor in that causal series in one respect—for his having been begotten. But, even so, each of them does his begetting without depending on any of his predecessors in *that* respect. A father's begetting, considered just as such, is no more dependent on his father's begetting him than this hammer's hammering is dependent on the most recently discarded hammer's hammering. Since the plurality of these independently operating causes is entirely accidental to the causality of any one of them, there is in theory no reason why the series of hammers, or even the series of begetters, should not have been beginningless, should not constitute a temporally infinite regress.

So, when Aquinas says in lines 6–7 that "one cannot go on ad infinitum in [a series of] causes," he doesn't mean that if we start with any doubly dependently existing thing, we can't in theory answer question Q1 ad infinitum in terms of a beginningless series of generating causes—an infinite regress of dependently existent, independently explanatory beings. In developing argument G2, Aquinas shows that he is occasionally willing to adopt the hypothesis of this world's beginninglessness for the sake of argument. Quite rightly, he takes the inclusion of that hypothesis to strengthen an argument for the existence of a first cause just because it poses a stiffer challenge to such an argument. So I propose adopting that hypothesis here in G6. I will suppose that for each and every thing that comes into existence, the answer to Q1—the explanation of that dependent being's coming into existence—can be correctly given in terms of the causality of at least one earlier dependent being. In other words, I'm supposing, for the sake of argument G6, that there actually is a beginningless series of dependent beings generated by earlier dependent beings. I'll call that series S. Theories of biological, geological, and cosmological evolution have given us good reasons to think that the uncountably many concurrent generatively causal series of dependent beings tend to converge as they are traced back in time, that these series branch only in one "direction"—from past to future. For simplicity's sake, I will suppose that we are dealing with just one many-branched causal series S in which can be found the answer to Q1 for any and every dependently existent thing to which Q1 applies.[307] S contains the hypothetically beginningless history of the natural world.

But Q1 obviously couldn't apply to the series S itself, because, by hypothesis, S never came into existence. If S itself is in some respect a dependently existent being, it isn't a *doubly* dependent being as I've been using that designation, because the question "What explains S's having come into existence?" has no application.

Sustaining Causes

A closer look at G6 should show that the kind of dependence at issue in this argument really is not every ordinary thing's dependence on something else for its having come into existence, but rather its dependence on something else for its remaining in existence, for its existing now, for its now becoming a component of the immediate future, which as of right now *isn't* yet. In some of Aquinas's cosmological arguments, he clearly is focusing on generative dependence, as he shows in ST's Second Way, when he explains that nothing can cause *itself* in the respect relevant to that argument because in order to do so, it would have to have existed before it began to exist. In G6, although he alludes to generability in order to establish the contingency of ordinary things, the kind of dependence he's concerned with is brought out in his denial of existential inertia and his claim that, consequently, a contingent being's presently existing requires an explanation (lines 4–6): "if *existing* is its status, *that* must be on the basis of some cause" (lines 5–6). Besides, since Aquinas expressly grants the possibility of an infinite regress of generating causes, we should, if we can, avoid interpreting his denial of an infinite regress here as if it concerned generating causes. And we can. I will, then, take argument G6 to be concerned not with generating but with sustaining or continuating causes.

The dependence of ordinary contingent things on sustaining causes is beyond dispute. But does series S itself need sustaining? Does it make sense to ask what explains beginningless S's remaining in existence, getting from the present instant into the immediate future? Does it make sense to ask why the world doesn't come to an end right now? Putting question Q2 in the form suggested by Aquinas's line in argument G6, does it make sense to ask what explains S's sempiternality, its beginningless, continuous ongoingness?

Question Q2 applied to series S seems ambiguous as between diachronic and synchronic considerations of S's persistence. The diachronic consideration—What explains S's having forever had new members?—is addressed in the answers to all the instances of Q1 asked about the generation of the particular doubly dependent beings that are the members of S, and so it doesn't constitute a question to be asked separately about S itself.[308] The synchronic consideration—What explains S's going on right now?—is a different question, one that amounts to a genuine application of Q2 to series S. As such, it may seem to require conceiving of S itself as a dependent being.

S's Instantaneous, Synchronic, Present Phase

Well, *is* series S a dependently existent thing in the sense of requiring a sustaining cause? Is it a thing at all? Since S's existence is successive, since there is no time at which all its members exist together, we might feel uncomfortable about regarding S as a thing in its own right.[309] I don't think worries of that sort are justified, but the issue doesn't have to be settled here. In asking about the explanation of S's going on right now, we're asking about the explanation of S's now having any members rather than none at all. And so in this case we're asking not for an explanation of S as a beginningless diachronic whole, but rather for an explanation of its instantaneous, synchronic, present phase, which I'll label S_n. Unlike S itself, S_n is not at all successive; all of S_n's members exist at once. And since each of S_n's members is, by hypothesis, a being that depends for its existing on the present operation of sustaining causes, the explanation of S_n can be construed as simply the sum of all the explanations of the existing of the dependent beings that are S_n's members. If such a construal makes sense, then the sum of all those particular explanations would explain S's now having not merely any elements at all but even the very elements it now has.

Such an explanation of S's going on right now in terms of explaining S_n would be enormously more complex than is needed for purposes of argument G6. And, besides, it may seem that all those particular explanations are too disparate to be summed into an explanation of S_n. After all, beings that depend on other beings for their existing have very different necessary conditions. Your presently existing needs the earth's atmosphere as part of its explanation; a mountain's or a star's presently existing doesn't. But S_n converges when traced up its chain of continuating causes as S converges when traced backward in time. Moving up several levels in the explanation of your continuing to exist, the existing of the earth's atmosphere requires earth's gravity, and so does the mountain's continuing to exist—though not the star's. And, moving up many more levels of explanation all at once, the continuing existence of earth's gravity, and of the sun, and of every other dependent being "we see . . . in the world" has the continuing existence (or obtaining) of natural laws as a necessary condition. For my immediate purposes, I can pause there, at the level of explanation at which a general reference to natural laws is the most or the only appropriate move to make. And, naturally, part of any generally correct answer to the question of what keeps the world going will have to be that natural laws continue to obtain. (By natural laws here I mean nature's actual governing regularities, of course, and not anybody's up-to-the-minute codified best estimate of what those regularities might be.)

So I maintain that question Q2 does apply to S in virtue of applying to S_n, and that Q2 applies to S_n in virtue of applying to each of S_n's members in such a way as to lead, through repeated applications, to an identifiable single condition necessary for S's going on right now: the persisting efficacy of natural laws. I am definitely not maintaining that the persistence of natural laws needs no explaining. At this point I want only to claim that although (in lines 6–7 of argument G6) Aquinas issues his denial of the theoretical possibility of going on ad infinitum only as regards applying Q2 to the existing of a particular observable dependent being, the denial can and should be construed as applying also to explaining S's presently continuing. But how, exactly?

A Synchronic Regress of Explanations

We've seen that Aquinas elsewhere accepts the possibility of a diachronically infinite regress of explanations in answer to repeated applications of

Q1. Here he is denying the possibility of a synchronically infinite regress of explanations in answer to repeated applications of Q2. Aquinas thinks that a causally linked series of efficient causes does not admit of an infinite regress just in case, for each cause in the series, its causally operating is required for its immediate successor's causally operating, so that the effect is not achieved unless all the causes in the series are operating simultaneously: "In connection with efficient causes a regress that is infinite *essentially (per se)* is *impossible*—if, that is, the causes that are essentially required for some effect were infinitely many. For example, if a stone were moved by a stick, the stick by a hand, and so on ad infinitum" (ST Ia.46.2, ad 7). If in asking question Q1 about S we picture a horizontal series of generating causes, stretching back infinitely into the past, then the series of sustaining causes we're considering now in asking question Q2 about S_n should be pictured as vertical, the series of causes all of which must be operating at once, right now, in order to explain the present existing of anything that is "on its own . . . related indifferently to . . . existing and not existing."

Aquinas says that the impossibility he's alluding to here "was proved above on the basis of Aristotle's reasoning" (line 7). At this point in SCG anything "proved above" has to have been proved in chapter 13, and chapter 13 does contain not just one but four Aristotelian arguments against infinite causal regresses—three as subarguments in argument G1 and one in G3. But only one of those four, the third one in G1, is clearly relevant to our case here: "That which is moved instrumentally cannot move anything unless there is something that moves it initially *(principaliter)*. But if one goes on ad infinitum as regards movers and things moved, all of them will be moving instrumentally, so to speak, because they are posited as moved movers; but nothing will be [operating] as the initial mover. Therefore, nothing will be moved" (13.95).

Like the Aristotelian example of the hand, the stick, and the stone, this argument has to do with causes of motion rather than with sustaining or continuating causes as such. But the relevant sort of causes of motion, considered just as such, obviously is a species of continuating cause: the stone stops moving as soon as the stick stops moving, and the stick stops moving as soon as the hand stops moving. This subargument from G1 insists that in such a synchronic causal series all the intermediate causes, however many they may be, must be merely *instrumental*, dependent for their causal operation on the causally prior but temporally simultaneous operation of some cause that is causally first in that series. So this inferred first cause cannot itself be an instrumental cause in the series but must instead be the originally operative cause relative to which all the others in the causal series are instrumental. Aquinas does not, and need not, concern himself with how many intermediate instrumental causes may be involved in explaining a dependent being's presently existing. When he says that "one cannot go on ad infinitum" in such a series, he means that it must be traceable to a first (or ultimate) cause, even if the causal distance between the first cause and the sustaining of the dependent being were *infinitely* divisible into simultaneously operating intermediaries.

The Impossibility of a Synchronically Infinite Regress of Explanations

But what entitles Aquinas to deny the possibility of going on ad infinitum in such a causal series? The most fully satisfactory answer I know is the one developed by Rowe. Suppose that A is a dependent being whose existing right now is explained by B's current sustaining activity, and that B's sustaining of A is explained by reference to C. "Can we now say," Rowe asks, "that the explanation for the fact that the causal activity of causing A to exist is now going on might be found in B? It seems clear we cannot."[310] In keeping with a later medieval tradition, Rowe calls a causal series of this sort "essentially ordered." "Now," he says,

> if C is causing B to be causing A to exist, then since we are operating within an essentially ordered series it also will be true that C is now causing A to exist. C, therefore, will be exhibiting that very sort of causal activity we are trying to explain. And if C is the first member of the series, we might be able to explain why the causal activity *causing-A-to-be-now-existing* is now going on by reference to C.[311] However, if C is an intermediate cause, if some other thing is now causing C to be causing A to exist, then we cannot find the explanation for the fact that this activity is going on by reference to C. What then if the series progesses to infinity? Each member of the series will be right now exhibiting the causal activity we are trying to explain. It will be true that every member of the series is exhibiting the causal activity in question and also true that the fact that the causal activity is going on cannot be explained by any member of the series. For any member we select, it will be true that it is caused to exhibit the activity in question by some other member and, therefore, true that we cannot explain the fact that this sort of causal activity is going on in the universe by reference to that member . . . [I]f the series proceeds to infinity there will be no explanation of the fact that a certain sort of causal activity [causing A to be now existing] is going on in the world.[312]

And, therefore, I would add, there could not in that case be a philosophically satisfactory, metaphysical explanation of the fact that A—or S—is now continuing to exist.[313] A's—and, therefore, S's—existing now would be a brute fact, theoretically inexplicable, "*if* the essentially ordered series of causes resulting in A's present existence proceeds to infinity, lacks a first member."[314]

Aquinas doesn't take the brute-fact alternative seriously, whether in G6 or anywhere else. As Rowe quite rightly observes, that fact about Aquinas shows that he assumes or considers self-evident some form of "the Principle of Sufficient Reason (PSR), a principle that in its strongest form maintains that no thing can exist and no fact can obtain without there being an explanation for that thing's existence or for that fact's obtaining."[315] Rowe argues convincingly that (PSR) is untenable in its strongest form, and I agree.[316] But I also agree with his claim that "no one has put forth any convincing argument for the falsity of (PSR2)," this weaker form of (PSR): "*Every existing thing has a reason for its existence either in the necessity of its own nature or in the causal efficacy of some other beings.*"[317] I subscribe to (PSR2), interpreting the expression "a reason for its existence" in the sense of a reason for its presently existing. Not only the history of science but even a fundamentally rational attitude toward ordinary reality presupposes (PSR2). And since there is no ordinary existing thing about which we could tolerate the blithe announcement that there simply is *no* reason for its existence, rationality forbids our abandoning the principle when the existing thing in question is extraordinary or all-pervasive—a thing such as the universe, or matter.

It may already be apparent, but it will become clearer, that the form of (PSR) presupposed in G6 is (PSR2). Even at this point it should be clear at least that in G6 Aquinas is assuming that *Every existing thing* that is related indifferently to existing and not existing *has a reason for its existence . . . in the causal efficacy of some other beings.*

It seems to me, then, that argument G6 is acceptable through the sentence ending in line 7. In any essentially ordered series of causes invoked to explain the presently continuing existence of any and every dependent being, there must be something that serves as a first, non-instrumental, independently operating cause.

Could that something be the natural laws themselves? Their persistence is a necessary condition common to the existing of all the dependent beings we've been considering, but the persistence of the laws—or, more precisely, of the governing regularities represented in them—certainly isn't self-explanatory. The necessity that has sometimes been ascribed to them isn't *logical* necessity but rather a kind of conditional necessity. Nor do the laws themselves, even sublimated and unified in the Theory of Everything, or the Final Theory, seem to constitute a plausible candidate for the role of first, noninstrumental, independently operating cause.[318] Anything that could count as Alpha would, obviously, have to have some intimate sort of relationship with natural laws, but identity goes too far.[319] Pointing to the laws counts as indicating part of the answer to the big question—"Why is there this sort of world rather than another sort, or nothing at all?"—but only the part that has to do with there being this sort of world rather than another, and not at all with the part that has to do with there being something rather than nothing.

Dependently Necessary Beings

Now, what about the subconclusion in lines 7–9 of the argument? It implies that "one must posit something the existing of which is necessary." A review of G6 up to this point shows that at least part of what can legitimately be meant here by saying of something that its existing is necessary is that it exists, but it couldn't have been generated and it cannot be destroyed. We've already seen that "altogether immutable" Alpha could never have begun to exist and can never cease to exist. Could Alpha on those grounds be identified as this necessarily existent thing that "one must posit?" No—or, at any rate, not yet.

Aquinas understands generation and destruction as including all the natural processes of being brought into and being taken out of existence. In his Aristotelian view of nature, some actually existent things—the sun, for instance—exist necessarily in the special, narrow sense of not being subject to any natural processes of beginning and ceasing to exist, and yet they exist dependently. Unlike all the other things "we see . . . in the world," a dependently necessary being is independent of all natural originating and sustaining causes. But the sun's nature doesn't entail its existence any more than the nature of the carrot I'm about to eat entails its existence. The (Aristotelian) sun's existing independent of natural generation and destruction warrants its being described as necessary in this special sense, while the fact that its nature does not entail its existence dictates its being described as having "the cause of its necessity in something else" (lines 9–10)—something else that sustains it in an existence that is not subject to the vicissitudes of nature.[320]

Although at least many of Aquinas's dependently necessary beings are scientifically discountable, his introduction of them in lines 9–11 of G6 is justified dialectically. The argument aims at showing that "one must posit some first necessary being that is necessary *through itself*." But since Aquinas and his contemporaries believed in *"necessary* beings that have the cause of their necessity *in something else"* (lines 11–12), he has first to rule out those lesser necessary beings. He does so by denying the possibility of an infinite regress of dependently necessary beings (in lines 11–12) along the lines of the analogous denial in line 5—the one we've already looked at. If we then move directly to G6's conclusion that "one must posit some first necessary being that is necessary through itself," we have arrived justifiably at an entity that can and must be identified with altogether immutable, beginningless, and endless Alpha.

Alpha as Existing Independently

But what does it mean to say that Alpha is necessary through itself *(per seipsum necessarium)*? It means that Alpha—that is, whatever ultimately explains the present continuing of S (the beginningless series of generating causes and their effects)—must itself exist *independently* as well as immutably, beginninglessly, and endlessly. The possibility of Alpha's having in any way begun to exist has been shown to be impossible. And Alpha considered simply in its explanatory relationship to S can't depend on anything else for its existing, because it has been identified as the requisite first cause in the essentially ordered series of causes that explains S_n's existing and thus S's going on right now. Such a first cause was shown to be required by the nature of an essentially ordered series of causes and (PSR2). Invoking (PSR2) in order to get to Alpha's existence in G6 and then discarding it would be unjustifiable, and Aquinas obviously has no inclination to declare Alpha's necessary existence inexplicable. All necessary existence is explicable, either on the basis of extrinsic necessitation or on the basis of intrinsic necessitation (lines 9–11). And the necessary existence that must belong to Alpha, the first cause, must of course be explained intrinsically (lines 11–13). Putting it in terms of (PSR2), Alpha must have *a reason for its existence* and cannot have it *in the causal efficacy of some other beings* and so must have it *in the necessity of its own nature*. Putting it as the conclusion of G6 puts it, a "first necessary being" must be "necessary through itself."

Summing Up G6

Summing up, let A be some existing thing that can also not exist—you, or this planet, or this galaxy, or all the galaxies taken together—

something that does actually exist but that on its own, in its own nature, is related indifferently to existence. And suppose that A is a present member of a beginningless series of generating causes and their effects. Then, since *every existing thing has a reason for its existence either in the necessity of its own nature or in the causal efficacy of some other beings*, there must be some reason for A's existing. That reason cannot be in the necessity of A's own nature, since A on its own is related indifferently to existence; and so the reason for A's existing must be in the causal efficacy of other beings. However many other beings may in their causal efficacy be contributing instrumentally to A's existing now, their operating causally would not constitute the reason for A's existing now if there were not some first cause at the head of that essentially ordered series of causes. Therefore, since A does exist, such a first cause—Alpha—must exist. As such, Alpha must be not an instrumental but an altogether independent cause, dependent on absolutely nothing else for its present causal operation that actualizes simultaneously the causal efficacy of all the instrumental causes in the series.

The Alpha whose necessary existence is argued for in G6 is a first sustainer; but I introduced Alpha into this discussion as the hypothetical first mover, the ultimate explanation of all change. Can Alpha the first mover and Alpha the first sustainer be one and the same? I think so. Since we have an argument for the first sustainer's existence, it's only natural to take the primary identification of Alpha to be that of first sustainer. What makes it also the first mover is that its sustaining of nature (involving all the natural laws) is what makes possible all the natural changes that occur when and as they do because of the natures of things. Alpha the first mover considered in this way need not initiate any change but must serve as the essential cooperating, enabling cause of every natural (and even volitional) change.

So, if Alpha the first sustainer is also the first mover, then it is as such altogether immutable, and therefore beginningless and endless. Alpha, by our initial hypotheses the first cause, must as such be at the head of an essentially ordered series of causes that explains the existing of any and every dependently existing thing. And, as the first sustaining cause, Alpha must be a first necessary being that is necessary through itself—that is, must exist altogether independently, in the sense that Alpha's existing is to be explained solely on the basis of Alpha's nature. Alpha's existing, then, is obviously independent of natural laws. But since those laws are inevitably referred to at some relatively elevated stage in the explanation of any dependent being's existing, natural laws must be intimately related to the nature of Alpha in some way (a relationship I will examine elsewhere).

The last word of this paper must be that even if, as I think, G6 provides good evidence for the existence of Alpha, it does not constitute an argument for the existence of God, simply because the characteristics essential to the entity in the conclusion of G6 don't constitute a condition sufficient for deity. However, as I'll try to show elsewhere, such a condition is fully developed in the course of Aquinas's natural theology in SCG I–III.[321]

11

On Plantinga's 1967 and 1983 Parity Defenses

George Nakhnikian

Alvin Plantinga has published three parity defenses of the epistemic rationality of theistic belief.[322] In this chapter, I shall focus on the first and second, and argue that they fail.

Plantinga tries to show that theistic belief is epistemically rational, even if there is no discursive reasoning by which its truth or probability can be shown. Both defenses deploy the same general tactic. Plantinga argues that theistic belief and belief in some suitable comparison class are on an epistemic par: they are epistemically rational or justified in analogous ways and to about the same degree. In the 1967 defense, the comparison class is belief in other minds; in the 1983 defense, it is perceptual belief. Plantinga assumes that beliefs in the comparison class are epistemically rational, and that once the relevant analogies between them and theistic belief are uncovered, it should be evident that theistic beliefs are epistemically rational in the same way and to (nearly) the same degree as the beliefs in the comparison class.

The 1967 Parity Defense

Since my objection to the 1967 defense does not require me to go into the massive analytical detail from which it is built, I shall simply sketch it before I turn to criticism. (All page references in this section are to *God and Other Minds*.)

The argument, in brief, is this: For each belief that *p* I have, there is an "epistemological question": How do I know, what are my reasons for believing, that *p*?, where only propositions can be reasons. The teleological argument is the best answer to the relevant epistemological question about the existence of God; however, it suffers "from a crucial and crippling deficiency," namely, that those propositions that constitute the teleological hypothesis are supported by evidence of a certain kind—the teleological evidence—but that evidence supports only *some* of those propositions. "But, then, of course," Plantinga says, "the conjunction of these propositions [that constitute the teleological hypothesis] is not . . . more probable than not on that evidence" (268). The comparison class is belief in other minds. The analogical argument for other minds is the best answer to the relevant epistemological question about other minds. It fails for reasons that are exactly similar to the reasons why the teleological argument fails: the analogical evidence—that is, the evidence that supports those propositions that constitute the other-minds hypothesis—supports only some of those propositions, and so the other-minds hypothesis is not more probable than not on the analogical evidence. (This is one respect in which belief in God and belief in other minds are epistemically on a par: both hypotheses have equally bad answers to their respective epistemological questions.) But now, obviously, belief in other minds is rational; so a belief can be rational even if there is no good answer to the relevant epistemological question. One might object that "although rational belief in other minds does not require an answer to the epistemological question, rational belief in God does" (270); for, after all, the teleological evidence used to support the teleological hypothesis does not coincide with the analogical evidence used to support the other-minds hypothesis. But, on reflection, the teleological hypothesis "is about as probable on the analogical evidence as it is on the teleological" (271). (This is a second respect in which belief in God and belief in other minds are epistemically on a par.) And, there is no other disparity on the point in question. "Hence my tentative conclusion: if my belief in other minds is rational, so is my belief in God. But obviously the former is rational; so, therefore, is the latter" (271).

What should we make of this argument? The key word is "rational." Of course, it is *non*epistemically rational to *behave as if* other human beings are not automata lacking feeling and consciousness. We ought morally and prudentially to act as if there are other minds. Some people, moreover, may be unable to act *as if* human beings are not automata without believing that they are not. They ought morally and prudentially to do whatever they can to retain that belief, or acquire it if they lack it. Perhaps belief in God is, for certain persons, likewise nonepistemically rational. Some people may be unable to act morally without believing in God. They, then, ought morally to believe that there is a God. And so they would be nonepistemically rational in believing that God exists. But in the present context the rationality has to be epistemic, not nonepistemic, and hence the just-mentioned similarities are irrelevant to Plantinga's aims.

Let us suppose, with Plantinga, that belief in other minds is obviously *epistemically* rational. What about the premise that if belief in other minds is epistemically rational, so is belief in God? Has Plantinga given us any reason to accept it, even tentatively?

Suppose we say that he has shown that the analogical argument is the only viable propositional evidence for belief in other minds. And suppose it fails for just those reasons that the teleological argument fails. Furthermore, suppose that the analogical evidence supports the teleological hypothesis just as well as it supports the other-minds hypothesis. Does *this* give us sufficient reason to believe that if belief in other minds is epistemically rational, belief in God is too? Of course not. An irreparably crippled inductive argument—even if it is the best we have—cannot confer any degree of probability on a proposition; and, even if it could, the degree of probability it could confer would not be sufficient to sustain the epistemic rationality of believing its conclusion.

Perhaps Plantinga had this in mind: the best discursive argument for other minds fails miserably, but belief in other minds is obviously epistemically rational, so there must be some *nondiscursive* grounds for belief in other minds that renders it epistemically rational. At least, *something* makes it epistemically rational. It is not magic or a brute fact. And the same goes for belief in God.

Herein lies the failure of Plantinga's 1967 parity defense. The belief in other minds *is* obviously epistemically rational, and, in light of Plantinga's judgments about discursive grounds for the belief, there must be some non-discursive fact that renders belief in other minds epistemically rational. We may not know what it is, but doubtless there is one. And here's the rub: *there is no comparable guarantee with respect to belief in God.* Unlike belief in other minds, you cannot say that belief in God is just *obviously* epistemically rational, and then, given the failure of theistic arguments, infer that there must be *some* nondiscursive fact that renders belief in God epistemically rational. For it is not just obvious that belief in God is epistemically rational. Indeed, nothing Plantinga says gives us any reason at all to suppose, even tentatively, that there is some nondiscursive fact that renders belief in God epistemically rational. With this disparity in mind, why should we accept on the basis of anything

Plantinga says that if belief in other minds is epistemically rational, belief in God is likewise rational?

The 1983 Parity Defense

Preliminaries

In his 1983 defense, Plantinga takes up the general strategy underlying his 1967 defense, with two major changes. First, the prominent comparison class is now the class of perceptual beliefs, rather than belief in other minds; and second, the alleged analogy is not that the best inductive argument for God's existence is on an epistemic par with the best inductive argument for the existence of physical objects, the objects of perception, but rather that belief in God can be *properly basic* in exactly the same way that perceptual beliefs can be. By Plantinga's definition, a belief is *basic* if its propositional content is not based on the propositional content of some other belief, even if it could be. *Properly* basic beliefs are basic beliefs that are epistemically justified, and answering a relevant epistemological question plays no part in their justification (since answering a relevant epistemological question requires basing a belief on other beliefs). The 1983 defense proposes that some basic beliefs can be epistemically rational in virtue of being acquired in circumstances such that experiential data play an indispensable causal role in acquiring the belief and at the same time cognitively attest to the truth or probability of the proposition believed. Plantinga undertakes to show that in this regard, justified basic theistic beliefs are exactly on a par with justified basic perceptual beliefs.

So, according to Plantinga, S's belief in God can be *properly basic* for S at t. A belief that p is properly basic for S at t if S's belief at t that p is *basic* for S at t, that is, at t, S accepts that p without appealing to some other proposition even if he could as evidence for the truth or probability of p, and in accepting at t that p (1) S is violating no epistemic duties and is within his epistemic rights in accepting at t that p, and (2) S's noetic structure is not defective by virtue of his accepting at t that p (79). (Unless otherwise noted references in this section are to the 1983 essay.) S is within his epistemic rights in accepting that p, because S's accepting that p is "grounded in justification-conferring conditions" (79, 91). If belief in God is properly basic, it is "entirely right, rational, reasonable, and proper . . . without any evidence or argument at all." (17). So, if belief in God is properly basic, it is epistemically rational. Plantinga proposes that the same goes for perceptual beliefs.

Plantinga and the Evidentialist Objectors

According to Plantinga, the main objection to his position comes from "the evidentialist objectors." In reply, Plantinga attempts to dismantle classical foundationalism. But that strategy assumes that there is some important connection between classical foundationalism and what the evidentialist objector says. This assumption, I shall argue, is false. But, first, what is classical foundationalism and what is an "evidentialist objector"?

Classical Foundationalism

Classical foundationalism says that if one believes a proposition in *scientia*, one is in principle *indefeasibly* epistemically justified and hence cannot be mistaken in believing it. Some of these propositions are basic and foundational, and properly so, in virtue of being self-evident or evident to the senses (Aristotle, Aquinas), or self-evident or incorrigible (Descartes). The propositions in *scientia* that are *not* properly basic are theorems, that is, they are deducible from properly basic propositions. *Classical evidentialism is the deducibility clause in classical foundationalism.* Classical evidentialism is not to be confused, or seen as being logically connected, with the evidentialism of the evidentialist objectors Plantinga names. He wrongly attributes to classical foundationalists the view that "in a rational noetic structure nonbasic belief is proportional in strength to support from the foundations" (55). This is the root cause of his confused attack on the evidentialist objectors, as I shall argue in the next two sections.

The Evidentialist Objectors

Plantinga initially says that the evidentialist objector holds both that "the strength of one's belief ought to be proportional to the strength of the evidence for that belief" (24) and that there is no sufficient evidence for theistic propositions, that is, propositions that assert or imply that God exists. Although this criterion fits Brand Blanshard and Bertrand Russell, it excludes W. K. Clifford, Michael Scriven, and Anthony Flew, all of whom appear on Plantinga's list of evidentialist objectors. Clifford's evidentialism is not committed to proportionalism. It is expressed in the following priniciple: "It is wrong, always, and for everyone, to believe on insufficient evidence." Now, suppose we put the proportionality principle as follows:

P. For any person S and for any proposition p, if S believes that p, then that belief ought to be based on sufficient evidence, and the degree of conviction with which S believes that p ought to be proportional to the degree to which the evidence testifies to the truth or probability of p.

Clifford's principle does not entail P, although P entails Clifford's principle. Flew and Scriven are self-proclaimed Cliffordians. So, to include Clifford, Flew, and Scriven in the class of evidentialist objectors, let "P-principle" name either principle P or some logical derivative of P; then, let us say that an evidentialist objector is one who adheres to some P-principle and holds that belief in God is justified and rational only if it is based on sufficient evidence, but there is no evidence sufficient for the truth or probability of theistic propositions.

Plantinga's Confused Attack on the Evidentialist Objectors

Plantinga launches his attack on the evidentialist objectors with compelling criticisms of Flew and Scriven. The criticisms are specific to faults Plantinga finds in them, and have no bearing on the P-principles definitive of the evidentialist objector. Next, Plantinga abruptly shifts his attack to classical foundationalism. This is bewildering. What does classical foundationalism have to do with P-principles?

By way of explanation, Plantinga says some astonishing things: "The vast majority of those in the western world who have thought about our topic [can belief in God be rational?] have accepted some form of classical foundationalism. The evidentialist objection to belief in God, furthermore, is obviously rooted in this way of looking at things" (48). Earlier on the same page we are told that "we can get a better understanding of Aquinas and the evidentialist objector if we see them as accepting some version of *classical foundationalism.*" Plantinga goes on to say that "the evidentialist objection *need* not presuppose classical foundationalism; someone who accepted quite a different version of foundationalism could no doubt urge this objection" (62). An evidentialist objector, moreover, "*need* not be a foundationalist *at all*" (63). True enough. But, then, how can the evidentialist objection to theism, based as it is on P-principles, be "rooted" in classical foundationalism? Clearly, there is confusion here.

Classical foundationalism says or implies nothing about proportioning belief to evidence. Such a notion is irrelevant to the kinds of propositions it accepts as being properly basic or properly based. A clear and attentive thinker can believe them with a degree of conviction that rules out his entertaining the possibility that they might be false. The evidence for them is supposed to be in principle indefeasibly conclusive. P, on the other hand, is quintessentially relevant to propositions the evidential support for which can vary in degree between being indefeasibly conclusive and none. Classical evidentialism and P can both be true, but the former does not entail P. Nor does it entail any of P's logical derivatives. Is there some other interesting way in which P-principles are "rooted" in classical foundationalism? I see none.[323]

If, in fact, there is none, then a successful wholesale refutation of classical foundationalism would leave P-principles intact.

Plantinga's (putatively) decisive argument against classical foundationalism—the argument from self-referential incoherence—does not apply to P-principles. At best that argument shows that a belief can be properly basic without being self-evident, incorrigible, or evident to the senses. But *this* has no bearing on the evidentialist objectors's P-principles. The P-principles are in fact false. It is important to see that they are false. They block understanding the nature, including the logic, of doxastic justification on epistemic grounds and on nonepistemic grounds.

The Refutation of P-principles

I shall argue against all P-principles in one fell swoop, with apologies to Quine. It will be instructive to focus on Clifford's principle: "It is wrong, always, and for everyone, to believe on insufficient evidence." Before proceeding, two observations are in order.

First, Clifford's examples illustrate that what he means by "evidence" certainly includes empirical facts that the believer can discern as attesting to the truth or probability of the proposition that he believes. By "empirical facts" we are to understand facts the discernment of which requires particular sense-contents. Determining that the ship is seaworthy requires observing that there are no leaks in its hull. It is important to note that Clifford's notion of evidence must allow for evidence that is not empirical. He means to use his principle against theistic belief. He cannot restrict evidence to empirical evidence, for then the argument would be that theism is absolutely unacceptable because there is no sufficient empirical evidence in its favor. To this the theist's obvious response would be that theistic propositions are not empirical. Clifford must work with a concept of evidence that will allow him to argue that there is no sufficient evidence of any kind in favor of theism. The other choice, to argue that theistic propositions are empirical, would not be promising.

Second, Clifford's argument for his principle clearly shows that "wrong" means *absolutely wrong*. His thinking is this: believing on insufficient evidence is epistemically wrong. In cases of conflict, epistemic considerations override any other considerations vis-à-vis justifying belief. Thus, if the evidence needed for a proposition is insufficient, there is no right way of believing it.

In light of these observations, we can unpack Clifford's principle as follows:

> it is *absolutely wrong* to believe that *p* unless one believes that *p* on the basis of evidence strong enough to indicate the truth or probability of *p*.

Now to my objections.

Objection 1

Clifford's principle conflates everything *epistemically* considered rational belief and everything *doxastically* considered rational belief. These are not the same thing. Doxastic rationality consists in doing the right thing, everything considered, with respect to our believings. Epistemic rationality consists in doing the right thing, everything considered, with respect to increasing our epistemic ratio (that is, with respect to increasing over time the ratio of our true beliefs over our false beliefs). We have a *prima facie* epistemic obligation to suspend judgment about unverifiable propositions. But, it is not hard to think of cases in which epistemic considerations do not trump all other considerations. For some people, it may be *prima facie* obligatory for prudential reasons to acquire unverifiable beliefs, and this *prima facie* prudential obligation may override (I didn't say "violate") the *prima facie* epistemic obligation.

Let me spell out four kinds of cases in which we can be mandated either not to believe propositions that we have a *prima facie* everything epistemically considered duty to believe, or to believe propositions for reasons that are not epistemic.

The first case shows that one can rationally choose to be irrational. This shows that epistemic requirements to be rational can be rationally overridden. Each of us has a *prima facie* epistemic obligation to maintain himself in a condition necessary for being able to think coherently. If that is too much to ask, then we have at least a *prima facie* epistemic obligation not to do anything purposefully that makes it impossible for us to think coherently. Imagine a Jew whom Torquemada wishes to convert to Catholicism. The Jew is very devout. The idea of giving up his

Jewishness is categorically unacceptable to him. Suppose that the only way he can prevent Torquemada from converting him into a sincerely repentant Jew and a passionate Catholic is to turn himself for the rest of his life into a madman incapable of coherent thinking. He can do that by swallowing a pill, and he does. Given his hierarchy of values, the Jew is rationally choosing to be irrational. His *prima facie* epistemic obligation to maintain his sanity conflicts with, and is overridden by, his weightier *prima facie* obligation grounded in his deepest preferences. He prefers becoming incapable of coherent thinking to being a convert from Judaism. This is not necessarily an irrational preference. Torquemada's sincere conviction that the right thing to do is to convert this man is not from the Jew's point of view a good reason why he ought to be converted. The Jew's autonomy is being threatened. He knows that it is, and he may be right to resist. The value he puts on his autonomy may be very great, and nobody can fault him for that. And nobody can fault him for defending it at the price of his sanity, even at the price of his life. If he dies, he loses his autonomy along with everything else as the price of refusing to live heteronomously. He does not lose his autonomy as the price of being able to live dishonorably. That would not do. Others may disagree that living dishonorably is worse than being dead. But they cannot prove to him that living dishonorably is better than being dead or unable to think coherently.

Here is another case. A mother who is perfectly normal mentally and emotionally may be confronted with convincing evidence that the apple of her eye, her only son, whom she never sees and who knows nothing of her existence, is an incorrigible delinquent. She may want to repress the evidence for perfectly good reasons. Suppose that believing the truth about her son would break her heart, and not believing it would assure her of peace of mind and leave her rational in every other respect. She will not act in unwise ways on her false belief about her son, nor will that one false belief impair her ability to reason with normal proficiency. Under these circumstances she has an indefeasible prudential right to her self-deception. She has a *prima facie* epistemic duty to believe the truth about her son. But, given all the relevant factors, she ought prudentially and everything considered to suppress the evidence and delude herself on this score. Given all the facts, including her scale of priorities, her *prima facie* prudential obligation overrides her *prima facie* epistemic obligation.

Another class of examples is William James's "will to believe" cases.[324] Suppose that no epistemic consideration whatsoever supports *p* and none supports not-*p*. It follows that we ought epistemically and *prima facie* to suspend judgment. Suppose, however, that suspending judgment will deprive some individuals of the reasonable likelihood of gaining some important good, for the reason that only by believing that *p* can they gain that good. Suppose, further, that someone's gaining that good will have no adverse effects on particular individuals and none on the community at large. Imagine that, on the contrary, the effects would be beneficial to other individuals and to the community as a whole. Under these circumstances it would certainly not be irrational for a person to abide by the prudential mandate to believe at the expense of the epistemic mandate to suspend judgment. Indeed, it would be everything considered irrational not to believe.

Another kind of example is the person Cardinal Newman describes: "The Word of Life is offered to a man and being offered, he has faith in it. Why? On these two grounds—the word of its human messenger, and the likelihood of the message. And why does he feel the message is probable? Because he has love for it. . . . He has a keen sense of the intrinsic excellence of the message, of its desirableness, of its likeness to what it seems to him Divine goodness would vouchsafe, did he vouchsafe any."[325] Unlike the doting mother, this man of faith is not suppressing evidence because, let us suppose, there is no evidence, pro or con, to suppress. This person is drawn to "The Word of Life" (presumably, the Catholic doctrine of salvation) not because he has evidence that it is true, but because he finds the message and those who deliver it to be loveable and trustworthy. The message sounds to him to be exactly what God would say, if God spoke to him. He is aesthetically moved to assent to it. This sense of "aesthetically" is not the narrow one of conforming to the standards of the fine arts. It is the broader sense of a person's allegiance to his own most deeply rooted sensibilities as to the fittingness, propriety, aptness, pertinence of his responses to the perhaps idiosyncratically but sincerely perceived nature of an object. To be sure, a person's sense of his own well-being may be enhanced greatly by his conviction that he has, at last, grasped the truth about his own salvation. This is the "will to believe" factor in his case. But let us set it aside and concentrate on the idea of a person who is moved to assent to a doctrine and to act on it for purely aesthetic reasons. Some secular idealists make enormous sacrifices, by giving up creature comforts, ease, security, even life itself, at the service of an ideal that is aesthetically so compelling for them that prudential considerations are not of primary importance. These people and Newman's "man of faith" have something in common. They are capable of serious commitment from aesthetic motives that by themselves can be sufficient for behavior that is predominantly other-regarding, hence not prudential.

Newman's "man of faith" has a *prima facie* epistemic obligation to suspend judgment about the Catholic message of salvation since (we are supposing) no epistemic considerations are influencing his belief. Nevertheless, he has a deeply rooted sense that the message comes from God. He loves it for its "intrinsic excellence." He wants to believe it. He hopes that it is true. In that case, he has a *prima facie* aesthetic obligation to believe. Does the epistemic ought to suspend judgment, as a matter of course, supersede the aesthetic ought to believe? Clearly not. A person who can think of God as a real possibility and can adore Him and hears a message as one that could come only from Him would be betraying himself if he discounted his deeply felt sense of the source of the message, his love of it, his wanting to believe it, and his hoping that it is true. If the only reason why he ought to discount these things is that he has no epistemic grounds to support them, then he is being told to treat his deepest sensibilities and aspirations as if they counted for nothing. One might as well tell him that there is something seriously wrong with the way he is put together as a human being. But is it not conceivable that this man's conversion to Catholicism would have no adverse effects on him, on the individuals whose lives touched his, and on the communities of which he was a member? Indeed, is it not conceivable that this man's conversion would have overall beneficial effects? If so, then it is conceivable that there is nothing seriously wrong with the way he is put together as a human being. The call for epistemic austerity is, then, a call for a man who is a well-constructed human being to act out of character for no reason other than the supposititious authority of epistemic austerity. This is nothing short of a call for self-betrayal; no person is legitimately bound to betray himself for such a reason. There are, in this kind of case, no nonepistemic factors that defeat the aesthetic *prima facie* obligation to believe, and the single epistemic *prima facie* mandate to suspend judgment is itself overridden by outweighing aesthetic considerations.

So, then, Clifford's principle is shown false by the principled Jew, the doting mother, James's "will to believe" cases, and Newman's man of faith. Crucial to all of these cases is the fact that nonepistemic considerations can trump epistemic considerations in determining what one ought to believe, all things considered.

Objection 2

Clifford's principle presupposes that it is *epistemically* rational to believe that p only if there is sufficient evidence testifying to the truth or probability of p. While this is sufficient, it is not necessary. We can be epistemically justified in believing that p if we have excellent inductive evidence that the doxastic practice of which believing that p is a product is reliable. By engaging in the practice we would have done something that we know is on that occasion causally sufficient for increasing our epistemic ratio, even though we have no independent evidence testifying to the truth or probability of p.

Perhaps we can tinker with Clifford's principle so that it gets past these worries. Suppose we say that it is *epistemically* wrong to believe on insufficient evidence. This is better, but still unacceptable: a person who knows inductively that a certain doxastic practice is reliable is epistemically justified in coming to believe that p by engaging in that practice, even if no independent evidence accessible to him at the time testifies to the truth or probability of p. Suppose we say it is epistemically wrong for anyone to believe on insufficient empirical evidence *or without inductive knowledge of the reliability of the relevant doxastic practice*. This will not do either. In the "will to believe" cases, one does no epistemic wrong while believing an unverifiable proposition. There is no need to go on. We have already reached a point where we are left with nothing that is characteristically Cliffordian. Clifford's principle is incorrigibly bad.

So, then, the situation is this. According to Plantinga, the evidentialist objector is committed to some P-principle. Those principles are unsubstantiated, he says, because they are "rooted" in classical foundationalism, which is self-referentially incoherent. But P-principles are not so rooted, hence Plantinga's reply to the evidentialist objector misses the mark. Still, he is right to reject P-principles, for the reasons I have just put forth. Where does this leave us? No evidentialist objection based on P-principles can be sustained; but, perhaps, an evidentialist objection based on classical foundationalism can. Here we need to examine Plantinga's attempted refutation of classical foundationalism. The attempted refutation fails, but even if it had succeeded, the proposition that classical foundationalism is self-referentially incoherent would lend no support to the proposition that evidentialist objections are "rooted" in it, and are, therefore, tainted.

Plantinga's Attempted Refutation of Classical Foundationalism

More than one critic of Plantinga's attack on classical foundationalism has observed that the attack fails.[326] Here I shall add my voice to theirs. Plantinga is right, however, that classical foundationalism is an unduly restrictive theory of proper basicality, as presented by the classical foundationalists themselves. But it is salvageable, and worth salvaging, as I explain below.

The Charge of Self-referential Incoherence

Plantinga takes the following proposition to be the fundamental hybrid principle of classical foundationalism:

(32) A proposition p is properly basic for a person S if, and only if, p is either self-evident to S or incorrigible for S or evident to the senses of S. (59)

Plantinga argues that (32) is self-referentially incoherent as follows. The foundationalist offers (32) as specifying the criteria for being a foundation for *scientia*. If (32) can be known "scientifically," then (32) is itself either properly basic or based upon (deduced from) properly basic foundations. Suppose it is properly basic. Then, it is either self-evident, incorrigible, or evident to the senses. It is none of these. So, if it is properly basic, (32) is self-referentially incoherent. Now, suppose it is properly based; but no foundationalist has deduced (32) from premises that are self-evident, incorrigible, or evident to the senses. Therefore, we have no reason for believing that (32) correctly specifies necessary and sufficient conditions for proper basicality in terms of which alone, according to foundationalism, we can have *scientia*.

Proposition (32) is self-referentially incoherent, all right, but it is not the fundamental principle of classical foundationalism. Plantinga takes (32) to be laying down necessary and sufficient conditions of classically proper basicality, but it does no such thing. Rather, it purports to specify the kinds of propositions that satisfy the conditions of classically proper basicality. In what follows, I shall argue that the *correctly* conceived fundamental principle is not self-referentially incoherent.

The Fundamental Principle

The fundamental principle of classical foundationalism is this:

FP. A proposition *p* is properly basic for S at t if, and only if, at t *p* is basic for S, and at t S is epistemically in principle indefeasibly justified, and hence, cannot be mistaken, in believing that *p*.

FP explains what proper basicality is in *scientia* by defining it. In form and by intention, FP is a real explicit definition. In form it specifies in the *definiens* necessary and sufficient conditions for the *definiendum*. The classical foundationalists intend it to be a real definition, assuming, as they do, that there are kinds of propositions that satisfy its conditions.

Whether FP is self-referentially incoherent can be sharply focused only with reference to the fact that FP is a definition. Is FP properly basic in *scientia* in terms of its own *definiens* of being properly basic in *scientia*? This is not a generally relevant question for appraising any definition that purports to be a real explicit definition. It is not generally true that in order to be an acceptable real explicit definition of its own *definiendum*, a definition must satisfy the conditions listed in its *definiens*. In order to be a good definition, "A father $=_{df}$ a male parent" does not have to be a male parent.

There is, however, something special about FP that makes it necessary that it satisfy the conditions mentioned in its own *definiens* in order to be acceptable as a definition of its own *definiendum*. FP defines the basic concept in the theory of *scientia*. Now either FP is itself a proposition in *scientia*, or it is a proposition about propositions in *scientia* but is not itself one of them. In the latter case, the question of its being self-referentially incoherent cannot arise. But if we view FP as being a properly basic proposition in *scientia*, the question of its self-referential incoherence does arise.

Let us suppose that we have *reformed* classical foundationalism: self-evidence, incorrigibility, or being "evident to the senses" are severally only sufficient conditions for proper basicality in *scientia*. If FP belonged to any of these kinds, then it would be classically properly basic.

FP is self-evident. Its *definiendum* is the notion of a proposition that is not based on any other proposition at all, and is such that anyone who believes it is epistemically justified in such a way that he cannot be mistaken in that belief. The *definiens* of FP explicates this notion in terms of being a basic belief that is epistemically in principle indefeasibly justified, from which it follows that the belief is true. Of course, this explication is not as clear as one would wish. There is much to be done in clarifying the idea of being epistemically justified, and the related ideas of epistemic justifiers and epistemic defeaters. But as definitions go, FP is not a bad start. The *definiens* and the *definiendum* are conceptually locked into each other.

The Specificatory Principles of Classical Foundationalism

The theory of *scientia* segregates the properly basic propositions of *scientia* from the ones that are properly based. In order to do this, the theory has to specify which kinds of propositions are classically properly basic, that is, satisfy the *definiens* of FP. Call such principles "specificatory principles." (32) is a composite specificatory principle. It conjoins the specificatory principle of the Aristotilean foundationalists,

SPC. At t p is basic for S, and S is epistemically in principle indefeasibly justified, and, hence, cannot be mistaken, in believing p at t if, and only if, p is self-evident to S at t or p is evident to the senses of S at t,

and Descartes's modern foundationalism

SPM. At t p is basic for S, and S is epistemically in principle indefeasibly justified, and, hence, cannot be mistaken, in believing p at t if, and only if, p is self-evident to S at t or p is incorrigible for S at t.

The conjunction of FP, SPC, and SPM entails (32). Note that every one of these four principles is in biconditional form. I have argued that FP's biconditional form is appropriate, since it is intended as a real explicit definition, and I have argued that FP is not self-referentially incoherent, since it is plausibly regarded as being a self-evident conceptual truth. The substantive question about FP is whether there are propositions to which it applies, and, if there are, whether any of them or any of their deductive consequences are important metaphysical truths.

I agree with Plantinga that the specificatory principles should not state necessary conditions for being properly basic in *scientia*. It is not possible to know *a priori* that a given list of kinds of propositions that satisfy the *definiens* of FP is exhaustive. Consider, therefore, a *reformed classical foundationalism* that specifies only sufficient conditions of proper basicality in *scientia*. SPM gives way to

SPM': If a proposition is basic and either self-evident or incorrigible, then it is properly basic in *scientia*.

Whereas SPM is self-referentially incoherent, SPM' is self-referentially confirmatory. For anyone who understands what it is to be self-evident, incorrigible, and properly basic in *scientia*, SPM' is self-evident. It satisfies one of the conditions it specifies as sufficient for a basic proposition to be properly basic in *scientia*. SPC, on the other hand, becomes

SPC'. If a proposition is basic and either self-evident or evident to the senses, then it is properly basic in *scientia*.

While Descartes would reject the "evident to the senses" part of this on the skeptical grounds adduced in the *Meditations*, within the framework of Aristotle's metaphysics it is not self-referentially incoherent. And there are other options for specificatory principles as well.

The fact of the matter is that neither the fundamental nor the competing specificatory principles of reformed classical foundationalism are self-referentially incoherent. As such, reformed classical foundationalism is a viable theory of *scientia*.

Theory of Scientia *and Theory of Doxastic Rationality*

FP is the fundamental principle of the theory of *scientia*. We must be careful, however, to allow that being properly basic in *scientia* is not the only way for a proposition to be properly basic. There are other ways of being properly basic, ways that do not require a properly basic belief to be epistemically in principle indefeasibly justified, hence, infallible. To suppose otherwise distorts the explanation of rational belief.

Belief that is rationally justified is doxastically rational. That is to say, it is belief acquired and retained in circumstances in which there are accessible cognitive grounds (reasons) why, everything considered, its propositional content ought$_i$ to be believed, where i indicates some mode of justification. In being doxastically rational, on a given occasion, we have fulfilled our doxastic obligations on that occasion. All epistemically indefeasibly justified beliefs are rationally justified, at least *prima facie*, but the converse is not true. A belief that is not epistemically justified in the least may be nonepistemically justified, and, on that account, rational to hold. Doxastic rationality is not confined to epistemic rationality. Moreover, an epistemically justified belief need not be infallible in order to be rationally justified, as the perceptual beliefs of a cognitively competent subject illustrate.

An acceptable account of proper basicality must, therefore, be more inclusive than FP. More on this below. But, first, let us examine Plantinga's conception of proper basicality.

Plantinga on Proper Basicality

Plantinga's conception of proper basicality is inadequate for the same reasons that P-principles are defective. In effect, Plantinga is a closet Cliffordian.

Recall that one of the two main defects of Clifford's principle is its conflation of everything considered doxastic justification and everything considered epistemic justification. This same defect appears in Plantinga's conception of proper basicality, rooted as it is in his notions of "a belief that is *justified* for a person at a time" and "a wholly, completely rational person." We need to examine these underlying notions to bring the Cliffordian defect to light.

The Underlying Notions

Plantinga characterizes "a belief that is justified for a person at a time" as follows: "Let us say that a belief is *justified* for a person at a time if (a) he is violating no epistemic duties and is within his epistemic rights in accepting it then and (b) his noetic structure is not defective by virtue of his then accepting it" (79). Let us take a closer look.

First, the (b)-component. By a "person's noetic structure," Plantinga means "the set of propositions he believes, together with certain epistemic relations that hold among him and these propositions" (48). What relations? These three: (1) believing a proposition on *the basis of* another, (2) the *degree* of belief (that is, how firmly one believes the proposition), and (3) a belief's *depth of ingression* (that is, how extensively a noetic structure would have to be adjusted if the believed proposition were removed from, or added to, the class of propositions in the noetic structure).

Why are these relations epistemic? Because, I suggest, they are indispensable to an explanation of epistemic justification. We are epistemically justified in believing p on the basis of q only if q is more or less strongly indicative of the truth or probability of p. We are epistemically justified in the degree of conviction that p, if it matches the strength of the truth-indicating support that q provides p (in the case of nonbasic beliefs), or if it matches the strength of the truth-indicating support that nonpropositional cognitive factors give p (in the case of basic beliefs). The depth of ingression of a proposition in a noetic structure partially determines whether and how epistemically justified we are in dropping it from, or adding it to, our noetic structure; that depends on which is more likely to make a positive contribution toward increasing our epistemic ratio.

Presumably a noetic structure is defective to the extent that in it some of the three epistemic relations mentioned above are not epistemically satisfactory. For example, p is believed on the basis of q when q is not indicative of the truth or probability of p.

Now we come to the (a)-component: a belief is justified only if one violates no epistemic duties, and one is within one's epistemic rights, in holding it. This applies to basic as well as nonbasic beliefs. Our interest here is basic beliefs.

Plantinga provides no a priori necessary and sufficient conditions of proper basicality in general. He proposes, instead, to look for patterns of conditions that are conjunctively sufficient for a basic belief to be *properly* basic, that is, *justified* and basic (79). The patterns of justification-conferring conditions may differ for different kinds of properly basic propositions. They may also coincide. According to Plantinga, a properly basic theistic belief and a properly basic perceptual belief are exactly alike with respect to those conditions conjunctively sufficient for proper basicality. In both cases, there are circumstances in which (1) accessible experiences testify to the truth or probability of the belief, (2) there are no accessible defeaters, (3) the very same items that justify the belief are also causally indispensable factors in its formation, and (4) the belief does not need to be based on any other belief, even if it could be. So, for example, the basic perceptual belief that that is a tree is *properly* basic because it is grounded, not on propositions but on characteristic experiential contents, for example, being appeared to treely, occurring in circumstances such that the phenomenal content of the experience instigates the belief and is indicative of its truth or probability. In the appropriate circumstances, such phenomenal contents "confer justification on the belief;" one who believes under those conditions is "within his epistemic rights." This alleged coincidence of patterns is the backbone of Plantinga's 1983 parity defense.

Finally, here is Plantinga's idea of "a completely rational person":

> To be completely rational, as I am here using the term, is not to believe only what is true, or to believe all the logical consequences of what one believes, or to believe all necessary truths with equal firmness, or to be uninfluenced by emotion in forming belief; it is, instead, to do the right thing with respect to one's believings. It is to violate no epistemic duties. From this point of view, a rational person is one whose believings meet the appropriate standards; to criticize a person as irrational is to criticize her for failing to fulfill these duties and responsibilities, for failing to conform to the relevant norms or standards. (52)

Plantinga means to be giving a definition here: "To be completely rational, *as I am using the term* . . . is to do the right thing with respect to one's believings" (my emphasis). What is the right thing to do? "It is to violate no epistemic duties [that one has]."

Note that to violate no epistemic duties we must have duties that we can fulfill or violate. The only such duties are duties that are overriding, hence, unconditional. Only they tell us what is the thing to do in the relevant circumstances. *Prima facie* duties never tell us what is the right thing to do. It is an everything epistemically considered *prima facie* duty to perform vivisection on a child, if that is the only way we know for finding out how that child responds to being vivisected. Obviously, this is not an everything considered unconditional epistemic duty, indefeasibly grounded in epistemic purposes. The *prima facie* epistemic duty to vivisect the child is not the everything considered thing to do. All sorts of nonepistemic considerations override (in this case) the *prima facie* everything epistemically considered duty to vivisect. To an everything epistemically considered *prima facie* duty there is a corresponding everything considered, hence, unconditional epistemic duty, if and only if, the everything epistemically considered *prima facie* duty is undefeated by any of its relevant potential defeaters. In this example, the everything considered unconditional duty is not epistemic. There is here no epistemic duty that one can violate or refrain from violating.

Inasmuch as for Plantinga to do the right thing with respect to our believings is "to violate no epistemic duties," by this expression he has to mean "to violate no *everything considered unconditional* epistemic duties that one has." This, on his view, constitutes being "completely rational." If this reading is accurate, then Plantinga is even more radical than Clifford, who holds the more modest view that a person is a completely rational *believer* if, and only if, he fulfills the everything epistemically considered obligations that he has. This amounts to saying "he fulfills the everything considered unconditional epistemic obligation that he has," because for Clifford, in matters of belief everything epistemically considered obligations are necessarily doxastically overriding, hence, unconditional.

So, at the very least, Plantinga is a closet Cliffordian. We have already seen that Clifford's position is unsupportable. Let us summarize the reasons why.

Coming Out of the Cliffordian Closet

Taken to be a definition of complete doxastic rationality rather than of complete rationality overall, Plantinga's definition leads to this:

B. one is everything considered doxastically rational *if and only if* one fulfills one's everything considered epistemic duties.

B can be weakened to either

N. one is everything considered doxastically rational *only if* one fulfills one's everything considered epistemic duties

or

S. *if* one fulfills one's everything considered epistemic duties, one is everything considered doxastically rational.

These principles presuppose what is plainly false: that doxastic rationality depends on or is a matter of fulfilling one's everything considered epistemic obligations. One can be everything considered doxastically rational for overriding reasons that are nonepistemic. Witness the "will to believe" cases, for example. In them all relevant *prima facie* epistemic obligations are overridden. Hence, there are no everything considered unconditional epistemic obligations to fulfill. Nevertheless, the believer is everything considered doxastically rational. So, N is false. Because everything considered doxastic obligations are not exhausted by everything considered epistemic obligations, fulfilling all of one's everything considered epistemic obligations is not sufficient for being everything considered doxastically rational. So, S is false. It follows that B is false.

I have been speaking of doxastic rationality. What about *complete* rationality? If fulfilling one's epistemic duties is neither necessary nor sufficient for everything considered doxastic rationality, it is neither necessary nor sufficient for complete (human) rationality since that involves more than doxastic rationality: actions, too, can be rational or irrational.

The same basic point above applies to Plantinga's conception of "a belief that is *justified* for a person at a time." Above we saw that this idea was the idea of a belief that is *epistemically* justified for a person at a time. But, for reasons already rehearsed, "will to believe" cases and others like them show that epistemic justification is neither necessary nor sufficient for everything considered doxastic justification.

Something else interferes with Plantinga's conception of "a belief that is *justified* for a person at a time." As we saw, according to that conception, one is justified in believing that *p* only if there are accessible cognitive factors testifying to *p*'s truth or probability. But, if one engages in a doxastic practice that one has excellent inductive reason to believe is reliable, one employs a means to increase one's epistemic ratio. From an epistemic point of view, belief so acquired is epistemically justified.

Nevertheless, the believer may have no independent reasons testifying to the truth or probability of the proposition that he justifiedly believes.

Now, as we might expect, the Cliffordian defects in those notions out of which Plantinga constructs his concept of proper basicality infect the latter as well. We can see it easily as follows: At a first approximation, Plantinga's notion of a *properly* basic belief is that of a basic belief that is defensible on *cognitive* grounds. So far so good. But, Plantinga goes wrong in restricting the cognitivity of the grounds to their ability to provide *epistemic* support for the proposition under consideration. This conception of proper basicality is unduly restrictive. While all epistemic support for belief is cognitive, not all cognitive support for belief is epistemic.

Toward a More Adequate Conception of Proper Basicality

Let us say that

Df 1. S's belief at t that p is *basic* for S if and only if S does not justify even if he could his accepting at t that p by invoking propositions other than p that testify to the truth or probability of p.

Then, we can put the generic idea of a properly basic belief in an explicit definition:

A proposition p is *properly basic* if and only if p is basic and there are decisive cognitive reasons why p ought, everything considered, to be believed.

In order to make "decisive cognitive reasons" more specific, we can use an open-ended disjunction of sufficient conditions.

Df 2. S's belief at t that p is properly basic for S at t if S's belief at t that p is basic for S at t, and either
(i) at t S's belief that p is epistemically and in principle indefeasibly justified and, hence, is true, or
(ii) at t S's belief that p is epistemically justified beyond reasonable doubt, even though that does not preclude its falsehood, or
(iii) at t S has some nonepistemic reason why he ought, everything considered, to believe that p.

The conditions (i), (ii), and (iii) may be exhaustive, but we have no *a priori* assurance that they are. The most one can say in defense of Df 2 is that it lists open-endedly plausible sufficient conditions for proper basicality, it accords with the fact that a belief may be either epistemically or nonepistemically rational or both, and that under each of (i), (ii), and (iii), we can list sufficiently specific kinds of propositions and explain why propositions of each kind satisfy the standards set forth by the sufficient condition of proper basicality that they instantiate.

Type (i) propositions include propositions that have certain intrinsic semantic properties in virtue of which believing them is epistemically in principle indefeasibly justified and, hence, cannot be mistaken. *Self-evidence* and *incorrigibility* are examples of such properties.[327] Aristotle agrees that self-evident propositions are properly basic, but he says nothing about incorrigible propositions, and he includes propositions that are evident to the senses. In Aristotle's hands, the latter category presupposes his anti-Platonic view of universals, and is, therefore, controversial. Moreover, to be "evident to the senses" in Aristotle's sense, a proposition has to be a special kind of empirical proposition. Concrete particular sense-contents are necessary for its formation and also for its being properly basic. Thus, to be properly basic, a proposition "evident to the senses" has to be hooked up with sense-contents and with at least one metaphysical principle, a very controversial one in this case. It is in principle indefeasible only within the bounds of that principle. None of these conditions enters into being self-evident or incorrigible. Self-evident and incorrigible propositions along with the rest of the propositions of type (i) have neither sense-connected nor metaphysically colored defeasibility conditions. They are *in principle indefeasible* independently of metaphysical presuppositions and empirical constraints. Type (i) propositions are the properly basic propositions of Descartes's classical foundationalism.

Type (i) propositions include another class of propositions, those with certain intrinsic pragmatic properties conclusively testifying to their truth. One subclass of this class consists of *self-certifying* propositions. A proposition is self-certifying if someone's asserting it, or believing it, or inferring it entails that it is true, for example, my belief that I have at least one concept. Another subclass consists of propositions that cannot be denied, disbelieved, inferred, or doubted without *pragmatic inconsistency*. If *p* is a contingent proposition, it is pragmatically inconsistent to assert, believe, infer, or doubt that *p* if, someone's asserting (or believing or inferring) that *p* entails that not-*p*, and someone's doubting that *p* entails that *p*. For example, someone's asserting (in English) that he himself can make no assertions in English is pragmatically inconsistent.

Every proposition in category (i) is such that we are epistemically, and in principle indefeasibly, justified and, hence, cannot be mistaken in believing it. We are epistemically rationally justified in believing it not in the weak sense that it is not epistemically irrational to believe it. We are justified in the strong sense that it is epistemically irrational not to believe it.[328]

Category (ii) includes contingent propositions that one is epistemically justified in believing at t not because they have intrinsic semantic or pragmatic properties that guarantee their truth, but because at t they are grounded on experiences that count as being cognitive factors testifying to their truth or probability. They are in principle defeasible. They have relevant potential defeaters, but at t none of them cancels or neutralizes the truth-testifying cognitive factors. In principle defeasible, but *de facto* undefeated perceptual propositions are paradigms of category (ii). Their cognitive ground is something other than themselves, and it need not be another proposition.

Corresponding to every such proposition there is a reliable doxastic practice. It consists of experiencing truth or probability supporting data while not experiencing data to the contrary. The converse, however, is not true. There can be a reliable doxastic practice in the absence of independently accessible positive epistemic support for what is believed. Imagine someone who is given a list of the horses running in the next race. He looks at the list, and then he looks into a crystal ball, and he invariably irresistibly believes the truth about which horse will win. He has no suspicion that he is an extraordinarily reliable predictor. Nor is he in a position to produce an independent epistemic justification for the truth or probability of what he believes. He is, nevertheless, epistemically justified in these crystal-ball beliefs. They are properly basic beliefs. They, too, belong in category (ii). Hence, every perceptual proposition delivered by a reliable doxastic practice, with or without independently accessible epistemic support for what is believed, is a constituent of a properly basic belief of type (ii).

Category (iii) includes propositions that may or may not have epistemic credentials. Since each one is everything considered doxastically rational to believe without needing a single epistemically cognitive factor that testifies to its truth or probability, every proposition in category (iii) is properly basic. Belief in other minds is in category (ii) and (iii); the pious Jew, the doting mother, James's "will to believe" cases, and Cardinal Newman's "man of faith" belong solely to category (iii).

We are now in a position to address Plantinga's 1983 parity defense.

Is Belief in God Properly Basic?

By "properly basic," we now mean properly basic in the sense specified by Df 2, above. As I have argued, theistic beliefs can be in category
(iii). But in that case, belief in God is properly basic not in virtue of its
epistemic credentials. If belief in God is to be properly basic *in virtue of
its epistemic credentials*, it must also be in category (i) or (ii).

Beliefs about God's nature and existence are not in category (i). That
God exists is not self-evident, incorrigible, or intrinsically possessed of
the pragmatic properties of being self-certifying or such that asserting,
believing, inferring, or doubting its denial are pragmatically inconsistent.
The very idea that belief in God could be in category (i) presupposes that
God is a possible being, which in itself is a problem.

We are left with category (ii). That God exists is not a garden-variety
perceptual judgment. Nor is it an ordinary memory belief, nor like an
ordinary belief about the existence of other persons, nor a deliverance of
a doxastic practice known to be reliable. There can be no such practice
because God is conceived as being mysterious and unpredictable.

Plantinga's second parity defense begins at this juncture. Take perceptual judgments as the class of comparison. The defense is that although
beliefs about God are not straightforward perceptual judgments, they are
"in the same boat" with perceptual judgments.

Two Ways of "Being in the Same Boat"

Plantinga holds that even though basic propositions are accepted
without being based on propositions other than themselves, the acceptance need not be epistemically unsupported. It may be epistemically
grounded, and, if it is *adequately* grounded, it is *properly* basic. What
makes a belief adequately grounded is that the proposition believed is
"grounded in justification-conferring conditions" (79, 91). Plantinga
proposes that basic beliefs about God, for example, that God is answering
my prayers, and basic perceptual beliefs, for example, that that is a tree,
are "in the same boat" in that although the contents of the justification-
conferring conditions differ in the two cases, the manner in which they
confer justification is identical. Speaking adverbially, the experience of
being appeared to treely confers *some* justification on the belief that a
tree is present. Roughly, if nothing legitimately casts doubt on the
judgment that a tree is present, then it is adequately grounded. Likewise,
an experience of being-appeared-to-Godly confers *some* justification on
the belief that God is presenting Himself; and, if nothing legitimately

casts doubt on that belief, then it is adequately grounded. This parity claim is Plantinga's *first line of defense* of the proper basicality of basic theistic beliefs.

Plantinga's *second line of defense* is that both types of belief can be "deliverances of reason," by which he means a proposition "accepted by all or nearly all rational persons" (70).

Plantinga sums up all this and more as follows:

> Everyone, whether in the [Calvinist] faith or not, has a tendency or nisus, in certain situations, to apprehend God's existence and to grasp something of his nature and actions. This natural knowledge can be and is suppressed by sin, but the fact remains that a capacity to apprehend God's existence is as much a part of our natural noetic equipment as is the capacity to apprehend perceptual truths, truths about the past, and truths about other minds. Belief in the existence of God is in the same boat as belief in other minds, the past, perceptual objects; in each case God has so constructed us that in the right circumstances we form the belief in question. But then the belief that there is such a person as God is as much among the deliverances of reason as those other beliefs. (89–90)

I shall dispute both lines of defense.

Why the First Line of Defense Fails

When in the first line of defense Plantinga says that belief in God and perceptual beliefs are "in the same boat," he means to point out that the *structure* of the justification-conferring conditions for properly basic perceptual belief is *identical* with the *structure* of the justification-conferring conditions for properly basic theistic belief. In both cases a certain experiential content is specified with reference to an independently existing entity. A tree-experience (being appeared to treely) causes one to believe that a tree is present. The experience confers some epistemic justification on the belief. If there are no actual defeaters, one is epistemically justified in believing that a tree is present. According to Plantinga, the same structure holds for acquiring properly basic theistic belief.

This would be right, if there were an *exact* structural similarity with respect to *defeasibility*. But, to the best of our knowledge, there is not. Thus, to the best of our knowledge, the justification-conferring conditions that obtain with respect to basic perceptual belief do not obtain with respect to basic theistic belief. The first line of defense, therefore, fails. Let me explain.

If a God-experience *epistemically* justifies the basic theistic belief it triggers, it must attest to the truth or probability of its propositional content. Within the sphere of perceptual experience, we can determine with reasonable certainty whether this is so. By careful observation under controlled conditions, we can determine that there are things in the jar. Further observation reveals that all the things in the jar are cookies. By counting them, we can find out that there are fifteen cookies. Further observation reveals that they are chocolate-chip cookies. Careful observation under controlled conditions has an exceedingly reliable track record for acquiring this sort of information about the contents of the jar.

That something like this is possible within the sphere of theistic experience is highly contentious. This is partly a matter of definition. We may (for certain purposes) define "perceptual proposition" as meaning a proposition that ascribes to physical objects (e.g., tables and chairs) or to physical phenomena (e.g., claps of thunder, flashes of lightning, rainbows, flames, afterimages) visual, or tactual, or gustatory, or auditory, or olfactory properties or relations. These, in turn, we define as being properties or relations whose presence in, or absence from, the objects or phenomena to which they are ascribed, it is logically possible to ascertain at any given time by looking, touching, tasting, listening, or smelling. So defined, only physical or material entities can be perceived. Being conceived as immaterial, God cannot be so perceived. Perhaps, however, God can be perceived by a cognitive process other than the sensory one that generates perceptual beliefs. Suppose there is such a process.

Now substantive issues arise. Can such a process be employed under carefully controlled conditions that are structurally on a par with the controlled conditions under which perceptual beliefs can be generated? We cannot answer this question unless we know enough about the structure of the theistic cognitive process and the nature of the associated control conditions for making an informed judgment. There is no satisfactory account of either in Plantinga's essay. Until we have intelligible proposals in sufficient detail, we are in no position to maintain that some basic theistic beliefs can be *properly* basic for reasons that are (almost) exactly analogous to the reasons why some basic perceptual beliefs can be *properly* basic.

Perhaps we can be epistemically justified in believing a theistic proposition without recourse to controlled procedures for distinguishing the veridical from the delusory among them. But that amounts to declaring that there is no structural similarity.

In a recent paper, William L. Rowe draws certain distinctions that make it easier to see the disparity between theistic and perceptual beliefs.[329] The issue is whether there are ways of distinguishing veridical from nonveridical theistic beliefs, and, if there are, whether or not they are exactly analogous in their structure to the ways in which we make that distinction in the sphere of perceptual beliefs.

My seeming to see a tree contributes something to my being cognitively justified in believing that I am seeing a tree. But that seeming is by no means enough to be cognitively sophisticated in believing that I am seeing a tree. My seeming to see a tree may be delusive. In order to be cognitively sophisticated in believing that I am seeing a tree, I must be in a position to know of no reason why *on this occasion* my seeming to see a tree may be delusive. This requirement is weaker than that I must be in a position to know that there is no reason why my experience may be delusive. The range of circumstances in which our experiences could be delusive is probably too large for us ever to be in a position to know that none of them obtains in a given perceptual situation. The weaker requirement appears to be the only reasonable option, and it conforms to our actual practice. The weaker requirement is, however, ambiguous. My failure to know of any reason why my present experience of seeming to see a tree may be delusive may be owing to my having no idea that delusory experiences can occur, or to my having no idea as to the conditions under which they do occur. Rowe calls this way of failing to be in a position to know *uninformed*. The uninformed way of not being in a position to know contributes nothing significant toward my being a reliable judge of perceptual matters. If I am right, it is serendipidously that I am right. If I am epistemically justified because delusive factors have not played a role in instigating my belief, it is serendipidously that I am epistemically justified. That is by no means enough for being a reliable judge of perceptual matters.

Now suppose that I know what sorts of conditions may cause delusions about trees. They include being very intoxicated, being too far away, being asleep and dreaming, being disoriented, having "potemkin" trees in the vicinity, and so on. On a certain occasion of having a tree-experience, I carefully attend to my situation and do not find any of the commonly recognized delusion-making factors to be present. Of course, I cannot make this determination exhaustively and with infallible certainty. The relevant background beliefs I need for an informed determination are, even in the best of circumstances, less than complete. I can, however, make a judgment with a degree of reliability that a reasonable person would find adequate for belief and action. This way of lacking knowledge that delusion-making factors are present Rowe calls *informed*.

To be so informed does not assure us of the truth of what we believe. Instead, it qualifies the belief as having been protected from delusion to a degree sufficient for its being an epistemically reasonable belief. If, after all the care we have taken to form an informed opinion, we happen to have made a mistake, we are all the same epistemically reasonable in forming it. Our assent to the proposition was as informed as it could be reasonably expected to be.

Rowe proposes that in theistic experience we are not in a position to have informed lack of knowledge that delusion-making factors are present. I think that he is right. This is the exact point at which Plantinga's analogy seems to break down. Within perceptual experience we can differentiate veridical from delusory, and informed from uninformed perceptual beliefs. Within theistic experience, there is no way of drawing distinctions between the veridical and the delusory, the informed and the uninformed, cognitive sophistication and cognitive competence and their contraries. Jimmy Swaggart scandalizes people by his behavior with prostitutes. He then tells the world that God tells him to continue his ministry. By what criteria, what standards, what conditions can a theist determine that Swaggart is deluded? Why should God not choose a sinner, a hypocrite, to be his messenger? Perhaps He is testing our faith. Is it not easier to believe a lovely message if the messenger is lovely too? These are reasonable speculations. But there are no controlled procedures that count as cognitive means of deciding where the truth lies.

In the Slavic world, but not confined to it, there is a tradition of revering "holy fools." Dostoyevsky describes such a man in the *Brothers Karamazov*. He is a mad hermit. He is revered, not in spite of, but because of, his madness. He rants and is taken seriously as being an oracle of God. A sober Anglican would frown on this, but on what cognitive grounds can the Slavic and Anglican communities resolve their differences on the issue? Even if both consult in the Bible a passage that they believe settles the issue and agree on its interpretation, they cannot offer this interpretation to themselves or to any other normal adult rational person as being cognitively significant. That the Bible and only the Bible speaks the truth on matters of religious propriety is an article of faith, not a cognitively established fact. There is no comfort in relativizing cognitive significance. "Cognitively significant for Christians" can only mean that Christians take it to be cognitively significant. That does not make it cognitively significant.

Intersubjective agreement cannot, by itself, be either a sufficient or a necessary condition of cognitivity. But intersubjective agreement *among cognitively sophisticated and competent people* can be at least a necessary condition perhaps even sufficient. With respect to the latter kind of intersubjectivity, perceptual judgments are, but theistic ones are not, intersubjective. Everyone in the community of theists believes that God exists. Membership in the community may be defined in terms of that agreement. The community of cognitively sophisticated and competent people in the sphere of perception, on the other hand, are not people who just agree about perceptual matters. The latter community is defined in terms of cognitive sophistication and competence in matters perceptual. Membership in that community is not just in virtue of the brute fact of agreeing with each other about perceptual matters. The members are in it in virtue of being cognitively qualified perceivers. It is not at all controversial that that class is not empty. The same cannot be said about the class of cognitively competent theists. The reason why it cannot is that we have no criteria for distinguishing cognitively competent theists from theists who are not cognitively competent.[330] Consider the following examples.

Lots of things are cognitively significant for mathematicians. They can tell you why what they think is cognitively significant is in fact cognitively significant; and if you understood them, you would believe them. You would see for yourself. But there is nothing a Christian can tell you to lead you to see for yourself that only the Bible is the source of truth about matters religious. You may "see for yourself" that the Bible is the truth about religion by having a conversion experience, say, by experiencing yourself as having a divine revelation. There is, however, no epistemically significant analogy between this and the way you see for yourself when you understand a mathematician. A mathematical explanation, if you understand it, lets you see that not to believe the explanation would be irrational. A Christian explanation can do no such thing. Just for a starter, not accepting a Christian explanation is not sufficient for being irrational. To deny this, as Plantinga does, by invoking his Cartesian conception of reason as a faculty capable of knowing that God exists, is itself a Christian explanation, one that is both questionable and question begging.

Now let the Slav and the Anglican begin with a disagreement about whether or not that thing by the lake is a tree. It is very easy to describe how they could go about resolving their disagreement by applying cognitive criteria they both accept as being the ones relevant to the case. A tree experience in a dream, or a waking and delusive tree experience, or a waking and veridical tree experience have something in common. In every one of them, the experiencer is appeared to treely, not goatly, or sheeply, or grassly. Now there are many different reasons why the Slav and the Anglican might begin with a disagreement about a tree. Perhaps one of them is appeared to treely and the other not. Perhaps both are being appeared to treely but within different background assumptions. One of them has reasons for wondering if the tree appearance is the appearance of a tree. He may know, while the other does not, that a theatrical company has planted some fake trees among the real ones, and from this distance he has no way of being sure that he is not looking at one of the fake trees. He may tell the other about the fake trees. Then they might both go to the place where the trees and the fake ones are and check each presumptive tree to see which are fake and which are real. And so on. Each thing they have done and could continue to do satisfies conditions that entitles them to believe that they are exercising informed control to make sure that they come up with an informed opinion about each "tree." They are being cognitively responsible.

Plantinga's first line of defense of the proposition that certain theistic beliefs can be properly basic relies on an alleged epistemic parity between perceptual and theistic beliefs. The alleged parity is that, in both, the factors that cause the belief are also its epistemically justifying grounds. I grant that in typical circumstances this is true of perceptual beliefs. I have argued that it is not true of theistic beliefs.

Let me add that the very notion of circumstances that are typical relative to theistic beliefs is elusive. The typical conditions, we are often told, must include that we have opened ourselves to God and that God chooses to reveal himself to us. By unveiling himself, God is supposed to cause us to believe that we are experiencing him, and the God-experiences we have are supposed to justify the belief that the experience is of God. Can we have an informed opinion that anything like this ever happens? Who knows? Could we have an informed opinion that it could happen? Even if we could, there would be no parity left.

Contrast this with counting the cookies in a jar to determine their number. The typical conditions are that we are sober, attentive, and know how to count; that we are not prevented from counting; that there are no disturbances in the immediate environment indicative of abnormalities; that everything looks normal; that if we needed to check this out we could, and more along similar lines. Under these conditions we count the cookies. We count fifteen of them. So, we believe that there are fifteen cookies in the jar. Does anything like this ever happen? Of course it does. I submit that Plantinga's first line of defense collapses.

The Second Line of Defense in More Detail and Why It, Too, Collapses

Plantinga's second line of defense of the proper basicality of certain beliefs about God is that they are deliverances of the reason implanted in us by God. Besides not sitting well with many modern intellectuals, this bit of theistic epistemology is, as a defense of the proper basicality of theistic belief, question begging, and as a flat assertion, dogmatic. Plantinga's beliefs about the noetic dispositions God has placed in us can be speculations permissible to a rational being, provided that he does not proclaim them as being rationally mandated. The belief that God has "so constituted us that in the right circumstances we believe that there is a tree out there" does not have to be true in order for it to be true that in the right circumstances our perceptual judgments are reliable.

Now take the experience of hearing the word of God while reading the Bible. That experience is certainly not an adequate *epistemic* ground for believing that God exists. That one is hearing the word of God is an interpretation, a theory. Moreover, it is a theory that most naturally would occur to those who have already formed habits of interpreting certain of their experiences in theistic terms. Why should that interpretation be taken for granted? Why should nontheists agree that the interpretation is the only one, or the best one, or even that it is a good one? Plantinga answers: because that interpretation is a deliverance of our God-given reason. This assertion, I believe, is not such that if anyone dissents from it, it must be because of a misuse of reason. Besides, this explanation presupposes that God exists; for, the right use of reason is the use intended by God. So this whole way of thinking is viciously circular. It assumes to be a fact the very fact that it is invoked to explain. As a Calvinist, Plantinga must believe that God "has so constructed us that in the right circumstances we [correctly] form" the appropriate theistic or perceptual belief. But as a rational being, Plantinga does not have to believe that he can form reliable perceptual beliefs only because God has created him with powers adequate to that task. The rationally acceptable criteria of perceptual reliability are logically independent of theological assumptions. To those of us who do not have an explanation as to why "properly basic" theistic beliefs are reliable, Plantinga's second line of defense offers an explanation that has all the earmarks of vicious circularity.

Plantinga may object that as someone speaking from within a theistic belief system, he is not in a vicious circle. Belief in God is the belief that identifies that system, and anyone speaking from "inside" that system would be inconsistent to believe anything that entails God's nonexistence. That much is true. But it does not support the suggestion that a theist is within his epistemic rights in proposing that the God-experiences he has in circumstances of certain sorts happen because God has created us in such a way that in those sorts of circumstances the God-experiences are experiences of God. Plantinga is convinced that all adult rational beings would, on reflection, acknowledge that they are all theists by nature, that acknowledging this to be true is a mark of genuine rationality, and a failure to do so can be explained only by man's originally sinful nature. None of this is obvious to me. In fact, none of it is at all credible to me. And I am convinced that I am a rational adult.

Plantinga believes that "theists and nontheists have different conceptions of reason" (90). Reason is "our natural noetic equipment," and, according to Plantinga, it is metaphysically loaded:

> The fact remains that a capacity to apprehend God's existence is as much a part of our natural noetic equipment as is the capacity to apprehend perceptual truths, truths about the past, and truths about other minds. Belief in the existence of God is in the same boat as belief in other minds, the past, and perceptual objects; in each case God has so constructed us that in the right circumstances we form the belief in question. But then the belief that there is such a person as God is as much among the deliverances of reason as those other beliefs.

I have already argued that belief in God and belief in perceptual objects are *not* "in the same boat." Moreover, Plantinga offers no reason for supposing that God gave us all a theistic reason. That He did presupposes that He exists. Why should we believe that God exists and that He gave us theistic reason? What about those of us who seem not to possess a theistic reason? Plantinga's answer is that this seeming is a false appearance. The reality is that we *have* that reason, but in some of us it is buried under a pile of sin. And how do we know that? We know it by exercising our theistic reason. Is it not clear that we are in a vicious circle?

There are other ways of conceiving what reason is that are not either viciously circular or dogmatic. Here is one. We all have certain purely intellectual powers. They form a logically interdependent family of powers. These are the power of discerning deductive relationships among propositions; the power of forming concepts; the power of forming beliefs; the power of asking and answering questions (i.e., to conduct inquiry); and relative to these, the second-order power of reflecting on these powers. Pure reason is the sum total of these powers.

Pure reason is not metaphysically loaded. Metaphysicians disagree on what the metaphysical truth is, but in order to invent their theories and to dispute about them, they have to exercise the powers of pure reason. These are the same in all, in varying degrees of acuteness. Reason and sentience informed by reason are the sum total of the human cognitive apparatus. This view of the structure of the human cognitive apparatus seems to me to accord better with firm data. Metaphysical hypotheses are the result of abductions from data. Rival metaphysicians often disagree about what the data are. They also come up with irreconcilably different metaphysical hypotheses. And none of the self-consistent hypotheses is verifiable. That God exists is a metaphysical hypothesis. That it is self-consistent is disputed. Even if it were, the problem of gratuitous evil is alive and kicking.[331]

In view of all this, it is highly implausible that there are circumstances in which God's existence is an indisputable deliverance of reason for any individual who is cognitively competent about matters theistic, which it must be, if it is to be properly basic. Plantinga's theist takes certain of his experiences as providing adequate grounds for his belief that God exists. It is indisputable that if God answers my prayers, then God exists. But is it clear that God answers my prayers, clear in the same kind of way that trees appear to me? What in the content of the God experience and in the circumstances in which the experience occurs shows that God answers my prayers? If there is parity between epistemically justified basic perceptual beliefs and epistemically justified basic theistic beliefs, then when the theist justifiably believes that God is answering his prayers, among the contents of the God-experience and in the circumstances in which the belief takes shape, there are factors that both cause the belief and are epistemically adequate grounds testifying to the truth or probability of the belief's propositional content, to wit, that God is answering my prayers. Unless I have overlooked something, I find no specification of such causative-justificatory factors in Plantinga's examples of experiencing God in prayer or while reading the Bible.

Take Plantinga's report that he experiences God while reading the Bible. I cannot see this as an example of a situation in which the belief in God is both basic and epistemically justified. I can, however, understand the situation clearly, if I think of it in Newman's terms. When Plantinga reads the Bible, he is suffused with a feeling that the message he receives is exactly what God would say if He deigned to speak to us. Plantinga is caused to believe that God is speaking to him. At that moment his belief in God is basic, perhaps even properly basic; but not in virtue of any of its epistemic merits.

Germane to the issue of the proper basicality of basic theistic beliefs are two facts. First, being a basic belief is relative to persons and to times. What is not basic to me now may become basic by tomorrow. Second, being *properly* basic is *not* relative to times, to persons, or to parochial belief systems, such as theism. The provisions for being properly basic are universal and objective.

A belief system such as theism can, of necessity, exist only within larger belief systems that are constructed by using human cognitive powers and only within which is it possible to understand the nature and scope of these powers. To attempt an elucidation of human cognitivity by appeal to basic theistic concepts and beliefs is to put the cart before the horse. Descartes tried it and was driven to incoherent verbiage.

I submit that Plantinga's second line of defense is a total failure. It construes the parity thesis as saying that basic perceptual beliefs and basic theistic belief can be *properly* basic for the exactly similar reasons, in fact, for one and the same reason. God made us in such a way that under circumstances appropriate for each type of belief (as decreed by God), we form perceptual and theistic beliefs that are properly basic. As a flat statement, the proposal is dogmatic. As an explanation of the proper basicality of theistic beliefs, it is question begging, and were it not question begging, it would be unacceptable for another reason.

It is in principle impossible to explain the nature of human cognition with reference to theological concepts. Once we have an explanation, we can go on to say, if we wish, that God gave human beings certain cognitive powers, namely, the ones that they have. Perhaps this is all that Plantinga means to say. He can present this as a part of what a theist might believe without being epistemically irrational, that is, without being epistemically culpable; but he cannot present it as a belief that a rational adult would be epistemically irrational not to hold. And it is this last condition that is necessary for proper basicality that is *epistemically proper*, as Plantinga would have it. It is epistemically irrational not to accept perceptual propositions that are beyond reasonable doubt on the part of individuals who are cognitively sophisticated and competent in the sphere of perception. An informed judgment that the plant in the flower-bed is a rose bush can be beyond reasonable doubt. But there is no comparable judgment beyond reasonable doubt that the voice heard by the saintly mystic and the mass murderer is God speaking to him. Hearing it *as* God's voice does not make it so. There are no grounds substantiating that way of taking that voice. The subject's *belief* that God has spoken to him may be a sufficient explanation of his behavior. The belief need not be true in order to be a causal determinant of conduct. There are those who believe that a certain mass murderer is a righteous man who belongs in heaven. There are those who see him as a fanatical killer. Who is right? One thing is certain. We cannot settle the dispute by a controlled empirical procedure comparable to those that would settle a dispute as to whether or not the plant in the flower-bed is a rose bush. Once more, let me emphasize: the Jew, the Christian, and the Muslim can hold their respective versions of theism in an epistemically inculpable way. But none of them can show that his version of theism is epistemically required. In that case, none of them can justifiably proclaim that his own version of theism is the true one, and that he has cognitive grounds for saying so. This stricture applies also to the central theistic core supposed to be common to their respective creeds. Insofar as there are no experiential indicators for distinguishing between informed and uninformed theistic beliefs, there can be no cognitively valid claim from experience to the truth of theism in any of its major manifestations.

Let me end with an intuition about parity defenses that rely on classes of comparison made up of propositions. A review of Plantinga's first and second parity defenses arouses the intuition that the stronger the positive epistemic status of the propositions in the class of comparison and of the cognitive mechanisms through which we come to believe them, the weaker is the relevant parity thesis; and the weaker the positive epistemic status of the propositions and mechanisms, the stronger is the parity thesis. In short, the strength of a parity defense based on classes of comparison made up of propositions is inversely proportional to the epistemic strength of the propositions in the class of comparison and of the mechanisms through which we come to believe them.

If this intuition is true, parity defenses that rely on classes of comparison consisting of propositions are not of much use.[332]

Notes

Chapter 1

1. L. Jonathan Cohen, *An Essay on Belief and Acceptance* (Oxford: Clarendon Press, 1992). Page numbers to this work will be cited in the text. For a somewhat similar distinction see Keith Lehrer, "The Gettier Problem and the Analysis of Knowledge," in George S. Pappas, ed., *Justification and Knowledge* (Dordrecht: D. Reidel Publishing Company, 1979).

2. See Robert Audi, "The Concept of Believing," *The Personalist* 53 (1972): 43–62, for a similar approach.

3. For a suggestion of a similar situation with respect to "want," see R. B. Brandt and J. Kim, "Wants as Explanations of Actions," *Journal of Philosophy* 60 (1963), 425–35.

4. Deciding how things are will be seen to fall on the "acceptance" side of my basic contrast.

5. What I call "feel that p is the case" is what is often termed, in the philosophical literature, "consciously believing that p" or "occurrently believing that p."

6. I am indebted to Dana Radcliffe for helping me to get straight about this.

7. For this to be a sound assessment it must be limited to *human* belief. When it is belief of sub-human creatures that is in question, the behavioral manifestations loom much larger. Since these creatures lack language, they cannot tell us how certain they feel.

8. For a more extensive survey of modes of voluntary control, with special reference to belief, see my "The Deontological Conception of Epistemic Justification," in *Epistemic Justification: Essays in the Theory of Knowledge* (Ithaca, NY: Cornell University Press, 1989).

9. H. Paul Grice, *Studies in the Way of Words* (Cambridge, MA: Harvard University Press, 1989), Chs. 2 and 3.

10. Note that Cohen speaks of accepting rules as well as propositions. I have no objection to that, but it will not figure in my discussion.

11. Here I am indebted to Jonathan Bennett.

12. Although H. H. Price in his magisterial treatise, *Belief* (London: George Allen & Unwin, 1969), explicitly draws a distinction between belief and the mental act of "assenting," he unfortunately takes the latter to be the acquisition of a *belief* (page 298).

13. A further complication is this. Acceptance can turn into belief. I may begin by adopting a positive attitude toward the proposition that p and then at some later stage find myself feeling it to be the case that p. Here it may be difficult to say exactly where the mere acceptance ends and where the belief begins.

14. The *Oxford English Dictionary* does list a subject-connected meaning of "faithful"—full of or characterized by faith. But it designates this sense as "obsolete."

15. *Belief*, 438–40.

16. See his *Dynamics of Faith* (New York: Harper & Brothers, 1957).

17. Another historically famous example of the way in which "faith" is used to express a particular thinker's basic perspective on religion is found in Kierkegaard's famous statement, "Faith is precisely the contradiction between the infinite passion of the individual's inwardness and the objective uncertainty." See Soren Kierkegaard, *Concluding Unscientific Postscript*, trans. D. F. Swenson & W. Lowrie (Princeton, NJ: Princeton University Press, 1944), 182.

18. For an illuminating account of this diversity, see William Lad Sessions, *The Concept of Faith* (Ithaca, NY: Cornell University Press, 1994).

19. *Summa Theologica* (ST) II, II, 2, 9.

20. Quoted from Philip Schaff, *The Creeds of Christendom* (Grand Rapids, MI.: 1993, reprint), 6th ed., Vol. II, 243.

21. ST II, II, 2, 10, ad 2.

22. *Essay Concerning Human Understanding*, IV, 18, 2.

23. ST II, II, 4, 5.

24. I have already acknowledged that one can be in an involuntary belief-like state with respect to p without feeling sure of p and without being free of doubt. But my present concern is to exhibit acceptance as an alternative to strong belief—feeling sure.

25. A powerful case for the satisfaction of needs as a basis for religious faith is made by Diogenes Allen, *The Reasonableness of Faith* (Washington: Corpus Books, 1968).

26. Kelly James Clark, ed., *Philosophers Who Believe* (Downers Grove, IL: InterVarsity Press, 1993); Thomas V. Morris, ed., *God and the Philosophers* (New York: Oxford University Press, 1994).

27. Later, I will briefly discuss some alternatives to belief that have been proposed in accounts of faith. But none of them are the same as "acceptance."

28. Louis P. Pojman, *Religious Belief and the Will* (London: Routledge & Kegan Paul, 1986).

29. ST II, II, 2, 9.

30. John Cottingham, Robert Stoothoff, Dugald Murdoch, trans., *The Philo-*

sophical Writings of Descartes (Cambridge: Cambridge University Press, 1984), Volume II. Page numbers in the text refer to this work.

31. The reader may think that I have already answered this question in the third section, where I insisted that one could lead a full Christian life even if one accepted, rather than believed, certain central articles of faith. But in saying that, I was expressing *my* sense of the matter. The present issue has to do with whether there are authoritative church pronouncements that require belief.

32. In this connection, Wilfred Cantwell Smith gives some interesting linguistic statistics concerning the Bible. See his *Belief and History* (Charlottesville: University Press of Virginia, 1977). Words in the *pistis* family occur 603 times in the New Testament. In only 4 percent of these occurrences is the word followed by a proposition. The noun *pistis* itself occurs 246 times, and in 217 of these occurrences there is no object, that is, the reference is just to *faith*, not to faith in something or faith that something.

33. For details, see Marion J. Hatchett, *Commentary on the American Prayer Book* (Seabury Press: 1980).

34. For these confessions I have drawn on Philip Schaff, *The Creeds of Christendom*.

35. *Faith and Belief* (Princeton: Princeton University Press, 1979).

36. I don't mean to suggest that this is typical of Shakespeare's use of "believe." Quite the contrary. My point is only that the earlier meaning can be found, atypically, as late as this.

37. *The Sufficiency of Hope* (Philadelphia: Temple University Press, 1979). See also the work by Pojman cited in note 28.

38. The reader may wonder how I square differentiating my thesis from Muyskens's with my earlier citation of Jordan, who says that his faith is best described as a hope rather than as a belief, as an example of one who *accepts* the articles of faith. It is like this. Acceptance is to be contrasted with hope as such. That does not mean that one who accepts Christian doctrines cannot also hope that they are true. Indeed, Jordan in the passage in question speaks of himself as *assenting* to the propositions of Christianity. This indicates to me that his characterization of his faith as hope is seriously incomplete, however prominent a place hope occupies in his total religious response.

39. "Faith, Belief, and Rationality," *Philosophical Perspectives* 5 (1991), 213–39, and "Rationality and Religious Commitment," in Marcus Hester, ed., *Faith, Reason, and Skepticism* (Philadelphia: Temple University Press, 1992), 50–97.

40. See the discussion of Audi in Dana M. Radcliffe, "Nondoxastic Faith: Audi on Religious Commitment," *International Journal for Philosophy of Religion* 37 (1995).

41. "The Virtue of Faith," in *The Virtue of Faith and Other Essays in Philosophical Theology* (New York: Oxford University Press, 1987).

42. *Resurrection: Myth or Reality?* (San Francisco: Harper, 1994), 237–38.

43. No doubt, Spong and like-minded thinkers would be just as confident

that the resurrection of Jesus could not be accepted in a literal way today as they are that it cannot be believed in a literal way today. Nevertheless, the point remains that for certain people acceptance might be a live option even if belief is not.

44. This paper has greatly benefitted from comments by Jonathan Bennett and Dana Radcliffe.

Chapter 2

45. Matthew 22:37–40. I use *The New American Bible*.

46. John 15:17.

47. Soren Kierkegaard, *Works of Love,* trans. Howard Hong and Edna Hong (New York: Harper Torchbooks, 1962), 35. Hereafter I identify quotations from this book by means of parenthetical page references in the body of my text.

48. Robert Brown, *Analyzing Love* (Cambridge: Cambridge University Press, 1987), 6.

49. Aristotle, *Nichomachean Ethics* 1158a 10–14.

50. Brown, *Analyzing Love,* 32.

51. Brown, *Analyzing Love,* 33.

52. Brown, *Analyzing Love,* 106.

53. Stephen E. Fowl and L. Gregory Jones, *Reading in Communion: Scripture and Ethics in Christian Life* (Grand Rapids: Eerdmans, 1991), 79–80. Fowl and Jones report in a note that this story is taken from Geoffrey Wainwright, *Doxology* (New York: Oxford University Press, 1980), 434.

54. I John 4:7.

55. I read an earlier version of this paper at a meeting of the Soren Kierkegaard Society and on the campuses of the University of Illinois at Urbana and Northern Illinois University. I am grateful to my audiences on those occasions for stimulating discussion. I am also indebted to Martin Andic, who commented on the paper at the Kierkegaard Society meeting, for asking whether love of neighbor is a distinctively Christian ethical doctrine. As he observed, ideals resembling it are commended in other religious traditions. Thus, for example, at *Bhagavad Gita* 12, 13–19 Lord Krishna says: "He who has no ill feeling to any being, who is friendly and compassionate, without selfishness and egoism, who is the same in pain and pleasure and is patient. . . . He who is alike to enemy and friend, also to honor and disgrace, who is alike to cold and heat, pleasure and pain, and is freed from attachment, He who is thus indifferent to blame and praise, who is silent and is content with anything, who is homeless, of steady mind and is devoted—that man is dear to Me." I quote from *The Bhagavad Gita,* translated by Eliot Deutsch (Lanham, Md.: University Press of America, 1968), 105. I see resemblance only, and not identity, between the non-attached benevolence dear to Lord Krishna and the love of neighbor commanded by Jesus Christ. More generally, as far as I can tell, love of neighbor, as Christian authors such as

Kierkegaard have fleshed it out in their works, is a distinctively Christian ethical doctrine.

Chapter 3

56. A complication: As Daniel Nolan pointed out to us, it is arguable that microphysical laws at a world do not supervene on the microphysical states at a world; and a materialist might say that mental properties are determined by microphysical states plus laws relating microphysical properties to each other (call them "micro-micro laws"). Fair enough. We invite materialists of that stripe to extend "microphysical states" to include micro-micro laws.

57. See Hilary Putnam's "The Meaning of 'Meaning,' " in his *Mind, Language and Reality* (Cambridge: Cambridge University Press, 1975) and Tyler Burge's "Individualism and the Mental," *Midwest Studies in Philosophy IV* (Minneapolis: University of Minnesota Press, 1979). Standard Twin Earth type cases, adduced to show that an individual's mental states do not supervene on the microphysical states of that individual, are cases where duplicate individuals are in different physical environments: such cases do not, then, have any force against the thesis that the distribution of mental properties supervenes on the global distribution of microphysical properties. The volume, edited by P. Pettit and J. McDowell, *Subject, Thought and Context* (Oxford: Oxford University Press, 1986) is devoted to this topic of externalism and mental content.

58. As Frank Jackson notes in "Armchair Metaphysics," J. O'Leary-Hawthorne and M. Michael, eds., *Philosophy in Mind* (Dordrecht: Kluwer, 1994), "Physicalists are typically happy to grant that there is a possible world exactly like ours but which contains in addition a lot of mental life sustained in nonmaterial stuff" (28), and thus, when they say that the distribution of mental properties supervenes on the microphysical properties, there must be some tacit restriction of the worlds considered. Jackson's suggested reformulation on behalf of the materialist: "Any world which is a minimal physical duplicate of our world is a duplicate simpliciter of our world" (28)—though he admits to there being no rigorous, noncircular definition of "minimal physical duplicate."

59. Again, angels share all of their microphysical properties (none), but have different mental properties. Thus the qualifier about immaterial beings.

60. Though we should pause long enough to acknowledge "nonstandard" breeds of compatibilism denying that freedom simply amounts to actions being appropriately causally connected to past beliefs and desires, even if those actions are contingent upon circumstances beyond the control of the agent. So-called multiple-pasts or altered-past compatibilism suggests that there is a relevant sense in which we can "affect" the past (that is, roughly: there are actions such that, if—contrary to fact—I were to perform them the past would have been different). So-called local-miracle or altered-law compatibilism suggests that there is a relevant sense in which we can have "power over" laws (roughly: there are actions such that, if—contrary to fact—I were to perform them, a law-breaking event

would have occurred). To the extent that they aim to capture some robust notion of power to do otherwise, these forms of compatibilism are not deflationary. (Whether the operative senses in which we can "affect" and "control" the past and laws of nature are relevant to ascriptions of freedom and moral responsibility is another question.)

61. See "How to Define Theoretical Terms," *Philosophical Papers, Volume I* (Oxford: Oxford University Press, 1983), 78–95, esp. 95.

62. As Michael Smith puts it (though he is not an agency theorist), freedom requires that we be the "authors" of our actions. See his "Freedom, Reason and the Analysis of Value," forthcoming.

63. The general picture is there in the earlier sections of the *Discourse on Metaphysics*, its connection with freedom coming in later sections, where Leibniz will say, for example, that "every substance has a perfect spontaneity, which becomes freedom in intelligent substances," and that all its actions are "the result of its own concept or being" (DM §32 at G, IV, 458: L, 324). Thus could Leibniz agree with Spinoza at least this far: a free agent is determined only by "the necessity of its own nature" (G, I, 150: L, 197).

64. *Noûs* 27 (1993): 191–203. Page references to this article will be included in the text.

65. See, for example, Peter van Inwagen, "When is the Will Free?," *Philosophical Perspectives* 3 (Atascedero, Calif.: Ridgeview Press, 1989), 399–422.

66. Peter van Inwagen, *An Essay on Free Will* (Oxford: Clarendon Press, 1983).

67. Van Inwagen's Principle ß is presented and discussed in *An Essay on Free Will*, 93–105. As worded, the principle needs (modest) repair; see, for example, David Widerker, "On an Argument for Incompatibilism," *Analysis* 47 (1987), 37–41, Timothy O'Connor, "On the Transfer of Necessity," *Noûs* 27 (1993), 204–18, and especially a recent discussion by Thomas McKay and David Johnson, "A Reconsideration of an Argument Against Compatibilism" (unpublished). The required repair does not substantially affect the content of this paper: assuming that one can proceed on the basis of a false principle that approximates a true one if the difference is irrelevant to the current line of inquiry, we continue with ß as formulated.

68. Of course, the altered-past and altered-law compatibilists (see note 60) will deny these platitudes, and so will deny their role with Principle ß in showing that determinism is incompatible with robust freedom.

69. Thus the strategy of altered-law compatibilism—of exploiting the fact that laws of nature are contingent in arguing for the power to do otherwise—is unavailable here, just as it is not available in arguing for the compatibility of human free will and divine omniscience (since God's existence and omniscience are reckoned necessary).

70. It is here that altered-law compatibilism will propose a noncausal sense in which the past is in our control, or up to us. The moral relevance of this innocuous sense of "up to me" is less obvious than that of the proposal to follow, below (see also note 71).

71. See *An Essay on Free Will*, 233–34. The thought that we don't exercise a high level of fine-grained control leads us to think that, say, I don't have a choice about whether I toss a six with the die, or that I don't have a choice about the exact trajectory T of my arm. Van Inwagen's point is that this latches onto the wrong sense of "up to me": there is a fair sense of "up to me," relevant to freedom and moral responsibility, that is at work in claiming that the particular trajectory T is up to me insofar as I can avoid arm-moving itself. Or, in van Inwagen's words, "Strictly speaking, Alfred does have a choice about whether he throws a six, at least provided he has a choice about whether he plays dice. He can avoid throwing a six by avoiding playing dice."

72. "Emergent Properties," *American Philosophical Quarterly* 31 (1994): 94–104.

73. See, for example, Hugh McCann, "Volition and Basic Action," *Philosophical Review* 82 (1974): 451–73.

74. "An Argument for the Identity Theory," *Philosophical Papers, Volume I*, 105.

75. There is one other way to try to blend agency theory with a claim of explanatory adequacy of science. Recall that Clarke's view is that agent causation contributes *nothing* by way of explanation. Perhaps, then, in response, the agent-causation theorist should deny that his theory provides explanations of microphysical happenings, thus leaving open the possibility that some body of scientific theories is exhaustive as far as explanation of physical phenomena goes. But that seems quite wrong. On a promising first pass, an explanation is an answer to a "why" question; and agency theory purports to provide us with answers to why questions. "Why was the agent in such-and-such microphysical states at that time?" "Because of such-and-such exercise of free will." If it is up to me whether I decide to do *a* at *t*, and if that will ensure that electron *e* is not at spacetime location *pt*, then it would appear to be appropriate, supposing I do refrain from deciding to do *a*, to explain the fact that electron *e* is not at *pt* by appealing to facts about agent causation.

76. Note that neither of these strictly entails the other. A sort of parallelism wherein the agent is immaterial is consistent with the supervenience thesis; meanwhile, an agent with wholly material parts might conceivably enjoy states that do not supervene on microphysical ones.

77. We shan't go into the metaphysics of states of affairs, here. In terms roughly hewn, they are the "truthmakers" (to borrow a term from D. M. Armstrong) for true propositions, and have their temporal specifications built in. The principle is thus meant to be, so to say, "at a time." We're grateful to Rod Bertolet for pointing out two flaws with an earlier formulation (his concern involved the conceivability of mutual causation, as illustrated by cases of symbiosis).

78. Note that the token-reductive materialist cannot comfortably say that the causal relation between the agent and the material event that is the willing is analyzable into groundfloor physical relations, and so even he will be committed to a sort of emergentism.

79. Conceivable at least in the sense that no semantic/analytic rule is violated by its postulation.

80. At any rate, we regard this as a compelling conjecture. See Sydney Shoemaker's discussion of nonrelational properties and causal powers of events in "Causality and Properties," ed. Peter van Inwagen, *Time and Cause* (Dordrecht: D. Reidel, 1980), 109–35; and consider also that if it is the purely accidental, external circumstances that place events into their causal nexus, events would emerge as the bare loci of change, with no subsequent events being excluded (save the logically impossible), since nothing intrinsic and essential to any event—nothing by its nature—precludes its entering into some causal relations and requires its entering into others. That, presumably, is not what we take genuine caused changes to amount to.

81. See, for example, "Mental Events," in *Essays on Actions and Events* (Oxford: Clarendon Press, 1980), 207–27.

82. The emphasis on "fundamental causal powers" is important and, we hope, intuitive enough. There is certainly a sense in which powers are context-dependent. A being on one planet may be able to see and a duplicate on another planet be unable to see. Why? Because of differences in light between one planet and another. We owe the example to Jonathan Bennett.

83. Of course, we can't assume that the boundaries of the agent will be unproblematic on every nonphysicalist ontology—though, it is a commonplace of traditional immaterialist accounts that minds or souls are simple.

84. We owe this point to Ted Warfield (in conversation).

85. Finally, this, for theists who may find themselves sympathetic with the Cartesian hunch that "it is above all in virtue of the will that I understand myself to bear in some way the image and likeness of God" (in *Philosophical Writings of Descartes*, eds. John Cottingham, Robert Stoothoff and Dugald Murdoch [Cambridge: Cambridge University Press, 1984], Volume II, 40), or with Leibniz's claim that "the root of human freedom is in the image of God in man" (Gr 300). We have volition as part of our nature. And so does God (since He loves us and is worthy of our praise, both of which imply freedom). The power to will marks out a joint in the world; it is, for lack of a better pair of words, a natural kind. It seems strange to claim that a natural kind supervenes on a certain set of properties in me, to which kind God also belongs but without its supervening on anything. It is strange to think that being a horse (consider Trigger) is a natural kind, but that horses might well have been made of nuts and bolts; it is strange to think that being an agent (consider God) is a natural kind, but that an agent might have been made of, well, nuts and bolts or flesh and bone. Of course, if willing were a boring high level property of functional architecture, then none of this would make much sense. But if, as the robust freedom theorist is wont to say, willing is one of the fundamental making relationships in the order of things, then the above consideration will surely have some weight.

86. A distant (historically thicker, philosophically thinner) ancestor of this chapter was presented to the Society of Christian Philosophers at the 1994 Pacific

Division APA meeting in Los Angeles. We are indebted to Rod Bertolet, Hud Hudson, Daniel Nolan, Tim O'Connor, Ted Warfield and Dean Zimmerman for helpful discussion and comments on an earlier draft. We're especially fortunate to have profited over the years from the good counsel and philosophical influence of Bill Rowe, whose work stands as an example of refreshing clarity and rigor.

Chapter 4

87. David Widerker, "Libertarian Freedom and the Avoidability of Decisions," *Faith and Philosophy*, 12 (1995): 113–18 and "Libertarianism and Frankfurt's Attack on the Principle of Alternative Possibilities," *The Philosophical Review*, 104 (1995): 247–61. Some portions of the discussion in this chapter of Widerker's argument are taken from my "The Principle of Alternative Possibilities: Widerker's Argument Against Frankfurt-Style Counterexamples," eds. Charles Manekin and Kellner Menachem, *Freedom and Moral Responsibility: General and Jewish Perspectives* (College Park, Md.: University of Maryland Press, 1996).

88. See, for example, Thomas Flint, "Compatibilism and the Argument from Unavoidability," *Journal of Philosophy* 84 (1987), 423–40. As Widerker points out, "morally responsible" in PAP shouldn't be taken to cover cases of derivative responsibility, where an agent is causally determined to do an action, but is himself responsible for the state of affairs that causally determined him to do the action.

89. See, for example, Harry Frankfurt, "Alternate Possibilities and Moral Responsibility," *Journal of Philosophy* 66 (1969): 829–39.

90. See my discussion in "Intellect, Will and Alternate Possibilities and Moral Responsibility," reprinted in *Perspectives on Moral Responsibility*, eds. John Martin Fischer and Mark Ravizza (Ithaca, N.Y.: Cornell University Press, 1993), 237–62.

91. John Martin Fischer, "Responsibility and Control," *Journal of Philosophy* 89 (1982): 24–40. Widerker focuses on this argument of Fischer's only in "Libertarian Freedom and the Avoidability of Decisions" but his strategy of arguing against Frankfurt-style counterexamples is the same in "Libertarianism and Frankfurt's Attack on the Principle of Alternate Possibilities."

92. Fischer, "Responsibility," 26.

93. Fischer, "Responsibility," 33.

94. Widerker, "Libertarian Freedom," 113. typescript, 1. In Widerker, "Libertarianism and Frankfurt's Attack on the Principle of Alternate Possibilities", he makes the claim this way: "an agent's decision (choice) is free in the sense of freedom required for moral responsibility only if (i) it is not causally determined, and (ii) in the circumstances in which the agent made that decision (choice), he could have avoided making it", 247.

95. Widerker, "Libertarian Freedom," 115.

96. Widerker, "Libertarian Freedom," 115.

97. Fischer doesn't think so, either. His response is in "Libertarianism and Avoidability: A Reply to Widerker," *Faith and Philosophy*, 12 (1995): 119–25.

Fischer's response includes a defense of Dennett's interpretation of libertarianism, according to which decisions for which agents are morally responsible are preceded by judgments that determine the decisions but that aren't themselves determined. On this way of thinking about moral responsibility, Black's neuroscope could operate once it detected the nature of the judgments. The problem with this response is that it enables Widerker to reply that the agent in question did have the ability to do otherwise, at least in the sense of having the ability to judge otherwise. Fischer attempts to block this rebuttal by arguing that the ability to judge otherwise can't be what grounds moral responsibility. But given the connection he himself makes between moral responsibility and reasons-responsiveness and the connection I argue for here between an agent's free will and her cognitive faculties, it isn't clear to me that Fischer's attempted rebuttal is on the right track.

98. William Alston has pointed out to me that it isn't necessary to go so far in order to get a Frankfurt-style counterexample that doesn't suppose mental acts are causally dependent on antecedent mental states. We might simply suppose that the mad neuroscientist of the counterexample intervenes whenever his monitoring leads him to think there is even a significant probability of the patient's making a decision the neuroscientist wants to prevent. But since some libertarians might object that even the assumption of such probabilistic correlations is incompatible with genuine libertarianism, it seems to me worth considering whether a Frankfurt-style counterexample might be constructed that doesn't posit the monitoring of mental states antecedent to the mental act the neuroscientist seeks to control.

99. Not every philosopher of mind, of course, supposes that there are any regular correlations, even nonlawlike correlations, between mental and neural states. If there are no regular correlations, or even if the regular correlations are violated, a certain amount of the time, then Grey's neuroscope won't work. In that case, to make a suitable Frankfurt-style neuroscope, we would need to postulate a very fancy neuroscope or a much smarter neurosurgeon, so that the neurosurgeon can tell in every case what mental state will exist at the completion of any given neural process. I don't see, however, that the degree of fantasy in the neurobiology fantasy story affects its ability to serve as a Frankfurt-style counterexample. Furthermore, I also think that research in neurobiology strongly suggests that there is a regular correlation between neural states and mental states for normal adult human beings, so that, for example, the mental state of seeing something regularly correlates with neural states in the occipital lobe. It doesn't correlate, even a very small percentage of the time, with states in, say, the cerebellum or the pituitary.

100. The example doesn't require this simplifying assumption. If each neural sequence were correlated with more than one set of mental acts, then the neurosurgeon's coercive mechanism would interfere with much more than it needs to interfere with for Grey's purposes, but this state of affairs doesn't alter the efficacy of the neuroscope in bringing about Grey's end.

101. This neuroscopic mechanism will thus abort many more actions than it needs to do in order to bring it about that Jones votes for Reagan. When

neurobiology is a complete science, no doubt neuroscopes in philosophy fantasy stories will be less clumsy.

102. See my "Non-Cartesian Substance Dualism and Materialism without Reductionism," *Faith and Philosophy.*

103. For discussion of the extent to which Descartes held Cartesian dualism, see, for example, Margaret Wilson, *Descartes* (London: Routledge and Kegan Paul, 1978), 177–85, and Tad Schmaltz, "Descartes and Malebranche on Mind and Mind-Body Union," *The Philosophical Review* 101 (1992): 281–325.

104. But notice that there are analogues of P1 and P2 that are true and yet compatible with libertarianism (understood as LR, as I explain):

P1'. The firing of neural sequence 2 in Jones's brain is (in the circumstances) a causally necessary condition of his deciding to vote for Carter

and

P2'. The nonfiring of neural sequence 2 in Jones's brain is (in the circumstances) causally sufficient for Jones's not deciding to vote for Carter.

105. Widerker considers an objection to his position that has some resemblance to the strategy behind RCE. Suppose, he says, that Fischer were to claim that inclinations don't causally produce decisions; rather, inclinations are just the first part of a temporal process that constitutes a decision. Nothing preceding the decision need causally determine the decision, but the temporal process of the decision itself would be enough to support FFC. Widerker's response is to claim that a decision itself (as distinct from what precedes a decision, such as deliberation) is a simple mental act and does not have a complex structure. Widerker may or may not be right about inclinations and decisions. But on most theories of the nature of the mind, mental states are at least implemented in neural states, and neural states certainly do have complex structures. Therefore, in a certain sense, there is a structure associated with mental acts as well. Since this is so, there is some purchase for the sort of coercive mechanism postulated in Frankfurt-style counterexamples.

106. See, for example, *Summa theologiae* I-II, q.6, a.1. There Aquinas says that for an action to be voluntary, the source of the action has to be intrinsic to the agent and the agent has to have some cognition of the end of his action, so that he acts for that end.

107. Eric Kandel, James Schwartz, Thomas Jessell, 3d ed. (New York: Elsevier, 1991).

108. Stephen M. Kosslyn and Olivier Koenig, *Wet Mind. The New Cognitive Neuroscience* (New York: Free Press, 1992), 33.

109. Stephen Jay Gould, "The Evolution of Life on Earth," *Scientific American* 271 (1994): 85.

110. See, for example, Alan Garfinkel, "Reductionism," and Philip Kitcher, "1953 and All That: A Tale of Two Sciences," *The Philosophy of Science*, eds. Richard Boyd, Philip Gasper, and J. D. Trout (Cambridge, Mass.: MIT Press, 1993), 443–59 and 553–70.

111. See, for example, Frederic M. Richards, "The Protein Folding Problem," *Scientific American* 264 (January 1991): 54–63. According to Richards, for relatively small proteins folding is a function of the properties and causal potentialities among the constituents of the protein, but "some large proteins have recently been shown to need folding help from other proteins known as chaperonins" (54).

112. John Dupré, *The Disorder of Things. Metaphysical Foundations of the Disunity of Science* (Cambridge, Mass.: Harvard University Press, 1993); see especially chapters 4–6.

113. Dupré, *Disorder*, 101.

114. Dupré, *Disorder*, 101.

115. Dupré, *Disorder*, 102.

116. See, for example, Zwei Huang, Jean-Marc Gabriel, Michael Baldwin, et al., "Proposed Three-Dimensional Structure for the Cellular Prion Protein," *Proceedings of the National Academy of Sciences* 91 (19 July 1994): 7139–143.

117. John Martin Fischer, "Responsiveness and Moral Responsibility," in *Responsibility, Character, and the Emotions*, ed. Ferdinand Schoeman (Cambridge: Cambridge University Press, 1987), 81–106. For an interesting recent argument to the same conclusion based on arguments about responsibility for failure to act, see Walter Glannon, "Responsibility and the Principle of Possible Action," *Journal of Philosophy* 92 (1995), 261–74.

118. See, for example, Fred Dretske, *Explaining Behavior: Reasons in a World of Causes* (Cambridge, Mass.: Bradford Books, 1988).

119. Dupré, *Disorder*, 216–17.

120. As I argued in "Intellect, Will, and Alternate Possibilities."

121. 2, of course, entails 1, so that 1 could be omitted, but I have spelled it out for the sake of clarity, because of the importance of 1 in the preceding discussion.

122. I am grateful to William Alston, John Martin Fischer, Daniel Howard-Snyder, Scott MacDonald, William Rowe, and David Widerker for comments on an earlier draft of this chapter; and I am especially indebted to Norman Kretzmann for many helpful questions and suggestions at every stage of this chapter.

Chapter 5

123. That D. Burrell calls a zero-sum ego contest. See A. Plantinga, *God Freedom and Evil* (Grand Rapids, Mich.: Eerdman's, 1974) and the extensive discussion of the "Free Will Defense."

124. "Redeploy" because these ideas are basic and explicit in both Augustine and Aquinas, for example, in *Summa Theologica* (hereafter, *ST*), I, 12, 5.c and 6.c.

Humans are "by essence" rational animals as a condition of their being at all; so humans are only *relatively* able to live with God. "Relatively" here means "the *sort* of thing that is able to live with God," although individually not being able to do so without divine intervention, for individuals lose that ability with sin, remaining responsible for what they do.

You can see why there would be such a debate, as there was, over the "corruption of human nature" by the Fall. Humans are unable to attain life with God by themselves in the way that Thalidomide babies are unable to grasp things, although they are the *sorts* of things that grasp things, in their full integrity. Nevertheless, Aquinas is explicit that even before sin, the intellect must be empowered by grace to see God.

125. Two notes here. First, Augustine and Aquinas held that (1) man is created in a supernatural condition aimed at life with God; (2) there is a "corruption" that follows from the Fall, but not a change of nature; (3) the Fall leaves humans responsible for what they do afterwards, exactly the same as before—and they remain the *sorts* of things suitable for life with God; and (4) humans have no other final end ever. Second, the medievals thought the supernatural *eminently* "contains" the natural in the way God's powers "contain" ours. A modern analogue is the way Dos 4.01 "contains" Dos 3.0.

126. For material life, flourishing is fulfillment. For rational beings, fulfillment specifically fits understanding and love. Biologically, flourishing that includes successful reproduction is fulfillment for animals. Some evolutionary biologists think that biological flourishing is "success" at adaptation, which simply is reproductive success. This is even narrower than they say Aristotle was, whom they criticized for saying that the function of birds was to make more birds.

Some scientists may deny that other living things have a fulfillment in nature. But "living well" and fortunately, in a hospitable environment with successful reproduction, and thus adequate animal functioning, is normally the foundation of human flourishing, but not fulfillment. Moreover, fulfillment can be attained without flourishing, for example, by the victimized, the defective, or infants. No pagan philosophy has ever been able to make a case in which fulfillment is available to all humans, regardless of whether the flourishing is.

127. Regarding (1), only remnants of true freedom remain, absent faith now, tattered remnants of spontaneity that looked to Andre Gide and Albert Camus like motiveless, reasonless spontaneity aimed as often at (what we regard as) evil as at the good. The existentialists discerned the burned-out hulk of the ark of fulfillment in man that other philosophers couldn't account for at all. It is as if they found the burned, cold, empty hearth where the last fire of love ignited by the presence of God had been, but could discern only the emptiness, and the bitter taste of ashes in human brokenness. Regarding (2), no material thing is capable of seeing God; some additional mode of being is required.

128. (1) raises the question of whether God might have evolved rational animals without our supernatural powers, rational animals that are not humans but prehumans, which have no fulfillment, only elusive flourishing that flickers out, even if attained. Regarding (2), see Ross, "Christians Get the Best of Evolution," in *Evolution and Creation*, ed. Ernan McMullen (Notre Dame, Ind.: University of Notre Dame Press, 1985), 223–51. Regarding (3), see Aquinas, *ST,*

q.27–43, for example: the First Covenant, by the Father; the Redemption by the Son (Logos); and Sanctification by the Spirit; also, *Compendium of Theology*, part I, chapters 37–66.

129. Which because of the Fall can only be understood through a redemption, so there is no adequate natural knowledge of God's freedom.

Apart from divine restoration of human freedom (in active redemption), by which we can act the way the redeemer acts, there is no way to understand what true freedom is. This is because we primarily understand God through God's effects (see Aquinas), and where the effect that is most appropriate, namely human freedom, has been impaired by sin, we have to look at its pure, proper exercise by a divine person who is human.

130. The spontaneity is emphasized by Duns Scotus from the perspective of man restored by Christ (see A. B. Wolter, trans., *Duns Scotus on the Will and Morality* [Washington, D.C.: Catholic University Press, 1986]) but is found in secular tatters among existentialist writers, for example, Sartre's self-making, and Gide's and Camus's notions of "free action" as unreasoned and unmotivated, entirely mysterious.

131. See Aquinas, *ST* 23, a. 2.c.

132. All living things have a *bias*, like a tilt in a spinning top, that delineates (but does not determine) the paths of their actions. Sometimes the bias is called "appetite"; it is regarded as a representation or a blueprint for future states. *How* the completion of a thing is present in it, so as to modulate its actions, varies with the kind of thing. "Tendency," "bias," "appetite," "disposition" are all protean notions, with different analyses in different contexts. In a human, the longing for "happiness" presents itself both as drive and as need (as missing). But hunger or sex present themselves in other ways.

133. There is animal voluntarism where there is animal cognition of its own good and animal desire biased toward that good, but there is no understanding of what the good is. See Aquinas, *ST*, I-II, q.6, a.2 on *Animal Voluntarism*:

> It is essential to the voluntary act that its principle be within the agent together with some knowledge of the end. . . . Imperfect knowledge of the end consists in mere apprehension of the end, without knowing it under the aspect of "end," or the relationship of an act to the end. Such knowledge of the end is exercised by rational animals through their senses and their natural estimative power . . . whereas the imperfect voluntary is within the competency of even irrational animals.

So animals are not moral agents even though they are capable of a kind of obedience/disobedience, wildness/compliance, and of being well-behaved/stubborn/docile and a whole range of other character traits that not only distinguish wild animals from domestic animals but distinguish one kind of domestic animal from another; trained lions are "willingly" compliant when they are, and "willy-nilly" indifferent or defiant when they are. Wildness in animals is like certain forms of insanity in humans.

134. Regarding the competing analyses, see Ross, *Truth and Impossibility.* Contemporary philosophy is twisted because of mistakes about truth, necessity, understanding and, therefore science, which were begun by Descartes and exacerbated with passing centuries. See also my "The Fate of the Analysts: Aristotle's Revenge," *Proceedings of the American Catholic Philosophical Association* (1990). Only a major reevaluation will put us back in touch with lost lines of inquiry and away from entrenched mistakes. See "First Lamentation," below, on disorders of the understanding.

135. Regarding (1), we think of such acts as "creative": composition (music or writing), design (painting, architecture), invention (mathematics or geometry, and so on), and "free expression" (dance, gesture, walk, talk). Regarding (4), many philosophers deny there is any such ability as freedom and say there is only a shadow of it, "wilful action," as described by materialists like Gide, Camus, and others. At the other extreme, there are *idealist* notions of "transcendental will," a response to Scotus's "spontaneity," for example, Kant, associated with the notion of a transcendental self (see Wittgenstein), where freedom has nothing to do with psychological or physical causation. Most philosophers deny that there is an active ability to attain human fulfillment, and even deny that there is such a reachable condition as genuine fulfillment, as opposed to temporary flourishing (which is denied circumstantially to most people and which ends for each of us at death).

136. It is a mode of love. And thus, each bodily sense is a mode of love, as Augustine observed.

137. *ST* I, 12, 5. See his reply to Objection 1, a "created light."

138. Plato, Aristotle, the Stoics, and the Epicureans; particularly as understood by Augustine.

139. It is a modern canard to tell that story about humans; it makes human fulfillment *attainable* by genetic accident or human cruelty or injustice. That is not so, no matter how much it appears to be so, from scriptural times ("the wicked prosper") to our own. Such "Wall Street people" are just achievers, not fulfilled.

140. In action habitually proceeding from the rational appetite in the absence of ignorance, fear, violence, or passion, in accord with the person's desire for the highest excellence of the understanding.

141. Remember that Augustine defined freedom as "the ability to act rightly" and Anselm defined it as "the ability to keep uprightness of will for its own sake." Only recent confusion thinks of wrongdoing as an exercise of the same ability by which we act rightly; it is as if overlooking something were an exercise of the power to *notice*, even though having the power to notice is *sine qua non* for overlooking.

142. So much is necessary for happiness, and so little is sufficient for unhappiness. These are paradoxes, of course, for Christians as well; notably, with the gratuitousness of divine gifts of faith and freedom.

143. One has to be lucky enough to come from a good family, and have good

health, practical wisdom, and a character that fits one's condition of life. One has to be additionally lucky not to be tried *beyond* one's character or be forced by one's outrage out of the human community (to be a dog): see Martha Nussbaum on Greek tragedy, *The Fragility of Goodness: Luck and Ethics in Greek Tragedy and Philosophy* (Cambridge: University of Cambridge Press, 1986).

144. After the Fall, that ability has to come by *restoration* for people in general (the redemption), and by *gift* to each in particular (salvation), as was the gift to Mary ("Immaculate") from the foreseen merits of her son.

You may ask *why*, to understand human freedom, do we have to understand divine freedom? Why don't we just study ourselves? The answer is that humans are not, even when restored in grace, able to understand the *full* human design in God's image because that condition was lost with the Fall and the condition of life with God (without *cognitio visionis*) has to be regained with practice; restoration presupposes nature, but nature has to be perfected by life with God.

145. An enlightenment about the original design of humans in the image of the creator. That original design is given to us by a story in Genesis and illuminated right through the Gospels. It *seems* that we can know by "figuring it out" that our fulfillment is in encounter with the divine essence, and also know that *we* lack the ability on our own, to encounter God, and so, can figure out that a divine enablement is *possible*. However, we cannot figure out its content or its manner, or that it is in fact available.

146. I read the later Wittgenstein to be convinced that there are disorders of the *understanding*, serious thought-disorders (analogous to neuroses and even sometimes psychoses) that can only be relieved by a distinctly philosophical therapy (or a metaphysical euthanasia); otherwise, the sufferers have to be abandoned to be intellectual "street people."

Typically, in philosophy, a fair start brings a bad end.

147. See Ross, *Truth and Impossibility*, and "Aristotle's Revenge," cited above.

148. And particularly virulently affects religious thinkers. See Ross, "Aristotle's Revenge," cited above.

149. Philosophers, for a long time, did not even attempt to explain animal consciousness, feeling and cognition. Descartes denied that animals are anything but robots. But animals are not machines; they are genuinely cognitive, and many actually see, hear, fear, rage, and desire. Everyone will cheer when we find out how matter can do that. Rather than do the *work*, philosophers promise to explain "intentionality" but in fact leave the entire task up to the scientists. Philosophers made *names*, "behaviorism," "functionalism," and now, "connectivism" (like the names of fictitious gold mines in the last century), for more promises that explain nothing.

150. See "Aristotle's Revenge," particularly the ideas that (1) there is "software everywhere"; (2) *we* have an ability to dematerialize things, to fluoresce the forms of things; and (3) the object of science is *comprehension*, to be "streetwise in the universe."

151. The fact is that for humans, intelligence is a constant transformation of animal consciousness, and that without sensation, there is no human understanding at all. See Aquinas *Q.D. De Anima*; *Q.D. De Veritate*; *ST*, q. 75–90.

152. See Gary Watson, ed., *Free Will* (New York: Oxford University Press, 1982). Also: "Free Action and Free Will," *Mind* (1987), 145–72; "Necessity and Desire," *Philosophy and Phenomenological Research* (1984), 1–13; see the criticism by Eleonore Stump, "Sanctification, Hardening of the Heart, and Frankfurt's Concept of Free Will," *Journal of Philosophy* (1988), 395–420, with copious references.

153. Like nasty childhood desires in the Freudian unconscious—not that I think there is one—or repressed adolescent fantasies that, to the conscious, seem "worn out," without erotic power, but which unconsciously pattern conscious arousal—in a more Jungian way; that I do think likely.

154. That is the English for what Aquinas had in Latin from the Arabic for Aristotle's *Metaphysics* IV, 5, 1010b, that says now, in English, "not everything that is imagined is true." I find the ex-Latin version more colorful and still true.

155. See Aquinas's *Commentary on De Anima* of Aristotle; his *Disputed Questions De Veritate* and his "Treatise on the Soul" in *ST*. For example, the whole of a physical thing is not presented in a visual glimpse but has to be "filled out" from memory, instinct, and imagination, in order for there to be a suitable "phantasm" (sensory appearance) for us to dematerialize. Yet this is *not* a representationalism, a cognition by "Holographic Heads Up Display" theory. See my *Truth and Impossibility*.

156. Reality falls short because the imaginary is idealized and without the defects and detail of the real. On the other hand, reality goes too far because it overflows the conditions of an image in all directions: it has hidden features and hidden properties, even dangerous ones, and properties that are unimaginable, like diameters of 10^{-19} cm.

157. Further, no imaginary objects can be a real individual because it can never be so particular as to be induplicable (as far as it goes).

158. Unfounded generalities, based on local instances, invite general belief: "Southern fundamentalists are hypocrites," or "Tinkers are cheaters"; even becoming so certain it becomes analytic: "A tinker is a cheat," with such falsities even occasionally "legitimized" by a dictionary entry.

159. A sure cause of neuroses, like exposing children to pornography.

160. *ST* Ia, 67, 68 and 70; *ST* 45, 2, ad 4.

161. In prison poetry, the verse could have a stark reality: "humilitatem meam" is "my poor ass," and the lion and the unicorn rule the cell block.

162. See the entertaining and also deeply informative discussion of the history of empty names in D. P. Henry's *That Most Subtle Question* (Manchester, England: University of Manchester Press, 1984).

163. Intentional logic is formulated as extensional, as over a range of individuals some of which are not actual or are "reached" by abstract surrogates. See Ross, "Crash," *Review of Metaphysics* (1989). How this was done and exactly

why it was needed are explained in "Crash" and "God, Creator of Kinds and Possibilities," cited above.

The canny David Hume attributed what he diagnosed as philosophical fictions, like the independent existence of physical things and the subsistent self, to runaway imagination, to "the mind's propensity to spread itself on things." And then, he fell for its trickery himself: saying that whatever we can consistently imagine is really possible. See my *Truth and Impossibility* and "Aquinas's Exemplarism, Aquinas's Voluntarism" on empty names, *American Catholic Philosophical Quarterly* (1990), 1–28.

164. Everything is in input-alignment with God's self-knowing the way every distinguishable thing-to-be-seen is within the one unified seeing I do at any given moment of looking.

165. David Lewis treats "to be" as a logical *product* of being, just as traffic is the logical product of things moving on a path.

166. This of course is talk in the fashion of one's opponents. There is no *domain* of possibility at all.

167. Still, that Neoplatonic "false imagining" of *abstract objects that exist forever and explain the truth of things and are the patterns of things* became part of "the collective intellectual unconscious" for two millennia and generated viral off-strains of iconic Neoplatonism as diverse as Augustine's "divine ideas which are the forms of things," Descartes's "eternal truths" by divine decree, and Spinoza's parallel infinite modes of extension and modes of thought, and spawned the even more outre recent atheist "idealist-materialism". See J. Passmore, *Recent Philosophy* (La Salle, Ind.: Open Court Publishing Company, 1985), 66–68, 100–101, and elsewhere, in which causally inert abstract numbers "make" arithmetic true (Quine) and abstract sets and objects make logic true (D. Lewis and many others); and some, furthermore, like D. Lewis in *On the Plurality of Worlds* (Oxford: Blackwell, 1986), who, skipping *divine* ideas and God altogether, think there is an eternal unmade array of everything that is possible, in parallel but physically inaccessible possible worlds: science fiction doing duty for theology.

168. "Most" here means "the ones one could easily semantically formulate; for example, "If the shot had been any closer, I would have been killed," and, "If I had been Oriental, I would have been female." Furthermore, I note from observation that the ones normally used by ordinary people involve suspension of causal or factual elements about *real* possibilities of which we have no knowledge at all; for example, someone says, "if I had not gone to that dance, I would never have met you," which is a probability estimate, or a person says, "if I had not grabbed your arm, you would have been killed," or "if I had not spoken up, he would have gotten away with it." Such probability estimates are made with only loose concern for the actual historical and physical causation involved.

169. As I explain elsewhere, and do not attempt to explain or illustrate here, disorders of the understanding (e.g., that there is no relevant difference between

human and animal intentionality [seeing] and that intentionality and consciousness are the same) become part of the intellectual *unconscious* of a *culture* (e.g., Western industrialized scientific culture), escaping the notice of those not taught to reflect *beyond* it. See Ross, *Truth and Impossibility*.

170. Though there might have been races of humans different from any that will ever be, and though "they" might have been Black or White, "they" could not have been transparent. Yet, there is no line of humans, like pickets on a fence, who could have *been* the members of such races.

171. "Middle Knowledge," knowledge "supposing-that," "contrary to fact knowledge that," purportedly covers every *consistent* description. One reason that there is no such thing is that consistency of description cannot *assure* real possibility, not even logical or metaphysical possibility. See my *Truth and Impossibility*.

172. For instance, I might have been a doctor, but it is entirely indeterminate where the office would have been, what speciality I might have practiced, and how long I would live doing it.

173. Of course, "antecedently impossible" is merely denominative: a predicate referentially *vantaged* in what *is* made, and, nevertheless, only an *imaginary* feature of actual things because it imagines (supposes) reference *before* being, like the imaginary "time before time" Aquinas criticizes.

Thus to say "what is made is antecedently impossible (because contentless)," may be informative; but it is not as if, antecedently, there is something contentless that comes to be made.

174. *De Primo Principio*, c.4, concl. 10, trans. E. Roche (St. Bonaventure, N.Y.: St. Bonaventure University Press, 1949), 147. I thank Fr. A. Maurer for pointing this out to me.

175. *De Potentia* 3, 16c. Also see *ST* Ia, 47, 1, and *CG* II, 35, 39.

176. *DP* 3, 17.c.

177. See F. Van Steenberghen, *Introduction a l'etude de la philosophie medievale, Philosophes medievaux*, vol. 18 (Paris: Publications Universitaires and Beatrice-Nauwelaerts, 1974), 555–70, and " 'Averroisme' et 'double verite' au siecle de saint Louis," in *Septieme centenaire de la mort de saint Louis, Actes des colloques de Royaumont et de la mort de Paris*, 21–27 mai 1970 (Paris: Societe d'Edition "Les Belles Lettres," 1976), 351–60; *Maitre Siger de Brabant*, Philosophes medievaux, No. 21 (Paris: Publications Universitaires, 1977), and *Thomas Aquinas and Radical Aristotelianism* (Washington, D.C.: Catholic University of America Press, 1980), on Aquinas's opposition to double-truth; and Martin Pine, "Double Truth," in *Dictionary of the History of Ideas*, vol. 2 (New York: Scribner's, 1973). See also Stuart MacClintock, "Averroism," ed. Paul Edwards, *The Encyclopedia of Philosophy*, vol. 1 (New York: Macmillan, 1967), 223–26; and Etienne Gilson, *History of Christian Philosophy in the Middle Ages* (New York: Scribner's Sons, 1955), and *Reason and Revelation in the Middle Ages* (New York: Scribner's Sons, 1938), 61–66, particularly on John of Jaudun.

178. *ST* Ia, 68, a.3. According to the text. Genesis 1:6 says, "Let there be a firmament made amidst the waters; and let divide the waters from the waters."

179. See the separation of explanatory roles from truth in Nancy Cartwright, *How the Laws of Physics Lie* (Oxford: Clarendon Press, 1983), reviewed by Geoffrey Joseph in *Philosophical Review* (1985): 580–83; and also Ian Hacking, *Representing and Intervening* (New York: Cambridge University Press, 1983).

180. D. Burrells's paper refers to Vatican II's acknowledgment of the lack of adequate models to make a scientific correlate for parts of the proclaimed faith in *Constitution on the Faith*—at least that is how I read that notion. There has always been a problem about the acts of Jesus, the divine person in history. However, because they are by way of his human nature, they present less problem than at first appears, except that *incarnation* cannot be eternal.

181. Besides, what counts as "science," occasionally, is just a tissue of obtuse abstractions, (1) made up to fit the observations (themselves made partially dependent on the artifacts that classify them), like Quantified Modal Logic; that is, really about nothing at all. (2) "Science" may turn out, as in the case of some recent highly mathematized physics, to be about the logical *shadows* of things and not about physical reality directly, however informative it may be. (3) Artless, incautious conjunction of imparately vantaged truths causes equivocal suppositions, and even outright contradictions and hostility to the religion it serves. As I said, this is recently the case with modal metaphysics (see "Crash"), where suddenly "logic" unrestrained makes *possibility prior to actual being*, the very antithesis of the Creator of Judeo-Christian religion.

182. See Ross, "Semantic Contagion," for theory, in *Frames, Fields and Contrasts: New Essays in Semantic and Lexical Organization*, eds. A. Lehrer and Eva Kittay (Hillsdale, N.J.: Lawrence Erlbaum and Associates, 1993), 143–69.

183. See A. Kenny's *The God of the Philosophers* (Oxford: Clarendon Press, 1979) and Richard Swinburne's books (cited in note 188), for many examples.

184. The same sort of dispute is in the open again: see M. Dummett's criticism of modern biblical science, in which he exaggerates the effect scholars have on believers. Of course, many believers do not keep their own place of authority, yielding too much to "advice" by the scholars. Further, scholars *do* often argue by a *non-sequitur* from the *absence* of data to the "later" composition of the Gospels.

185. But some people learn to *see* a wave passing *through* the water while others, like me, are usually confused, especially by waves crashing on the shore; the stopped train in the station seems to move when another passes on the other side of the platform.

186. These two notions, "standpoint" and "perspective," pick out the *referential* and the *semantic* dimensions (the two kinds of content and potential opposition) among observations.

187. However, see Paul Churchland, *Scientific Realism and the Plasticity of Mind* (Cambridge: Cambridge University Press, 1981).

188. Just to name a few: A. Kenny, *The God of the Philosophers*; N. Kretzmann, "Omniscience and Immutability," *Journal of Philosophy* (1966): 63; E. Stump & N. Kretzmann, "Eternity," *Journal of Philosophy* (1981): 453f; E. R.

Wierenga, *The Nature of God: An Inquiry Into Divine Attributes* (Ithaca, New York: Cornell University Press, 1989); R. Swinburne, *The Coherence of Theism* (Oxford: Clarendon Press, 1977), *Faith and Reason* (Oxford: Clarendon Press, 1983), *The Evolution of the Soul*, (Oxford: Clarendon Press, 1986), and *The Evidence for God* (Oxford: Published by Mowbray for the Christian Evidence Society, 1986); and assorted articles in *Faith and Philosophy*.

189. Everyone knows that, when they say, "I was talking about his *character*, not his actions, when I said, 'He's honest.' "

It is only the philosophers who have failed to work out neat accounts of "conceptual systems" as systems of truth-dependence and evidence relative to a *base* of references and assumptions, and to distinguish that from "conceptual systems" as *meaning*-systems based on different referential and conceptual bases (the Quine-Davidson-Kuhn aforementioned debate).

190. Preferring Aristotle over Aristarchus, for instance, on the motion of the stars.

191. Nowadays, theologians, unaware of the attacks on the pretensions of science (and of the even more pretentious "deconstruction" of all objective attitudes), are tempted to even greater fancies on the analogue of the arctic navigation system, in which to fly from Australia to Antarctica, an *artificial* chart is used that has the pilot steering "due north" on his instruments at crucial times when he is flying directly toward the South Pole. (Those charts are made-up devices to create a course that corrects for the South Pole magnetic field disturbances.) Theology imbibes those impulses too: to supply a made-up world-chart (usually borrowed from some secular discipline, say, psychology) on which to plot the scriptural realities of sin, redemption, and salvation, to guide our thinking. That is dangerous business, whether we use historical, psychological, hermeneutical, political, or even philosophical artifacts. We may get more falsity imported from the "secular discipline," than we preserve and expand religious truth, as I say happened to theology based on recent modal metaphysics, and to modernism of the twenties, and to the neo-orthodoxy of the fifties (Tillich), that combined psychological, existential, and religious notions into a freehand meaningless account of sin. Nevertheless, that, in crucial part, is what theology *is*, as Tillich said: the exfoliation and explanation of the faith in secular categories imposed by secular questions (from secular science and arts). So my criticism is not against the activity in principle, but against exaggerations that make secular-natural pictures the world-chart *on which* religious realities are supposed to be fitted and found. That is *not* at all how the interaction must happen.

192. See Ross, "Aquinas on Annihilation," in *Studies in Medieval Philosophy*, ed. John Wipple (Washington, D.C.: Catholic University of America Press, 1986), 177–99.

193. See Ross, "Creation II," in *The Existence and Nature of God*, ed. A. J. Freddoso (Notre Dame: University of Notre Dame Press, 1983).

194. See Watson, *Free Will*.

195. We tend to think another adult does not *truly* love us because we do not

merit such devotion and interest, not noticing that *we* love without regard to prior merit, at least sometimes, and without realizing that God loves us more than we love anything, even ourselves, because it is by God's love that we exist and do all our loving.

Chapter 6

196. Edwards's principal discussions of the relevant issues are located in the "Miscellanies," a number of which can be found in *The Philosophy of Jonathan Edwards from His Private Notebooks*, ed. Harvey G. Townsend (Eugene, Ore.: University of Oregon Press, 1955), hereafter cited as Misc. T; in *The Nature of True Virtue* and *Concerning the End for Which God Created the World* (in *Ethical Writings*, ed. Paul Ramsey [New Haven, Connecticut: Yale University Press, 1989], hereafter cited as *TV* and *EC*, respectively; and in "Observations Concerning the Trinity and the Covenant of Redemption" and "An Essay on the Trinity" (in *Treatise on Grace and other Posthumous Writings*, ed. Paul Helm [Cambridge: James Clarke & Co., Ltd., 1971]), hereafter cited as *OT* and *ET*, respectively. Other relevant material can be found in *Religious Affections*, ed. John E. Smith (New Haven, Conn.: Yale University Press, 1959), hereafter *RA*; in *Freedom of the Will*, ed. Paul Ramsey (New Haven, Conn.: Yale University Press, 1957), hereafter *FW*; and in *The Works of President Edwards*, 10 vols., eds. Edward Williams and Edward Parsons (Edinburgh, 1817, 1847; New York: B. Franklin, 1968), hereafter *Works*.

197. See Misc. 461 (T 134) or Misc. 243 (T 129) where Edwards argues that "to make happy is not goodness if it be done purely for another, superior end."

198. Edwards's treatment of goodness is somewhat inconsistent. Misc. 445 (T 130–32) contrasts God's goodness and His other moral attributes. His justice, for instance, is a disposition to act justly in those situations that demand it. Its exercise is thus conditional upon the existence of situations in which just actions are called for. But justice *doesn't* include an inclination to *create* situations in which it should be exercised. Goodness, on the other hand, not only includes a disposition to communicate good or happiness; it also includes a disposition to create occasions for its communication. By the time he had written Miscellany 1218, Edwards had assimilated goodness to the other divine virtues, treating it as a disposition to bestow happiness upon "particular minds" *once they have been created*. Edwards's final word on the matter is presumably expressed in *End in Creation* (EC 438f) where he distinguishes benevolence or goodness "in a larger sense" from benevolence or goodness "in the most strict and proper sense." The former is "that good disposition in his nature to communicate of his own fullness in general," and does not presuppose an existing object. The latter does. (The two are closely related, however. For both have "the same general tendency and effect in the creature's well-being." Furthermore, the underlying disposition is the same. The disposition that disposes God to communicate His goodness also

disposes Him to communicate good or happiness to particular beings once they have been created.)

199. Although I think that these two strands in Edwards's thought reflect the eros and agape motifs in the Christian tradition (see Anders Nygren, *Agape and Eros* [London: S.P.C.K., 1957]), benevolence can't be straightforwardly identified with the latter. Benevolence's object is "being in general," that is, in the first instance, beings *qua* beings and, in the second, "virtuous being." Agape's object is *needy* being.

200. Views like these aren't peculiar to Edwards. In *The True Intellectual System of the Universe* (London, 1678), Ralph Cudworth maintained "that the reason why God made the world was from his own overflowing and communicative goodness, that there might be other beings also happy besides him. . . . Nor does this at all clash, with God's making of the world, for his own Glory and Honour." God made the world "to communicate his Goodness, which is chiefly and properly his Glory, as the light and Splendor of the Sun, is the glory of it" (886). John Smith says that "God himself being infinitely full, and having enough and to spare is alwaies overflowing; and Goodness and Love issue forth from him by way of redundancy. . . . When he is said to seek his own glory, it is indeed nothing else but to ray and beam forth, as it were, his own lustre." (*Select Discourses* [London, 1660], 142). Edwards was familiar with both Smith and Cudworth, although these claims are commonplace in Christian Platonism. There is an important Platonic strand in British and American Puritanism.

201. It should be remembered, however, that *God's* self-love is a love of His own infinite perfection, that is, it is a love of the Good. For God *is* the Good. It is not a form of selfishness or partiality.

202. Quoted in Robert W. Jenson, *America's Theologian: A Recommendation of Jonathan Edwards* (New York and Oxford: Oxford University Press, 1988), 42. Compare Malebranche who argues that "even if man had not sinned, a divine person would not on that account have failed to conjoin himself with the universe in order to sanctify it . . . to render it divine, to endow it with an infinite dignity in order that God . . . should receive from it a glory which perfectly corresponds to His action" (*Dialogues on Metaphysics and Religion*, trans. Morris Ginsberg [London: G. Allen Unwin, Ltd., 1923], 231–32). Christ alone makes the world "perfectly worthy of its author." But the body of Christ includes its members. God's end in creation is thus "the establishment of His church," of which Christ is the head. The world is created for the church and the church for Christ (*Concerning Nature and Grace*, included in *Father Malebranche's Treatise Concerning the Search after Truth*, vol. 2, trans. Thomas Taylor [London: 1694], 3–4). While there is no evidence that Edwards was familiar with the *Dialogues*, he may have been acquainted with *Nature and Grace*. (He appears to have read the *Search after Truth*. However, Norman Fiering argues that Edwards probably read the Richard Sault translation, which was also published in London in 1694 rather than the more popular Taylor translation. The Sault translation did not include *Nature and Grace* (Fiering, *Jonathan Edwards' Moral Thought and its British Context* [Chapel Hill: University of North Carolina Press, 1981], 43).

203. The notion that the Son or Logos is God's perfect idea of Himself is well entrenched in the Christian tradition. Edwards's idealistic metaphysics gives it a new twist, for, on his view, the perfect idea of a thing is the thing itself.

204. More formally:

1. It is necessarily true that God has an inclination to diffuse His own fullness.
2. It is necessarily true that God is able to satisfy His inclination.

Assuming that

3. It is necessarily true that people satisfy their inclinations when they are able to satisfy them and have no reason for not doing so,

and that

4. It is necessarily true that God has no reason not to diffuse His own fullness,

it follows that

5. Necessarily, God diffuses His own fullness.

Edwards explicitly asserts 1 and 2; 4 follows from the excellency of the good in question (viz., God diffused). The only reason God could have for not diffusing His own fullness would be that doing so is incompatible with a greater good. But no good is greater than Himself diffused. Edwards would also subscribe to 3, for he believes that action is necessarily determined by the strongest motive. To fail to satisfy an inclination that one is able to satisfy and has no reason not to satisfy is to fail to do what one has the strongest motive for doing. So Edwards is committed to 3 and 4 as well as to 1 and 2. He is therefore committed to 5.

205. Isn't the Son an adequate expression of the Father's goodness? Miscellany 104 suggests that He is but adds that *creation* is needed to express the *Son's* goodness, that is, to express the Son's propensity or inclination to diffuse *His* own excellence. Miscellany 553 (T 136f) contends that while the "act of God within Himself and towards Himself" involved the exercise of His perfections, it "was not the same kind of exercise" that was involved in creation, and that God not only delights in exercising His perfection, He also "delights in all the kinds of its exercise." The implication is that God must not only diffuse and communicate Himself, He must diffuse and communicate Himself *ad extra*.

206. Thomas A. Schafer, "The Concept of Being in the Thought of Jonathan Edwards," Doctoral Dissertation: Duke University (1951), 285.

207. Malebranche, *Concerning Nature and Grace*, in Taylor, *Father Malebranche*, 22.

208. The last claim requires explanation. Locke distinguished an object's powers from the non-relational properties underlying those powers in virtue of which the object produces its effects. A body's powers, for example, must be distinguished from its microscopic structure. It is the latter that accounts for the body's effects. An object's nonrelational properties are real properties. Its powers are not. Powers are merely relations between (some of) the object's real properties and its effects. See Reginald Jackson, "Locke's Primary and Secondary Quali-

ties," in *Locke and Berkeley*, eds. C. B. Martin and D. M. Armstrong (Notre Dame, Ind.: University of Notre Dame Press, 1968), 55–60. Edwards's view is similar. In Miscellany 94, he asserts that "power always consists in something— the power of the mind consists in its wisdom, the power of the body in plenty of animal spirits and toughness of limbs, etc." (T 257f). Miscellanies 94 and 259 identify the real property that underlies God's power with "the essence of God," or "the Father," or the divine being itself (T 258 and 259). *An Essay on the Trinity* identifies it with His understanding and will. "God's power . . . is not really distinct from His understanding and will; it is the same but only with the relation they have to those effects that are, or are to be produced" (ET 118f). (The relation in question is presumably "[possible] cause of.")

209. Edwards is an occasionalist, a subjective idealist like Berkeley, and a mental phenomenalist like Hume. God is the only true cause of phenomena. He is also the only substance "underlying" the sensible ideas, and the "thoughts" and "perceptions," of which bodies and minds, respectively, are constituted.

210. But while God's happiness isn't *causally* dependent on creatures, it *is* logically dependent upon them. Edwards thinks that (1) if God is perfect, He will diffuse Himself *ad extra*, and that (2) if God were less perfect, He would be less happy (i.e., His happiness would not be "complete" or infinite). But 1 and 2 entail 3, namely, if God's happiness is infinite, He will diffuse Himself *ad extra*. Since 1 and 2 are necessary, so is 3. It is quite possible that Edwards would have regarded logical dependency as innocuous.

211. At least one passage suggests that Edwards would also reject 1—at least in so far as it pertains to God. "God has no more by making His creatures that they may be happy. He hath in His Son an adequate object for all the desires of that kind that are in His heart, and in His infinite happiness He sees as much happiness as can be. When new beings are made . . . God sees not the sum of happiness increased" (Misc. 1218, T 150f). This passage implies that if God hadn't created, He would be just as happy as He is. Can this be squared with the claim that God places part of His happiness in His self-communication *ad extra*? Only if we add that God's happiness is so great that if part of it (e.g., His delight in diffusing Himself) were removed, His happiness would be undiminished. But Edwards never suggests that this is true, and it isn't especially plausible. If the set of odd numbers is subtracted from the set of natural numbers, the remaining set is still infinite. On the other hand, if God is unable to perform just one possible task, His power isn't infinite (i.e., perfect or complete); although there may be an infinite number of tasks He can perform (e.g. create one duck, create two ducks, create three ducks . . . , etc). Now it is at least as reasonable to suppose that God's infinite happiness should be construed on the second model as on the first, that is, it is at least as reasonable to suppose that "God's infinite happiness" refers to God's complete or perfect happiness as to suppose that it refers to an infinite quantity of happiness (e.g., an infinite number of pleasurable moments). Yet this has an important implication, for while an infinite quantity can be diminished without ceasing to be infinite, it is doubtful that a perfect or complete whole can lose one of its parts without losing its completeness or perfection.

212. And, *pace* (e.g.) Hartshorne, that A entails B doesn't logically imply that B is an ontological part of A. Logical inclusion doesn't entail ontological inclusion.

213. Nevertheless, even if God needs creatures, He isn't "needy." God's pleasure in creatures is pleasure in communicating His own infinite fullness. This hardly argues "indigence." " 'Tis no argument of the emptiness or deficiency of a fountain that it is inclined to overflow" (EC 448).

214. It is perhaps significant that Edwards frequently compares the end state of God's creation to music. (See Jensen, *America's Theologian*, 19–20.)

215. Edwards certainly didn't *think* of his views as unorthodox. "Untraditional" might be a better word. Whether Edwards clearly saw that his views committed him to the necessity of creation is a moot point. Norman Kretzmann argues that Aquinas, too, was more or less unwittingly committed to the necessity of creation. See his "A General Problem of Creation: Why Would God Create Anything at All?" and "A Particular Problem of Creation: Why Would God Create This World?," in *Being and Goodness*, ed. Scott MacDonald (Ithaca, N.Y.: Cornell University Press, 1991), 208–49.

216. Edwards says of sin, for example, that "if God sees that good will come of it, and more good than otherwise . . . God . . . must permit it—for if this sum total be really the best, how can it be otherwise than that it should be chosen by an infinitely wise and good being, whose holiness consists in always choosing what is best?" (*Works* VIII 386).

217. Thus in *Freedom of the Will*, Edwards quotes George Turnbull with apparent approval: "Of all possible systems he [God] hath chosen the best" (*FW* 408fn). See Malebranche who argues that God needn't create but that if He does, He "must produce the perfectest possible" (*Nature and Grace*, 22).

218. Edwards clearly believes that at least some normative propositions are necessary (see *Freedom of the Will*, 153). Now the only normative propositions that clearly *aren't* necessary are those that (like "The United States Government's support of Batista and Somoza was morally wrong") entail the existence of contingent states of affairs. "Charly is the best possible world" doesn't do so. (Note that "Charly" would pick out our world even if our world weren't actual.)

219. "God creates Charly" entails "Charly exists." Since the first is necessary, so is the second. Now "Charly exists" can be regarded as the conjunction of "F1 obtains," "F2 obtains," . . . "Fn obtains," where F1, F2, . . . , Fn are the facts that would obtain if Charly were actual. But if a conjunction is necessary, so are its conjuncts. It follows that "F1 obtains" is necessary, "F2, obtains" is necessary, and so on, that is, there are no contingent facts.

220. William Rowe, "The Problem of Divine Perfection and Freedom" (paper presented at the Philosophy of Religion Society meeting, San Francisco, 1993), 15. Most of this paper appears under the same title in *Reasoned Faith*, ed. Eleonore Stump (Ithaca, N.Y.: Cornell University Press, 1993), 223–33.

221. As I have argued in *Philosophy of Religion* (Belmont, Calif.: Wadsworth Publishing Co., 1988), 84–86.

222. Rowe has objected to me that "the crucial issue . . . is not whether the factors necessitating choice are outside us or inside us. The crucial issue is whether these factors are beyond our control. And God has no more control over his nature than we do over conditions that existed before we were born" ("Response to William Wainwright," paper presented at the Philosophy of Religion Society meeting, San Francisco, 1993, 1). I agree that God doesn't possess libertarian freedom on this view. My point, though, is that our resistance to compatibilist conceptions of freedom in the human case partly rests on the fact that the sufficient causes of our actions are outside us. *This* reason for resisting compatibilism doesn't apply in God's case. On views like Edwards's, God isn't manipulated by outside forces.

223. Creatable worlds are those possible worlds God can actualize. On Edwards's or Leibniz's view, creatable worlds and possible worlds are coextensive. If creatures possess libertarian freedom, however, and some counterfactuals of freedom are true, then not all possible worlds are creatable. For example, if it is eternally true that Adam would freely sin if he were created, then even God can't actualize a possible world in which he exists and doesn't sin.

224. Thomas Aquinas, *The Summa Theologica*, vol. 1, trans. Fathers of the English Dominican Province (New York: Benziger Bros., 1947), part I, question 25, article 6.

225. Rowe, "The Problem of Divine Perfection and Freedom."

226. I have argued for this in *Philosophy of Religion*, 90. Rowe accepts my reasoning.

227. Rowe, "The Problem of Divine Perfection and Freedom," 17–18. I have relabeled Rowe's principles B and C, I and II respectively.

228. Or so I would argue. What creatable worlds there are depends on what counterfactuals of freedom obtain, and counterfactuals of freedom are contingent. It seems to me likely, however, that *whatever* counterfactuals of freedom obtain, no creatable world is such that God couldn't have created a world that is better in *some* morally relevant respect. (Perhaps it might have been more beautiful, for example, or its members happier.)

229. Let S stand for the supposition that for every creatable world there is a better one, and let G represent the proposition that an essentially omnipotent, essentially omniscient, and essentially perfectly good being exists. Proof:

1. Necessarily, S (Assumption)
2. Necessarily, I (Assumption)
3. Necessarily, II (Assumption)
4. (S & [I & II]) —> ~ G (Rowe's argument)
5. Necessarily, (S & [I & II]) (from 1, 2, and 3)
6. Necessarily, ~G (from 4 and 5)

230. See Hartshorne's *Divine Relativity* (New Haven, Conn.: Yale University Press, 1948), 19ff. That God is surpassable by Himself doesn't entail that it is possible for Him to grow in perfection. For God might surpass Himself in two

ways—by being more perfect at later than at earlier times or by being more perfect in one possible world than another. The first is endorsed by Hartshorne but seems inconsistent with traditional notions of divine perfection. (A God who is more perfect at later than at earlier times seems less worthy of worship than a God who possesses His perfection from the beginning. In any case, if God is timeless, He *can't* grow in perfection.)

231. This clearly isn't sufficient. No being can be called "perfect" that fails to exhibit a superlatively high degree of those perfections lacking intrinsic maxima. It seems impossible, however, to fix a precise minimum.

232. This assumes identity across possible worlds. If the God in world 2 who is better than the God in world 1, is identical with the God in world 1, then the God of world 2 obviously isn't a *different* possible being than the God of world 1. Rowe's remarks on an earlier version of this argument suggest that he might respond to my point as follows. Let P be a being that is perfect in the second sense. If there is a possible world, W1, in which P exists and is better than P is in the actual world, there is also a possible world, W2, in which there is a being, Q, distinct from P that is better than P is in the actual world. But this seems doubtful. Since P is perfect in the second sense, P necessarily exists and is essentially omnipotent. It also has the essential properties of being creator and lord of whatever other beings happen to exist. It follows that, in W2, Q is dependent on P and limited in power. (See my "Monotheism," in *Rationality, Religious Belief, and Moral Commitment*, eds. Robert Audi and William J. Wainwright [Ithaca, N.Y.: Cornell University Press, 1986], 289–314.) Furthermore, given that P is good *enough* in the actual world, it isn't obvious that Q *can* be better than P is in the actual world. Note that there are different *kinds* of moral goodness—that of a child, for example, and that of a mature adult. It isn't clear to me but that the moral goodness of a superlatively good but not maximally perfect adult is better than that of a perfectly good child. By parity of reasoning, even if a limited and dependent being were perfect of its kind, it wouldn't clearly follow that it was better than a superlatively good being that infinitely surpassed it in power and upon whom it was absolutely dependent.

233. This presupposes that an omnipotent, omniscient, and good being's love of a person can logically precede its creation of her. I *think* this makes sense. Parents sometimes love their unborn children. One cannot, of course, love someone whom one can't identify. Prospective parents cannot, therefore, love a child before she is conceived. But given that Linda Zagzebski and others are right in thinking that each possible person has a singular essence, an omniscient being *can* identify individuals before they are created. See Linda Zagzebski, "Individual Essence and the Creation," in *Divine and Human Action*, ed. Thomas V. Morris (Ithaca, N.Y.: Cornell University Press, 1988), 119–44. See also Jeffrey S. Coombs, "John Poinsot on How to Be, Know, and Love a Non-existent Possible," *American Catholic Philosophical Quarterly* LXVIII (1994), 321–35. If Coombs is right, however, Poinset (who is also known as John of St. Thomas) thinks that although God can *know* nonexistent possibles, He can't *love* them.

234. Rowe, "Response to William Wainwright," 4.

235. Even if every creatable world is surpassable, a superlatively good, omnipotent, and omniscient agent would be unwilling to settle for a world that didn't meet a very high standard of goodness.

236. At the very least, any omnipotent, omniscient, and superlatively good being would refuse to create worlds that are bad on the whole.

237. Of course, if all worlds are surpassable, then no matter how high an omnipotent, omniscient, and superlatively good being sets its standard, there remain an infinite number of opportunities for exercising gratuitous love. The fact remains that more opportunities are available to omnipotent, omniscient, and superlatively good beings who set their standards lower.

238. This presupposes that the worlds containing less worthy vessels have less objective value, and this may be doubted. Isn't it possible that the better worlds contain the less worthy vessels, that is, that (for example) the beings in w2 whom G2 loves are less worthy than the beings in w1 whom G1 loves? Indeed, mightn't w2 be better than w1 just because the act of grace G2 exercises in creating w2 is more splendid? I suppose it might. But the *belief* that it is therefore better can't be G2's *reason* for creating w2, for, if it is, its motive isn't gratuitous love but to produce objective value. Furthermore, if the objective value of grace isn't (part of) G2's reason for creating w2, then the objective value of grace isn't included in the "calculations" G2 makes to determine whether w2 meets its minimal standard. For if it is, the objective value of G2's act of grace in creating w2 *will* be part of its reason for creating it. (Part of its reason for creating w2 is that w2 is creation worthy [i.e., meets its minimal standard]. If that is partly determined by the value of God's act of grace in creating it, then the latter is part of God's reason for creating it.) Hence, even if w2 is better than w1 because the act of grace G2 exercises in creating w2 is more splendid, it won't follow that w2 is better than w1 when measured by G2's standard for evaluating worlds (for G2's standard abstracts from the value its gracious actions add to a world). So if w2 is better than w1 only because G1's act of grace in creating w1 is more splendid than G1's act of grace in creating w1, w2 is not better than w1 in the relevant sense (viz., that it meets a higher minimal standard).

239. One must be careful here. If I am correct, God's motive for creating (some world or other) is His desire to glorify Himself by communicating Himself *ad extra*—which He does by (among other things) exercising gratuitous grace. This is a desire to produce or maximize a certain kind of good, and must be distinguished from His motive for creating one world rather than another. I have argued that the latter is plausibly construed as gratuitous love (grace). The desire to exercise gratuitous love, which is (part of) God's motive for creating some world or other, shouldn't be confused with the gratuitous love that is (part of) God's motive for creating the particular world He does.

Chapter 7

240. *Lectures and Essays* (London: Macmillan, 1879). Variously reprinted.

241. Shortly after this chapter was written, Louis P. Pojman published the

anthology *The Theory of Knowledge: Classical and Contemporary Readings* (Belmont, Calif.: Wadsworth, 1993), which contains "The Ethics of Belief." It should be noted that Pojman is a Christian philosopher who has written extensively on the epistemological problems of religious belief; his writings display an abiding interest in the issues raised in "The Ethics of Belief."

242. Versions of this chapter were read at the 1993 Chapel Hill Philosophy Colloquium and to departmental colloquia and student groups at the University of Alabama at Tuscaloosa, Tufts University, and the University of Miami (Coral Gables). I wish to thank those who were present on those occasions for their questions and comments, especially Simon Blackburn, Jarrett Leplin, William G. Lycan, H. Scott Hestevolt, George Smith, Daniel Dennett, Susan Haack, and Eddy Zemach. I also wish to thank David Lewis, both for conversation and correspondence, over many years, that have had a profound influence on my ideas of the nature of philosophy, and for conversations on the specific topic of this chapter. Some of the ideas in this chapter—and, indeed, some of the paragraphs in this chapter—appeared in my essay "Quam Dilecta," which was included in Thomas V. Morris, ed., *God and the Philosophers* (New York and Oxford: Oxford University Press, 1994).

Chapter 8

243. For formulations and defenses of the argument from evil, the work of William L. Rowe is as instructive as any in the literature. See, for example, his "The Empirical Argument from Evil," in *Rationality, Religious Belief, and Moral Commitment*, eds. Robert Audi and William J. Wainwright (Ithaca and London: Cornell University Press, 1986); "Ruminations about Evil," *Philosophical Perspectives* 5 (1991), collected in *The Evidential Argument from Evil*, ed. Daniel Howard-Snyder (Bloomington: Indiana University Press, 1996), and "The Evidential Argument from Evil: A Second Look," also in *The Evidential Argument from Evil*.

244. See, however, Ernest Nagel, "Philosophical Concepts of Atheism," in *Basic Beliefs*, ed. Johnson E. Fairchild (New York: Sheridan House, 1966) for an indication of how a philosopher of science views the issue of the harmony of theism and science.

245. Among the best short treatments of the nature of science and scientific explanation is the title essay of Carl G. Hempel's *Aspects of Scientific Explanation* (New York: Macmillan, 1965).

246. It is attacked by, for example, Saul Kripke, *Naming and Necessity* (Cambridge, Mass.: Harvard University Press, 1982).

247. For an instructive example of how eliminative materialism might proceed, see Paul M. Churchland's "Eliminative Materialism and the Propositional Attitudes," *Journal of Philosophy* 78 (1981). The folk psychology presented there is not comprehensive with respect to the ordinary notion (or the range of ordinary notions) of the mental, and I think it may be argued that in some of the cases

Churchland considers, for example, action-explaining generalizations, there is no reason to expect massive disconfirmation. For explication and defense of one such generalization see my "The Concept of Wanting," in my *Action, Intention, and Reason* (Ithaca and London: Cornell University Press, 1993).

248. For both critical discussion and defense of functionalism see Part 7 of *Mind and Cognition*, ed. William G. Lycan (Oxford: Basil Blackwell, 1990). Also instructive is Lynne Rudder Baker's *Saving Belief* (Princeton: Princeton University Press, 1987), esp. chapter 3.

249. For a statement and defense of nonreductive materialism (with references to much literature on the topic), see John F. Post, *Metaphysics: A Contemporary Introduction* (New York: Paragon House, 1990), and for critical discussion of the position, see Jaegwon Kim, "The Myth of Nonreductive Materialism," *Proceedings and Addresses of the American Philosophical Association* 63 (1989).

250. See, for example, some of the papers in *Mental Causation*, eds. John Heil and Alfred Mele (Oxford and New York: Oxford University Press, 1992). The previous two paragraphs are drawn from my own contribution to that collection, "Mental Causation: Sustaining and Dynamic."

251. Some readers may tend to dismiss Cartesian dualism (or indeed any kind of substance dualism) out of hand. But the view has surely not been shown to be incoherent and indeed has recently been ably defended. See, for example, Richard Swinburne, *The Evolution of the Soul* (Oxford and New York: Oxford University Press, 1986); and Charles Taliaferro, *Consciousness and the Mind of God* (Cambridge and New York: Cambridge University Press, 1994). For critical discussion of both (especially the latter) see William Hasker, "Taliaferro's *Consciousness and the Mind of God*," forthcoming. For Hasker's own dualist conception of mind see his "Concerning the Unity of Consciousness," forthcoming in *Faith and Philosophy*.

252. It may also be possible to construe perception in a way that requires less than I am here imagining in the way of sensory impressions. For extensive discussion of what perception is, with a number of relevant points about the divine nature, see William P. Alston, *Perceiving God* (Ithaca and London: Cornell University Press, 1991).

253. On this problem see Hugh J. McCann, "Divine Sovereignty and the Freedom of the Will," forthcoming in *Faith and Philosophy*.

254. For a widely discussed account of how bodily resurrection might be plausibly conceived, see John Hick, *Philosophy of Religion*, 2d ed. (Englewood Cliffs, N.J.: Prentice-Hall, 1973). I have assessed several important aspects of this account in "Eschatological Verification and Personal Identity," *International Journal for the Philosophy of Religion* 7 (1976).

255. For a sketch of a theistic anti-realism, with discussion of some difficulties facing non-theistic versions of anti-realism, see Alvin Plantinga, "How to Be an Anti-realist," *Proceedings and Addresses of the American Philosophical Association* 56 (1982): 47–70.

256. For detailed discussion of the possibility of God's having a body see

William Wainwright, "God's Body," *Journal of the American Academy of Religion* 62 (1974).

257. This is the kind of view we find in James M. Gustafson, *Ethics from a Theocentric Perspective*, vol. 1 (Chicago: University of Chicago Press, 1981). Gustafson is quite critical of the anthropomorphism he finds in personal conceptions of God. I have critically assessed some aspects of his naturalism in "Science, Theology, and Ethics in James M. Gustafson's Theocentric Vision," in *James M. Gustafson's Theocentric Ethics: Interpretations and Assessments*, eds. Harlan R. Beckley and Charles M. Swezey (Macon: Mercer University Press, 1989).

258. In places Gustafson seems to portray God in this way; see *James M. Gustafson's Theocentric Ethics*, chapter 5, section II.

259. This chapter is dedicated to William L. Rowe, who over the years has contributed greatly to both my understanding of the philosophy of religion and my interest in studying the subject. An earlier version has benefited from discussions with Hugh McCann and Richard Swinburne. The essay draws heavily on my contribution to Philip L. Quinn and Charles Taliaferro, eds., *The Blackwell Companion to Philosophy of Religion* (Cambridge: Basil Blackwell, 1996), and I gratefully acknowledge the publisher's permission to reuse that material.

Chapter 9

260. An ancestor of this chapter was read to the Indiana Philosophical Association in 1990 and to a joint meeting of the Central States and Illinois Philosophical Associations held in the same year. The commentator on the latter occasion was William Wainwright, who gave me much to think about. I've also been fortunate over the years to have had Bill Rowe as a colleague and a friend and it is to Bill that this chapter is dedicated, with respect, gratitude, and affection.

261. See, for example, Hume's "accurate definition": *a transgression of a law of nature by a particular volition of the Deity, or by the interposition of some invisible agent*, in *An Enquiry Concerning Human Understanding*, 3d ed, eds. L. A. Selby-Bigge and P. H. Nidditch (Oxford: Clarendon Press, 1975), 115, n. 1. In the text of Section X of the *Enquiry*, titled "Of Miracles," Hume says simply that "a miracle is a violation of the laws of nature" (114). Hume's reason for consigning the "accurate definition" to a footnote was that its main feature, the condition of supernatural causation, was irrelevant to his skeptical argument. Hume's own treatment of miracles in Section X of the *Enquiry* seems to conflate epistemological issues with ontological ones. On page 115, for example, Hume writes, "it is a miracle, that a dead man should come to life; because that has never been observed in any age or country." Presumably, what Hume meant was that we justifiably believe it to be a law of nature that dead men do not come to life on the basis of exceptionless past experience. Hume often refers to arguments based on absolutely uniform past experience as *proofs* as contrasted with *probabilities* (based on past experience that is not absolutely uniform) and *demonstrations*

(valid deductive arguments with premises all of which are relations of ideas, known with intuitive certainty). For good discussions of Hume's classification, see M. Jamie Ferreira, *Scepticism and Reasonable Doubt* (Oxford: Clarendon Press, 1986), and David Owen, "Hume's Doubts About Probable Reasoning: Was Locke the Target?," in *Hume and Hume's Connexions*, eds. M. A. Stewart and John P. Wright, (University Park: Pennsylvania State University Press, 1995), 140–59.

262. See William Rowe, *Philosophy of Religion*, 2d edition (Belmont, Calif.: Wadsworth, 1993), 127, n. 12. The claim by Hume and many others that it is logically possible for an event to violate a law of nature without that event having any cause, whether natural or supernatural, rests on the presumed contingency of the principle that every event has a cause. Unlike Samuel Clarke, Hume regarded the causal principle as at best a contingent truth, not a necessary truth. See David Hume, *A Treatise of Human Nature*, 2d ed, eds. L. A. Selby-Bigge and P. H. Nidditch (Oxford: Clarendon Press, 1978), book 1, part 3, Section 3. For a critique of Hume's argument for the contingency of the causal principle see G. E. M. Anscombe, " 'Whatever Has a Beginning of Existence Must Have a Cause,' " *Analysis* 34 (1974): 145–51.

263. Rowe, *Philosophy of Religion*, 127, note 12.

264. Hume supposed otherwise. As Alasdair MacIntyre has recently noted, Hume rather cavalierly assumes that every event in nature falls under at least one law of nature. (See, for example, Hume's frequent appeals to the universality of law in his essay "Of Suicide" and his attack on the libertarian concept of free will in the *Enquiry*.) Some authors (such as MacIntyre and Fogelin) claim to detect a naturalistic argument for the impossibility of miracles in "Of Miracles" that does not depend on Hume's appeal to the weakness of testimony. Needless to say, this claim has been disputed (by Flew and Penelhum, among others). See Robert J. Fogelin, "What Hume Actually Said about Miracles," *Hume Studies* 16 (1990): 81–86; Antony Flew, "Fogelin on Hume on Miracles," *Hume Studies* 16 (1990): 141–44; Joseph Ellin, "Again: Hume on Miracles," *Hume Studies* 19 (1993): 203–12; Alasdair MacIntyre, "Hume, Miracles, Nature, and Jansenism," in *Faith, Scepticism and Personal Identity*, eds. J. J. Macintosh and H. A. Meynell (Calgary: University of Calgary Press, 1994), 83–99, and Terence Penelhum's reply to MacIntyre in the same volume, 257–63. The assumption that if an event does not violate any law of nature then that event must be covered by laws in such a way that the event has a complete, lawlike explanation is commonly made, usually without any supporting argument. For example, Nicholas Everitt writes that "if an alleged miracle does not violate the laws of nature, it will be explicable in terms of those laws" (349), assuming, apparently, that naturalism entails that everything that happens is governed by laws. See Nicholas Everitt, "The Impossibility of Miracles," *Religious Studies* 23 (1987): 347–49.

265. Historically, theistic sects appealed to miracles and prophecies mainly to authenticate their rival claims concerning revealed religion rather than as evidence for theism. Clarke, Locke, Paley, and others assumed that there were conclusive

proofs of God's existence. The issue, for them, was the truth of Christianity as opposed to Judaism and Islam; the truth of Trinitarianism as opposed to Unitarianism. But if miracles can be evidence for theistic claims, then they must also be evidence, however inconclusive, for God's existence. Modern writers such as Richard Swinburne regard miracles as weakly confirming theism. See Richard Swinburne, *The Existence of God* (Oxford: Clarendon Press, 1979), chapter 12.

266. Versions of this argument can be found in Alastair McKinnon, " 'Miracle' and 'Paradox,' " *American Philosophical Quarterly* 4 (1967): 308–14; Norman Swartz, *The Concept of Physical Law* (Cambridge: Cambridge University Press, 1985), Chapter 9; and, Nicholas Everitt, "The Impossibility of Miracles," *Religious Studies* 23 (1987): 347–49. The problem of explaining how miracles are logically possible is also discussed by Rowe, Smart, Swinburne, and others.

267. For the sake of brevity, I omit consideration of statistical laws and the problem of defining counterinstances of them. The difficulty is an obvious one: if the law says that some percentage of A's are B, then no single event of an A that is not a B, nor any set of such events, is logically incompatible with the law.

268. For challenges to the traditional interpretation of Hume as a regularity theorist see A. J. Jacobson, "Does Hume Hold a Regularity Theory of Causality?," *History of Philosophy Quarterly* 1 (1984): 75–91, and T. L. Beauchamp and A. Rosenberg, *Hume and the Problem of Causation* (Oxford: Oxford University Press, 1981), chapter 1.

269. In "Miracles and the Laws of Nature," *Faith and Philosophy* 2 (1985): 333–46, George Mavrodes attempts to argue that laws of nature possess a kind of necessity according to which "necessarily all A's are B" does *not* entail that all A's are B. But, as Joshua Hoffman points out in his comments on Mavrodes's paper, in *Faith and Philosophy* 2 (1985): 347–52, it is hard to see how "the fact that a statement is nomically necessary [is] supposed to *weaken* the force of that which is asserted to *be* nomically necessary" (350). Mavrodes regards laws of nature as having the same kind of prescriptive force as legal statutes, which humans can and do violate. Hoffman rightly objects that this ignores a fundamental disanalogy between statutes and laws of nature: statutes have prescriptive force precisely because they are mere imperatives, whereas laws of nature have descriptive content.

270. Del Ratzsch, "Nomo(theo)logical Necessity," *Faith and Philosophy* 4 (1987): 383–402.

271. Douglas Odegard, "Miracles and Good Evidence," *Religious Studies* 18 (1982): 37–46.

272. See, for example, James Gilman, "Reconceiving Miracles," *Religious Studies* 25 (1989): 477–87.

273. John Stuart Mill, *A System of Logic*, ed. J. M. Robson (Toronto: University of Toronto Press, 1974), book 3, chapter 25, sections 2 and 3.

274. Mill, *A System of Logic*, book 3, chapter 22.

275. This thesis, that laws of nature are conditional propositions that apply only when natural forces are present, has been embraced by several authors. See,

e.g., Robert A. Larmer, *Water into Wine?* (Kingston: McGill-Queens University Press, 1988); David Basinger, "Miracles as Violations: Some Clarifications," *Southern Journal of Philosophy* 22 (1984), 1–7. Both Larmer and Basinger conclude from this thesis that we should drop the violation of law condition from the definition of a miracle.

276. This point is argued with great vigor in William Lane Craig, *The Historical Argument for the Resurrection of Jesus during the Deist Controversy* (Lewiston, N.Y.: Edwin Mellen Press, 1985), 480–91. Craig is expounding and responding to the arguments in Stephen S. Bilynskyj, "God, Nature, and the Concept of Nature" (Ph.D. dissertation, University of Notre Dame, 1982).

277. That, in essence, is the strategy adopted by Larmer, Basinger, and Craig.

278. Ninian Smart, *Philosophers and Religious Truth* (London: SCM Press, 1964), chapter 2; Richard Swinburne, *The Concept of Miracle* (London: Macmillan, 1970), chapter 3.

279. Smart's own example of the "law of rolling bodies" being derivable from the principle of gravitation plus relevant initial conditions actually requires Newton's laws of motion for its derivation.

280. Smart, *Philosophers and Religious Truth*, 41.

281. This terminology is used by Swartz in *The Concept of Physical Law*. As Swartz cautions when introducing these terms, scientific laws are not a subset of laws of nature since, unlike the latter (which are true as a matter of definition), many of the former are, at a given time, likely to be false.

282. For an expression of these doubts see Andrew Rein, "Repeatable Miracles?" *Analysis* 46 (1986): 109–12.

283. Swinburne's own way of putting this choice is a little odd since he talks about L being a law of nature "operative in the field" and E being a counterinstance to L's "occurrence." Laws of nature do not "operate" or "occur," they just (timelessly) are. Perhaps Swinburne's language is a symptom of an underlying theistic commitment that sees laws of nature as an expression of God's will "operating" on matter.

284. Swinburne, *The Concept of Miracle*, 27.

285. In *The Existence of God*, Swinburne writes: "To say that a generalization 'all A's are B' is a universal law of nature is to say that being A physically necessitates being B, and so that any A will be B—apart from violations" (229). This suggests that he recognizes that on his account a law of nature can have more than one counterinstance.

286. Hume, *Treatise*, 31.

Chapter 10

287. See also Aristotle, *Metaphysics* I 1, 981a28–b6; and Aquinas's commentary *In Met.* I: L1.24-28; also *Metaphysics* I 2, 982a-30–b4; *In Met.* I: L2.49. For a full account of Aquinas on wisdom see Eleonore Stump, "Wisdom: Will, Belief, and Moral Goodness," forthcoming.

288. *Metaphysics* II 1, 993b29–30 (translating the medieval Latin text): "For that reason it is necessary that the principles *(principia)* of existing things be absolutely true *(verissima)*, for it is not the case that they are true at some times and not true at other times. Nor do they have any cause for their existence; instead, they [are the causes for the existence] of other things." See also *In Met.* II: L2.298.

289. Scott MacDonald, "Aquinas's Parasitic Cosmological Argument," *Medieval Philosophy and Theology* 1 (1991): 119–55.

290. 13.83 (G1); 108 (G2); 113 (G3); 114 (G4); 115 (G5).

291. In these circumstances it may be worth remembering that G5 is the only one of the arguments in chapter 13 that isn't drawn from Aristotle. Aquinas attributes it to John Damascene and Averroes. And so it is the only one that can be characterized as an argument "by means of which . . . Catholic teachers have [or, more precisely, one Catholic teacher has] proved that God exists" (13.81).

292. "It is impossible that contrary and discordant things coexist *(concordare)* in a single order always or for the most part except under someone's governance, on the basis of which all and each will be brought to tend toward a definite goal. But in the world we see things of diverse natures coexisting in a single order, not rarely or by chance, but always or for the most part. Therefore, there must be someone by whose providence the world is governed, and him we call God" (9.115).

293. Naturally, I don't intend this claim of replaceability to extend to the use of "God" (or "Lord") in the Scriptural passages he appends near the end of some of those chapters, for example, 14.119, 15.126.

294. This may be seen in the variants of this claim used as premises in later chapters: "altogether without motion" (15.122); "altogether impassable and immutable" (16.132; cf. 23.215 and 217). The claim itself is invoked in, for example, 15.121, 17.138, 19.152, 20.156, 23.215.

295. Aquinas does open chapter 14 with an announcement of an existential result: "Therefore, having shown that there is a first being *(est aliquod primum ens),* . . . we have to investigate its characteristics" (14.116). But I think it is clear that this particular existence claim is important to him only as an announcement that he has fulfilled the Aristotelian precondition for going on to investigate the *nature* of the first being that is his science's subject. What makes me think it is clear is that at the end of chapter 14 it is only immutability, and not existence, that he deliberately cites as the basis from which to go on.

296. The argument in 15.123 is perhaps clearer than the one in 15.121 as regards beginninglessness, but I think that it is less clear as regards endlessness, and that the argument to the same conclusion in 15.121 is generally the better of the two.

297. The editors of the Marietti edition of SCG suggest that this Latin expression stems from Avicenna's Arabic, and they distinguish it typologically (although not in all its occurrences). See their note to this passage. But they offer no evidence that Aquinas derives the expression from the medieval Latin translation of Avicenna, and I see no reason why he should have had to do so.

298. Aquinas's claim here that it has been shown that God is the First cause should perhaps be construed as going beyond the starting point he cites at the end of chapter 14, in which case he may be drawing here on G3 more directly than on G2 (or G1).

299. "Eternal" means only sempiternal (beginningless and endless) in 15.121 and 123. In 15.125 God is not called eternal at all, but only sempiternal. Only in 15.122 is there an argument explicitly and unmistakably for God's atemporality. But Argument G6 as I interpret it may indeed imply the atemporality of the being whose existence it argues for: see note 320 below.

300. Although the title of chapter 15 contains the proposition "God is eternal" and although the chapter contains five arguments (including the one in 15.124) concluding either that God is eternal or that God is sempiternal, the derived propositions in chapter 15 that matter most to Aquinas in the following chapters are the conclusion (lines 12–13) and the subconclusion (lines 7–9) of this argument G6 (as distinct from the full argument in 15.124). He uses these G6 results as premises at least eleven times through chapter 28: 16.130 (twice), 18.143, 19.150 (twice), 19.151, 22.203, 22.205, 22.206, 24.223, and 26.240. In those same chapters he cites "God is sempiternal" just once (16.128) and "God is eternal," meaning no more that that God is sempiternal, twice (16.127 and 26.242).

301. The literature on the cosmological argument(s) is vast. The best philosophical treatment of it I know is William L. Rowe, *The Cosmological Argument* (Princeton, N.J.: Princeton University Press, 1975). William Lane Craig, *The Cosmological Argument from Plato to Leibniz* (London: Macmillan, 1980), provides a very helpful historical account.

302. Fernand van Steenberghen, *Hidden God. How Do We Know That God Exists?* (Louvain: Publications Universitaires de Louvain, 1966), 126. He considers this "version" clearly better than the Third Way itself and useful in refurbishing it: "When set right with the help of the *Summa contra Gentiles*, the *Third Way* doubtless gives us a satisfactory proof" (127). "Why St. Thomas ever abandoned the simpler and more satisfactory formulation of the proof given in the *Contra Gentiles* (begun in 1258) to become involved in the curious and complicated considerations of the *Third Way* (written towards 1266) is a historical enigma to which we shall return" (127, n.9; cf. 149–50). For a later, more detailed discussion along these same lines, see van Steenberghen's *Le Problème de l'existence de Dieu dans les écrits de S. Thomas d'Aquin* (Louvain-la-Neuve: Éditions de l'Institut Supérieur de Philosophie, 1980), 126–30 and 187–205.

303. Being related indifferently to existing and not existing must apply only to an existing contingent thing considered on its own, as is suggested in the wording of lines 5–6—"if *existing* is its status, *that* must be on the basis of some cause"—and even by G6's opening words: "we *see* things *in the world.*" Aquinas is not suggesting that any nonexistent contingent being considered on its own, such as my twin brother, could suddenly show up among existing things. My existing must have some explanation; no explanation is needed to account for the nonexistence of my twin.

304. For this reason, the contingent things Aquinas describes as being "related *indifferently* to . . . existing and not existing" (lines 4–5) might be described more precisely as having no inherent tendency *to exist,* a characteristic strongly suggested by his going on to claim only as regards the *existing* of such a thing that *that* "must be on the basis of some cause" (lines 5–6).

305. *The Tempest,* Act I, Scene ii.

306. See, for example, *SCG* II.30–38 and *ST* Ia.46; also, specifically, his treatise *De aeternitate mundi.*

307. This sort of convergence is at least in keeping with an Aristotelian proposition Aquinas invokes as an unsupported premise in 18.147: "Prior to every multitude [of things some] unity must be found."

308. It is this diachronic consideration that lies behind the extensive, sophisticated medieval discussions *de aeternitate mundi*—on the possibility of a beginningless universe. Participants in that discussion who, unlike Aquinas, denied the possibility would not have taken this view of the applicability of Q1 to S.

309. This sort of question has been admirably dealt with in Rowe's analysis and appraisal of the metaphysical status of a beginningless causal series in Rowe, *Cosmological Argument,* esp. chapter 3, 115–67, "Two Criticisms of the *Cosmological Argument,*" and my discussion here owes something to his. In private correspondence (1993), Bernard Katz has suggested to me that, despite Rowe's worries on this score, there is no particular difficulty associated with treating the exhaustive collection of dependent beings as an object. I'm inclined to share Katz's view:

> It is quite plausible to regard the universe as a mereological sum of . . . the dependent beings that make up or made up the natural universe. . . . In fact, it seems to me that is exactly what the universe is, the mereological sum of all the things that make it up. (What else could it be? Surely not something set-theoretic?) Moreover, it would be quite reasonable to suppose that the mereological sum of dependent beings would itself be a dependent being. But what about your objection that there is no time at which all of S's members exist together? . . . . [W]e can raise the very same question about things that we clearly do regard as concrete objects but which also seem to lose and gain parts: for example, an automobile or, for that matter, any persisting physical object. . . . So, I don't think that the observation that S's existence is successive, or that there is no time at which all its members exist together, is a good reason for concluding that S cannot be construed as a concrete being.

310. Rowe, *Cosmological Argument,* 33. In these passages Rowe is in fact developing an interpretation of Aquinas's attempt to block an infinite regress, but the attempt Rowe is focusing on is the one in the Second Way, which can be read along these lines only if the Second Way is interpreted as concerned not with coming into existence but rather with remaining in existence, an interpretation Rowe adopts, ascribing it to G. H. Joyce (27, n.9). I think Joyce's line of

interpretation is badly suited to the Second Way but fits G6 well, and so I think Rowe's explanation of the blocking of the infinite regress of sustaining causes is better suited to G6 than to the Second Way.

311. Only the first two hyphens in the italicized phrase occur in Rowe's text; I've supplied the others.

312. Rowe, *Cosmological Argument*, 34, 35.

313. Rowe carefully distinguishes between "two different items: *i. the fact that A now exists, and ii. the fact that a certain sort of causal activity (causing A to exist) is now going on*" (33). His apparent reason for doing so is that "Someone might argue that, even though B is not the first member, we can still explain item (i) by reference to B and B's causal activity vis-à-vis A. I do not wish to dispute this point. To say that we have not really explained the present existence of A until we explain why B is causing A to exist, tracing each step backward until we arrive at an ultimate first cause, may be nothing more than a confusion as to the nature of explanation" (33; see also the sentence on 34–35). But the situation Aquinas is concerned to characterize as no explanation at all is not one in which an ordinarily adequate sort of first-level explanation has been captiously rejected as insufficient. It is, instead, one in which the first-level explanation is in terms of something that is itself theoretically inexplicable. In such a situation, no one with a philosophical interest in understanding A's presently existing could consider its being referred to B's causal activity to constitute any explanation at all.

314. Rowe, *Cosmological Argument*, 35–36.

315. Rowe, *Cosmological Argument*, 36–37.

316. Rowe, *Cosmological Argument*, 60–114.

317. Rowe, *Cosmological Argument*, 261.

318. A paradigm of the distinction between a necessary condition and the sustaining cause that supplies the condition is (a) nourishment as a necessary condition of life and (b) the source of the nourishment as the cause sustaining life.

319. Cf. Paul Davies, *God and the New Physics* (New York: Simon and Schuster, 1983), 45:

> The God who is outside time is regarded as "creating" the universe in the more powerful sense of "holding it in being at every instant." Instead of God simply starting the universe off (a belief known as deism rather than theism), a timeless God acts at all moments. The remote cosmic creator is thus given a greater sense of immediacy—he is acting here and now—but at the expense of some obscurity, for the idea of God being above time is a subtle one. The alternative roles of God in time, causing the creation, and a timeless God holding the universe (including time) in being, are sometimes illustrated schematically in the following way. Imagine a sequence of events, each one causally dependent on the preceding one. They can be denoted as a series ..E3, E2, E1, stretching back in time. Thus, E1 is caused by E2, which in turn is caused by E3 and so on. This causal chain can be denoted as follows:

$$L \qquad L \qquad L$$
$$\ldots \longrightarrow E4 \longrightarrow E3 \longrightarrow E2 \longrightarrow E1$$

where the L's remind us that one event causes the next through the operation of the laws of physics, L. The concept of a causal God . . . can then be illustrated by making God, denoted G, the first member of this series of causes:

$$L \qquad L \qquad L$$
$$G \longrightarrow. \ . \ . \longrightarrow E4 \longrightarrow E3 \longrightarrow E2 \longrightarrow E1$$

By contrast, if God is outside time, then he cannot belong to this causal chain at all. Instead, he is above the chain, sustaining it at every link:

$$G \qquad G \qquad G$$
$$| \qquad | \qquad |$$
$$L \qquad L \qquad L$$
$$\ldots \longrightarrow E4 \longrightarrow E3 \longrightarrow E2 \longrightarrow E1$$

and this picture could apply equally well whether the chain of causes has a first member (i.e., a beginning in time) or not (as in an infinitely old universe). With this picture in mind, we may say that God is not so much a cause of the universe as an *explanation*.

See also David Braine, *The Reality of Time and the Existence of God* (Oxford: Clarendon Press, 1988).

320. Human souls and angels are among the things Aquinas thinks exist necessarily in this sense because he takes them to involve no matter and, therefore, to be invulnerable to natural disintegration. But since their natures do not entail their existence, they, too, exist dependently. For a helpful critical survey of Aquinas's views on this topic, see Patterson Brown, "St. Thomas' Doctrine of Necessary Being," *The Philosophical Review* 73 (1964): 76–90.

321. For comments on earlier drafts, I'm grateful to William Alston, Christopher Hughes, Anthony Kenny, Scott MacDonald, Richard Sorabji, Eleonore Stump, the members of my 1994 Aquinas seminar at Cornell, and especially to my old, dear friend Bill Rowe.

Chapter 11

322. The first is in *God and Other Minds* (Ithaca, N.Y.: Cornell University Press, 1967). The second is in "Reason and Belief in God," in *Faith and Rationality*, eds. Alvin Plantinga and Nicholas Wolterstorff (Notre Dame, Ind.: University of Notre Dame Press, 1983). The third is in Plantinga's trilogy on warrant: *Warrant and Proper Function* and *Warrant, the Current Debate* (Oxford and New York: Oxford University Press, 1993), and *Warranted Christian Belief* (forthcoming).

323. Locke may be an exception. But Locke is not a classical foundationalist in the way that Aristotle, Aquinas, and Descartes are. Moreover, Locke is extremely muddled. No clear and coherent sense can be made of his foundationalism. I think it best to separate him sharply from the classical foundationalists. My hypothesis is that the classical foundationalism of Aristotle, Aquinas, and Descartes is logically independent of P-principles.

324. "The Will to Believe," in *The Will to Believe and Other Essays on Popular Philosophy* (Dover edition, 1956), 1–31.

325. Cardinal Newman, *Oxford Sermons*, 203.

326. See in *Thomistic Papers IV*, ed. Leonard A. Kennedy, C.S.B. (Notre Dame, Ind.: University of Notre Dame Press, 1988), 6–93, the essays by Henry B. Veatch and Joseph M. Boyle, Jr.; also, Phillip L. Quinn, "In Search of the Foundations of Theism," *Faith and Philosophy*, October 1985: 469–85; and William P. Alston, "Plantinga's Epistemology of Religious Belief," and Plantinga's reply in *Alvin Plantinga*, eds. James E. Tomberlin and Peter van Inwagen (Dordrecht: Reidel, 1985).

327. For more details on incorrigibility and the pragmatic properties, see my essays, "Incorrigibility," *The Philosophical Quarterly*, July 1968, and "On the Logic of *Cogito* Propositions," *Nous*, May 1969. See also my *An Introduction to Philosophy* (New York: A. Knopf, 1967) or (Bloomington, Ind.: TIS Press, 1982), 70–82.

328. Here's a worry. Category (i) propositions are doxastically irresistible and epistemically mandated. That is, no rational adult who is thinking clearly and attentively can refrain from believing them and every rational adult ought to believe them. But how can this be? If we have no choice about something, it can't be that we have an obligation to do it. "Ought" implies "can." I haven't the space to address this worry here.

329. William L. Rowe, "The Rationality of Religious Belief," *Contemporary Philosophy* 14, no. 6 (1992): 3–9.

330. Very young children are adept at making correct perceptual judgments in typical circumstances. In them there is very little likelihood that delusion-making factors are present. Children's perceptual judgments are typically epistemically justified. But children are not cognitively sophisticated to the degree that adults are. Their lesser capacity to make informed judgments puts them at a disadvantage when the circumstances are atypical. They are less reliable than informed adults.

331. A powerful argument from gratuitous evil is in William L. Rowe, "The Evidential Argument from Evil: A Second Look," *The Evidential Argument from Evil*, ed. Daniel Howard-Snyder (Bloomington: Indiana University Press, 1996).

332. This is by no means the end of the story. Plantinga's books on warrant, cited in note 322, and William P. Alston's *Perceiving God* (Ithaca, N.Y.: Cornell University Press, 1993) continue to argue for the epistemic soundness of theistic beliefs. These books are already subjects of critical scrutiny. An example is Mark S. McLeod's *Rationality and Theistic Belief* (Ithaca, N.Y.: Cornell University Press, 1993).

My thanks to Roger Gustavsson and to Alvin Plantinga for commenting at length on the earliest predecessor of this essay. Their responses were very helpful in showing me where I needed to explain my position more clearly. I deeply appreciate their help. William P. Alston deserves special mention. He read versions before this one and other material I sent him. Given our serious differences, his criticisms were an exemplar of generosity of mind and spirit, and an act of supererogation. I am grateful to George Pappas for very helpful correspondence, and to my colleague, David McCarty, who helps me whenever I turn to him for advice on the logical issues involved in the philosophical issues I happen to be working on. Thanks also to my colleagues Paul Eisenberg and Anil Gupta, and to William L. Rowe for good conversation and again to Eisenberg for knowing what I am up to and steadfastly encouraging me to go on. Daniel Howard-Snyder also deserves special mention for editing expertly to printable size a much longer paper I submitted at first. In the course of shortening the paper he improved the clarity and cogency of two of my arguments and made the paper easier to read. I am grateful.

Index

acceptance, 3, 8–12, 17–27
Aquinas, Thomas, 8, 15, 20, 78, 80, 85–6, 88, 90, 93, 96, 100, 101–9, 111, 112, 128, 185–204
Aristotle, 34, 83, 91, 93, 94, 96, 101, 112, 185–86
Audi, Robert, 24, 241n2

basic actions, 7–8, 165
basic beliefs, 208–12, 217–23, 225–28
belief (belief that), 3–14, 16–24; belief in, 3, 14, 22;
degrees of belief, 6; voluntary control of believing, 7–8, 11, 20–25
belief in other minds, 206–8
Brown, Robert, 32, 36–37, 244n48–52

causal dependence, 192–93
Christianity, 21–24, 29–44
Clarke, Randolph, 53–58
Clifford, W.K., 137, 140, 143, 144–47, 209, 223. *See also* Clifford's Principle
Clifford's Other Principle, 146–47
Clifford's Principle, 145–53, 210–16. *See also* Clifford's Other Principle
Cohen, L. Jonathan, 3, 5, 7, 8, 9, 10, 241n1, 241n10
Conversational Implicatures. *See* Grice, H.P.
creation, 119–33, 165; and the "best of all possible worlds", 126–33

Descartes, René, 20–21, 78, 130, 163, 238
despair, 33–34
Determinism, 47, 74–77. *See also* freedom
disposition, 4, 9, 10
divine embodiment, 164–66
Double Truth Theory, 101–9
dualism (Cartesian), 78, 85, 87, 163–64
Dupré, John, 83–84, 86

Edwards, Jonathan, 119–27, 133
evidentialism, 137–53, 209, 223

faith, 14–16, 22–24; faith in, 12–14; faith that, 12–13
Feigl, Herbert, 69–70
Fischer, John Martin, 74–81, 85, 87–88
foundationalism, 209, 216–20
Frankfurt-style Counterexamples, 73, 79–81
freedom, agency (free will), 50–71; compatibilism, 50–51, 85–88, 127–28; divine, 90, 127–33; libertarian free will, 73–81, 85–88
functionalism, 161–62

Geach, Peter, 115–16
Grice, H.P., 8, 241n9

Hume, David, 68, 97, 160, 174, 183

283

Contributors

William P. Alston is professor of philosophy emeritus at Syracuse University, having previously served on the faculties of the University of Michigan, Rutgers University, and the University of Illinois. His main interests are philosophical psychology, epistemology, and the philosophy of language. His most recent books are *Divine Nature and Human Language* (1989), *Epistemic Justification* (1989), *Perceiving God* (1991), *The Reliability of Sense Perception* (1993), and *A Realist Conception of Truth* (1995).

Robert Audi is professor of philosophy at the University of Nebraska, Lincoln. He works in epistemology, including religious epistemology; ethics, theoretical and applied; and the philosophy of mind and action, especially the theory of rational action. He is author of *Practical Reasoning* (1989), *Action, Intention, and Reason* (1993), and *The Structure of Justification* (1993), and is currently working on projects in epistemology, ethical theory, and the theory of rationality.

J. A. Cover is an associate professor at Purdue University, with research interests in history of early modern philosophy and metaphysics. Coauthor of *Theories of Knowledge and Reality* (1990) and coeditor of *Central Themes in Early Modern Philosophy* (1990), he has published articles on Leibniz, space and time, and causality.

Martin Curd, an associate professor at Purdue University, works mainly in the philosophy of science and epistemology. He has articles on conclusive reasons, the logic of discovery, the direction of time, and incongruent counterparts, and is the author of *Argument and Analysis* (1992).

Peter van Inwagen is John Cardinal O'Hara Professor of Philosophy at the University of Notre Dame. Before teaching at Notre Dame, he taught for many years at Syracuse University. Van Inwagen works in the areas of metaphysics, epistemology, and the philosophy of religion. He is the author of *An Essay on Free Will* (1983), *Material Beings* (1990), *Metaphysics* (1993), and *God, Knowledge and Mystery: Essays in Philosophical Theology* (1995).

Norman Kretzmann is the Susan Linn Sage Professor Emeritus at Cornell University. He has written widely on medieval philosophy and philosophy of religion and was the principal editor of *The Cambridge History of Later Medieval Philosophy* (1981), and coeditor of *The Cambridge Companion to Aquinas* (1993).

George Nakhnikian is professor of philosophy emeritus at Indiana University, having retired in 1988. Prior to teaching at Indiana University, he was professor and chair at Wayne State University. He was a Fulbright Lecturer at St. Andrews during 1965–66, and a visiting assistant professor and Carnegie Intern in General Education at Brown University in 1955–56. His philosophical work has been in moral philosophy. In the last few years he has been working in the epistemology of theism.

John O'Leary-Hawthorne is an associate professor at Syracuse University. He has published articles in philosophy of mind, philosophy of language, metaphysics, epistemology, history of early modern philosophy, and philosophy of religion. He is coeditor of *Philosophy in Mind* (1994), and coauthor of the *The Grammar of Meaning* (forthcoming). He is presently working with Jan Cover on *Leibnitz on Substance and Individuation*.

Philip L. Quinn is John A. O'Brien Professor of Philosophy at the University of Notre Dame and was formerly William Herbert Perry Faunce Professor of Philosophy at Brown University. He is the author of *Divine Commands and Moral Requirements* (1978) and of over a hundred articles and reviews. He has served as editor of *Faith and Philosophy* (1990–95) and as president of the American Philosophical Association's Central Division (1994–95).

James F. Ross is professor of philosophy and law at the University of Pennsylvania. He works primarily in the areas of medieval philosophy, cognitive voluntariness, the philosophy of language, the philosophy of religion, and philosophical theology. He is at work on a book on metaphysics, entitled *Hidden Possibilities*. Ross is the author of *Philosophical Theology* (1969), *Introduction to Philosophy of Religion* (1969), and *Portraying Analogy* (1981).

Eleonore Stump is the Robert J. Henle Professor of Philosophy at St. Louis University. She is the author of many articles in philosophy of religion and medieval philosophy and has written or edited several books in those fields, including *Dialectic and its Place in the Development of Medieval Logic* (1989), and *Reasoned Faith* (1993).

William J. Wainwright is professor of philosophy at the University of Wisconsin, Milwaukee and editor of *Faith and Philosophy*. He has authored and edited books and articles in the philosophy of religion and the history of philosophy, including *mysticism* (1981), *Philosophy of Religion* (1988), and *Reason and the Heart* (1995).